DIVERGENT PATHS OF THE RESTORATION

DIVERGENT PATHS OF THE RESTORATION

A History of the Latter Day Saint Movement

Fourth Edition, Revised and Enlarged

Steven L. Shields

Herald House
2001

ISBN 0-8309-0569-3

First Edition, April 1975
Second Edition, Enlarged, August 1975
Third Edition, Revised and Enlarged, 1982
Fourth Edition, Revised and Enlarged, 1990
Second Printing, 1998
Third Printing with Corrections, 2001

Material contained in this volume is accurate only insofar as the author has been able to verify information. Any errors are completely unintentional and will be corrected in any future editions upon receipt of verfied factual information. Address the author at 6055 East Lake Mead Blvd., Suite A183, Las Vegas, Nevada 89115-6909 USA. All correspondence received will be considered as having been submitted with permission for possible publication. Individual replies are not possible.

TABLE OF CONTENTS

Extant Movements Founded During the Fragmentation Period, 1844 to mid-1860s

Part Three: The Church of Jesus Christ, *Alpheus Cutler*, 1853...........60

Part Four: The Reorganized Church of Jesus Christ of Latter Day Saints, 1851-1860....65, 283

Part Five: The Church of Jesus Christ, *William Bickerton*, 1862.......89

INTRODUCTION

This all new edition of *Divergent Paths of the Restoration* brings this unique catalog of Latter Day Saint churches up-to-date. While retaining the main body of the text of the third edition, which was published in 1982, this edition presents a number of new features. First, and foremost, is an additional section, which provides updated material on primary entries in the main body of the book, but more importantly includes information on more than 60 groups not included in previous editions. A new table of contents provides better access to the material; the new index is more comprehensive than before and of course, includes entries for the updated section.

The manner in which the table of contents is organized is compatible with the bibliography for this work, which is published in a separate volume (see the Bibliographical Note at the end of the book). While no one method of organization will make everyone happy, the history of the Latter Day Saint movement lends itself quite well to a number of chronological divisions. This method has thus been used in formatting the table of contents. Groups prior to Joseph Smith's death are listed first, then a series of movements that developed during the fragmentation period of 1844 to mid-1860s, but have not survived, are listed. The major section of the contents occupy the section containing the six movements which were founded during the fragmentation period that still function today, including all groups which have evolved from one or more of those six. Under each section, groups are listed in as near chronological order as possible. This has often been difficult because some movements evolve over a period of time.

The criteria for inclusion in this volume has been a matter of contention for many of those herein listed. Some groups have been offended that dates of organization are pinpointed, especially when the beliefs of the group acknowledge only the initial dates of the Latter Day Saint movement in the early 1800s. Thus, in certain cases, the date of organization would refer to the point in time when a group was identifiable as independent of other organizations. The same is true for key leaders. Listing an individual's name in no way makes a statement regarding the faith of the particular group. In order to be objective, the author must detach himself from the particular tenets of that faith as much as possible. Further, inclusion in this volume is not a defacto proclamation that all groups herein are churches per se. Many groups are not churches in the typical sense of the word, either by their own admissions and statement of purpose, or simply by the dynamics of their particular movement. It is frankly quite difficult given the unique nature of the Latter Day Saint movement to make a blanket statement or to develop criteria which determine what is a church and what is not. Some general ideas are involved, however. First, when an individual proclaims revelation that sets him or her in a course different from the church they are currently a member of often indicates the beginning of a new movement. Second, when an individual or group of people incorporate according to the laws of the land. Third, when an individual proclaims a new church.

The rationale by which a church or organization has been categorized in the section with one of the six major movements is not always clear-cut. Some leaders have been involved in more than one Latter Day Saint church. In most cases, a new group is listed with the parent organization from which the prime leaders have most recently been a part. Sometimes, though, doctrinal style has been a determining factor. This method does not adequately deal with the problem of third, fourth or later generation movements, but it does provide a grouping of the genre.

As always, this work is not currently complete, nor can it ever be. As will be noted from the opening statements in this introduction, more than 60 different organizations have come to light or have been organized since the publication of the third edition in 1982. The author sincerely hopes that the information contained herein will provide insightful understanding into the complexity that is the Latter Day Saint movement. So often historians, researchers and reporters confine their explorations and studies to only one segment of the Latter Day Saint movement, and promote that one particular style as being generally indicative of the entire movement. As this book proves, the honest historian, researcher or reporter must consider the Latter Day Saint movement in the broad terms that it really is.

A unification of the various churches which make up the Latter Day Saint movement will not likely ever come to be. The author's purpose in this volume is not to make such a proposition. As we come to understand other fellow Latter Day Saints, though, perhaps some of the animosity which has been so prevalent in the past will be replaced by mutual respect and understanding.

For Christopher

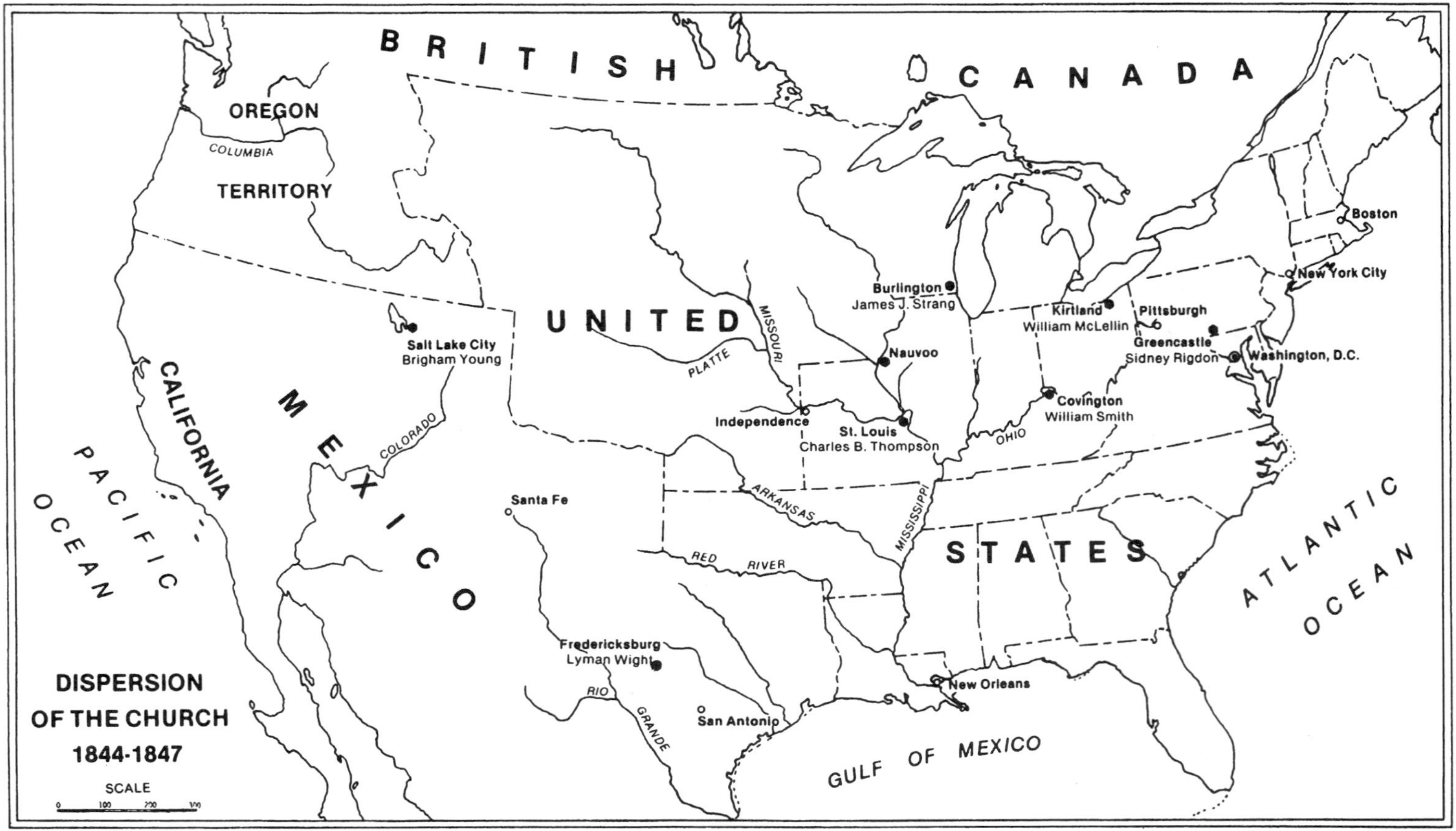

Cartography by Dale Broadhurst

INTRODUCTION TO THE THIRD EDITION

Although I would like to think of this edition of *Divergent Paths of the Restoration* as definitive, it is not. I believe it is the most complete and up-to-date volume to be published in this field, but the task of discovering and assembling material is ongoing. Continually some previously unknown group comes to light or additional details about other groups are being discovered. There is much work yet to be done in order to preserve this rich historical heritage. The material in this volume is of necessity brief—containing but basic presentations and introductions. Many of the groups will actually require one or more volumes to fully cover the subject of their history and doctrinal development.

Prior to my work in this field, there existed but a handful of very sketchy publications. Several years ago Russell R. Rich, Brigham Young University, had two of his lectures on the topic printed in booklet form. Others borrowed from him, but did not add to his research. The Daughters of Utah Pioneers published a more detailed booklet in the 1960s, but again, it did not significantly add to the information in this field.

In my extensive and ongoing research, I have been able to correct the inadequacies of their reports and greatly amplify the information contained therein. A point of note is that each of these previous works were written from a strictly pro-Utah Mormon point of view. In this volume I have diligently attempted to maintain an objective presentation, particularly when reporting on those organizations still functioning.

I hope to have produced herein a comprehensive volume of readable material and to have corrected any previously published errors or inadvertant misrepresentations. I have carefully consulted source material and individuals representing various groups as much as possible in an effort to maintain accuracy.

Steven L. Shields

INTRODUCTION TO THE FIRST EDITION

For some reason as yet unexplored and unexplained, the Restoration Movement has shown a schismatic tendency from its very first. From the difficulties with such men as William McLellin and Hiram Page, to the full scale battle for the successorship after his death, the movement started by Joseph Smith has never been a single unified organization.

For more than one hundred years, the writing of one group on another was largely a matter of "anti-your group, pro-our group" pamphleteering. The label of "damned apostate," "heretic," etc., is largely a thing of the past, and thank goodness for that. Today we are in the midst of a refreshing and honest search for the points that unite us in a common religious and historical heritage.

There have been only a few rather broad and somewhat limited studies of the various groups in the Restoration Movement. Dr. Russell Rich, BYU, published two booklets of lectures he gave, both from the LDS viewpoint. A few others have published material, mostly borrowed from Dr. Rich.

Steven L. Shields is now completing his Freshman year at Brigham Young University, and has for some time been interested in the "other" Mormons. His first work was a small booklet done for a Seminary class. This has now been expanded into a full scale book dealing with as many of the groups as information is available on. Along with the groups, there are many individuals who on their own wrote tracts advocating one position or another, but belonged to no organized group. These, too, have been added. There are many groups whose information is very sketchy, or non-existent, but they have been listed in hopes that someone, somewhere, can help. We would ask that those of you who have information would share, rather than keep it buried in your personal files, as the scholarly community is wont to do.

The Restoration Movement is growing, both in numbers and in groups. Someone should keep some kind of track of what is going on. Our thanks goes out to Steven for his pioneering in this heretofore neglected field.

David C. Martin, Provo, Utah, February 2, 1975

INTRODUCTION TO THE SECOND EDITION

To the best of our knowledge, this is the first book printed and published in Nauvoo, Illinois, since the Mormons left in 1846.

August 1975

ACKNOWLEDGEMENTS

Without the kind assistance from scores of individuals, this volume would not be as complete as it is. A few of these people include: David C. Martin, George Windes, Bruce Flanders, Chad Flake, Richard P. Howard, William A. Sheldon, Joseph Calabrese, Holland J. Davis, Raymond T. Bronson, James W. Savage and Stanley M. King. In addition, appreciation is extended to all others who have contributed to this work. I am also grateful to my family.

THE BEGINNINGS OF THE LATTER DAY SAINT MOVEMENT

As we view the history of the world we find that the various religious philosophies extant are as diverse and seemingly numerous as the stars in the sky. Since time immemorial people have found comfort in holding something or someone in awe. Some have worshipped the sun, some the moon. Others found it more intriguing to build monuments, or idols, to represent the governing forces ruling natural phenomena.

A sizeable portion of the world population today has found their comfort in revering a man called Jesus, the Christ. And to this deity, who came among men to dwell, is ascribed the very creation of the world and all things therein. Through his short life on this earth, this man did more to promote good and peace than perhaps any other one individual. His church, which he started in Palestine, spread throughout the whole world and has changed the lives of countless millions. And yet, there are probably more kinds of "Christians" in the world today than one can possibly imagine. No single Christian-oriented movement has been without "splinters."

With any group of people, no matter what the size, there will be individuals of varying intellect, education and personality. Each will interpret an idea or philosophy somewhat differently than the next person.

In Christianity, there have been intelligent, studious, thinking individuals who bravely fought for their interpretation of theology, authority and practice. Martin Luther, John Calvin, John Wesley and others boldy proclaimed their differences with the then accepted "one" church. And through time, others have proclaimed their own interpretations.

Another bold individual in this relgious melee, perhaps even bolder than the others due to his youthfulness and lack of formal education, was Joseph Smith, Jr. The son of a poor New England farmer, this boy learned from the Bible that he could receive an answer to his questions from God. Inasmuch as he had been struggling over which church to join, he approached the Almighty with his problem. To his amazement, the very God of the Universe appeared to him, with Jesus Christ, who instructed him to join no church.

As the years passed, Joseph learned that through him the true church of Christ was to be restored. In 1827 an angel named Moroni delivered a record inscribed on golden plates to Joseph and bestowed upon him the power to translate it into English.

The record, published in 1830 as the Book of Mormon, purported to be a record of an ancient civilization that had migrated from the Holy Land to the American continent several hundred years earlier.

Joseph claimed numerous heavenly visitations and revelations, and on April 6, 1830 he and a handful of believers, organized the Church of Christ. The name of the church was changed in 1834 to the *Church of the Latter Day Saints,* and finally in 1838 to the *Church of Jesus Christ of Latter Day Saints.*

The church grew and after several forced migrations and countless tribulations, settled in what became known as Nauvoo, Illinois in 1839.

The history of the church was not unlike the situations of Luther, Calvin or Wesley. Within a few months of its organization others in the church began promoting divine inspiration, or a better interpretation of church government, but these forms of "apostasy" were relatively low key when compared with the "great apostasy" of 1837-38, when most of Smith's early associates denounced him and left the church. The reasons were numerous and complex. It is not my intent to detail these at this time. Of all the different religious groups sprouting from infant "Mormonism" before Joseph Smith's untimely death in 1844, none have survived to the present day.

At Joseph Smith's death, the church was faced with a new problem. Joseph's early associates, who might have succeeded him in the leadership—and some of whom had been publicly designated for successorship—had formally disassociated themselves with the church. There was no scriptural precedent for this particular situation. Many dynamic individuals came forth to claim the leadership of the church by virtue of the office they currently held, or by some other means of either pretended or real appointment from the Prophet Joseph himself.

So the church, instead of losing small groups from the mainstream became severly fractured into many pieces. And as long as there are intelligent, thinking individuals in the Latter Day Saint Movement, I believe that the future will see various leaders come forth and lay claim to a divine call or interpretation of what the Latter Day Saint gospel is all about.

SECTION 1

CHURCHES AND ORGANIZATIONS

In this section will be presented, in as near chronological order as possible, each church, organization or leader with an informally organized following, that has existed from the very beginning of the Latter Day Saint Movement up to the present time. A few, for whom no date of beginning has been determined, appear at the end of this section.

Several of those to be discussed do not necessarily consider themselves a church per se, or in some cases, even a religiously oriented organization. I have tried to be very specific in pointing this out to the reader.

Every effort has been expended to be as complete in coverage as space has allowed, but many groups were short-lived, never published any literature, and left nothing but second-hand information in the historical record. Others have desired not to respond to inquiries to obtain detailed information.

PART 1—1830-1844

PURE CHURCH OF CHRIST (Wycam Clark)

The only information concerning this church comes from two references made by George A. Smith, an apostle of the LDS Church, in remarks presented on two different occasions, once in Salt Lake City and another in Ogden, Utah.

"I think the first church attempted to be established in opposition to Mormonism was that established by Wycam Clark, in Kirtland. He was baptised about the same time as Sidney Rigdon, and, in company with Northrop Sweet and four others, seceded from the Church, and said they could carry the whole world with them by preaching Mormon principles. They had two or three meetings; but the society would never have been known in the world, had not a few of us remembered the circumstance and told of it." (*Journal of Discourses,* Volume 7, Liverpool, England, 1860, p. 114—quoting a discourse delivered January 10, 1858 in Salt Lake City, Utah.)

"...when Joseph [Smith, the Prophet] came to instruct these Saints in relation to the true spirit, and the manner of determining the one from the other, in a short time a number of those who had been influenced by those foul manifestations, apostatized. Among the number was Wycom [sic] Clark; he got a revelation that he was to be the prophet—that he was the true revelator; and himself, Northrop Sweet and four other individuals retired from the Church and organized the *Pure Church of Christ,* as they called it, composed of six members, and commenced having meetings, and preaching, but that was the extent of the growth of this early schism." (*Journal of Discourses,* Volume 11, Liverpool, England, 1867, p. 4—quoting a discourse delivered November 15, 1864, in Ogden, Utah.)

Clark's action took place circa 1831.

JOHN NOAH

The year 1831 saw another prophet, John Noah, making claims of divine calling. In accordance with church procedure he was excommunicated for that claim. It is said that one of his followers, a Mr. Hawley walked "barefooted six hundred miles from New York to tell Joseph Smith that because he had permitted the women to wear caps, men to wear cushions on their coat sleeves, and had permitted John Noah to be cut off from the church, that he, Joseph, was no longer the prophet. Mr. Hawley claimed the Lord had given him this message." (Carter, Kate B., *Denominations that base their beliefs on the teachings of Joseph Smith, the Mormon Prophet,* Salt Lake City: Daughters of Utah Pioneers, 1969, pp. 8, 9)

THE INDEPENDENT CHURCH (Hoton)

In 1832, a man by the name of Hoton withdrew from the LDS Church and organized the Independent Church. He denounced the Prophet, Joseph Smith and also the Book of Mormon.

Himself as President of this new church, Hoton called a man by the name of Montague to the office of bishop.

According to Kate B. Carter, who did not leave us any references to original source material, "Persons who had apostatized from the Latter-day Saint Church could become members of this group by entering the room, shaking hands with every member and consecrating their property to the common cause. After two or three months there arose a difficulty between the president and the bishop. The bishop who had charge of the temporal things accused the president of visiting his pork barrel and the president accused the bishop of visiting his wife. These accusations resulted in a split between the two head officers and the organization fell apart." (Carter, *Denominations...,* p. 9)

CHURCH OF CHRIST (Warren Parrish)

Perhaps the most serious crisis to affect the church in its formative years, was the demise of the church's financial institution, the Kirtland Safety Society, and the establishment of a powerful, though short-lived, opposition group led by Warren Parrish. Organized during the summer and fall of 1837, the Church of Christ and its proponents insisted that Joseph Smith and other leaders of the church, then in Kirtland, Ohio, had strayed from the gospel by calling the church *The Church of the Latter Day Saints.*

According to the Elders Journal, published at Far West, Missouri, Parrish, cashier of the Kirtland Safety Society, had been engaged in embezzling money from the bank for a period of several months, which compounded the problems of the period. (*Elders Journal,* Volume 1, Number 4, Far West, Missouri, August, 1838, pp. 57-59)

Parrish took with him three members of the quorum of the twelve apostles: Luke S. Johnson, John F. Boynton, and Lyman E. Johnson. Others involved in the movement were Leonard Rich, Stephen

Burnett, Sylvester Smith, Cyrus P. Smalling and Joseph Coe.

According to B. H. Roberts, Mormon historian, this group met in the temple at Kirtland and claimed ownership thereof. On occasion they allegedly resorted to violence to support their claims.

The church's printing house was taken by the sheriff on instructions from the county court and on January 14, 1838, was sold to these reformers, but on the very night of the sale the printing office was burned. (See Roberts, B. H., *A Comprehensive History of the Church of Jesus Christ of Latter-day Saints,* Volume 1, Provo, Utah: Brigham Young University Press, 1965, pp. 403-407)

In the *Journal of Discourses,* George A. Smith reported:

"One of the First Presidency, several of the Twelve Apostles, High Council, Presidents of Seventies, the witnesses of the Book of Mormon, presidents of Far West, and a number of others standing high in the church were all carried away in this apostacy; and they thought there was enough of them to establish a pure religion that would become universal.

"This attempted organization was under the direction of Warren Parrish, who had been a Travelling Elder in the Church, and who sustained a high reputation in the Southern States as an eloquent preacher, and had for a short time been employed by Joseph [the Prophet] as a clerk...

"They were going to renounce the Book of Mormon and Joseph Smith, and take Mormon doctrines to overthrow all the religions in the world, and unite all Christian churches in one general band and they to be its great leaders.

"What success did this great apostacy meet with? Brother [Heber C.] Kimball, when on a mission in 1844, (this apostasy took place in 1837-38), while crossing Fox River on the ferry, encountered Warren Parrish. He was a grave-looking man—a straight-jacketed fellow, dressed in black, with a white handkerchief around his neck. Says he, 'Elder Kimball, will you have the goodness not to say to the people here that I ever was a Mormon. I am a Baptist minister. I am preaching in that meetinghouse for a salary of $500 a year. If they find out I have been a Mormon, it would hurt my influence very much indeed." (Smith, George A., reported in *Journal of Discourses,* Volume 7, Liverpool, England, 1860, p. 115.)

THE ALSTON CHURCH (Isaac Russell)

Isaac Russell, an English convert to the church, capitalized on the troubles of the church in Missouri during the final expulsion of the saints in the winter of 1838-1839. Many of the members of the church desired to remain rather than follow the directives of Joseph Smith to leave.

Russell began issuing revelations which favored their position. He gained a few followers there, and attempted to gain support from members of the church in and around the town of Alston, England, where he had recently completed successful missionary work.

He stated that the Lord had told him to take his Church into the "wilderness" so that directions could be given pertaining to ministering to the Lamanites. In addition, the Lord was to send the Three Nephites to the group and they would prepare a Zion.

A letter written to the Saints in Alston by Russell, dated January 30, 1839, from Far West, Missouri, is recorded in the History of the Church (LDS) Volume 3, pp. 343-344:

"To the Faithful Brethren of the Church of Latter-day Saints in Alston:

"Dear Brethren:

"Inasmuch as wisdom is only to be spoken amongst those who are wise, I charge you to read this letter to none but those who enter into a covenant with you to keep those things that are revealed in this letter from all the world, and from all churches, except the churches to whom I myself have ministered, viz.—the church in Alston and the branches round about, to whom I have ministered, and to none else; and to none but the faithful amongst you; and wo be to the man or woman that breaketh this covenant.

"Now the Indians, who are the children of the Nephites and the Lamanites, who are spoken of in the Book of Mormon, have all been driven to the western boundaries of the States of America, by the Gentiles, as I told you; they have now to be visited by the gospel, for the day of their redemption is come, and the Gentiles have now well nigh filled up the measure of their wickedness, and will soon be cut off, for they have slain the people of the Lord, and scattered the rest; and for the sins of God's people, the Gentiles will now be suffered to scourge them from city to city and from place to place, and few of all the thousands of the Church of Latter-day Saints will stand to receive an inheritance in the land of promise, which is now in the hands of our enemies. But a few will remain and be purified as gold seven times refined; and they will return to Zion with songs of everlasting joy, to build up the old waste places that are now left desolate.

"Now the thing that I have to reveal to you is sacred, and must be kept with care; for I am not suffered to reveal it at all to the churches in this land, because of their wickedness and unbelief—for they have almost cast me out from amongst them, because I have testified of their sins to them, and warned them of the judgements that have yet to come upon them; and this thing I tell you, will not come to the knowledge of the churches until they are purified.

"Now the thing is as follows—The Lord has directed me, with a few others, whose hearts the Lord has touched, to go into the wilderness, where we shall be fed and directed by the hand of the Lord until we are purified and prepared to minister to the Lamanites, and with us the Lord will send those three who are spoken of in the Book of Mormon, who were with Jesus after His resurrection, and have tarried on the earth to minister to their brethren in the last days.

"Thus God is sending us before to prepare a place for you and for the remnant who will survive the judgements which are now coming on the Church of Latter-day Saints, to purify them, for we are sent to prepare a Zion, (as Joseph was sent before into Egypt), a city of peace and a place of refuge, that you may hide yourselves with us and all the Saints in the due time of the Lord, before His indignation shall sweep away the nations.

"These things are marvelous in our eyes, for great is the work of the Lord that He is going to accomplish. All this land will be redeemed by the hand of the Lamanites, and room made for you, when you hear again from me. Abide where you are, and be subject to the powers that be amongst you in the Church. Keep diligently the things I have taught you, and when you read this, be comforted concerning me, for though you may not see me for some few years, yet as many of you as continue faithful, will see me again, and it will be in the day of your deliverance. Pray for me always, and be assured that I will not forget you. To the grace of God I commend you in Christ. Amen.

"Isaac Russell. P. S. We have not yet gone into the wilderness, but we shall go when the Lord appoints the time. If you should hear that I have apostacized, believe it not, for I am doing the work of the Lord. I.R."

THE CHURCH OF JESUS CHRIST, THE BRIDE THE LAMB'S WIFE
(George M. Hinckle)

The noted bibliographer, Dale L. Morgan, has left the following report of this group, established in 1840, by George M. Hinckle.

"Hinckle had been prominent among the early Mormon elders

and had attained to positions of responsibility, including the colonelcy of the Caldwell County militia. When the Saints were besieged by the Missouri state militia in October 1838, it fell to him to negotiate a surrender. Ever since, he has been regarded by the Saints as something of a Benedict Arnold, but his own view was that he had been made a scapegoat, and his side of the story, printed in *The Ensign* for August, 1844, has received insufficient attention. Whatever the merits of his case, the feeling against Hinkle made impossible his continuance in the church. Like many another man unchurched who still answers to the emotional need which had made him a member, Hinkle brought into being an organization of his own. In effect, and this is a familiar phenomenon in Mormon history, his church was the Mormon faith but with the Book of Mormon, Joseph Smith and his revelations excised.

"This church Hinkle named *The Church of Jesus Christ, the Bride the Lamb's Wife,* and the date of its organization is stated to have been June 24, 1840. The first conference was held at Moscow, Muscatine County, Iowa, on November 20, 1842, with subsequent meetings on April 14, June 17, July 14 and September 16, 1843—all these apparently at Moscow—and a sixth conference at Buffalo, Scott County, Iowa, on June 24, 1844. Thereafter headquarters was maintained at Buffalo.

"How delicate were the distinctions which gave separate identity to so many of the lesser Mormon churches is shown by the effect upon Hinkle's church of Joseph Smith's death. An old friend of Sidney Rigdon, he was immediately attracted to the new church Rigdon erected in Pittsburgh; on invitation from Rigdon and by authorization of his own organization, Hinkle attended the Rigdonite conference in April, 1845. Merger of the two organizations followed, although a separate conference of Hinkle's church was held as late as June 16, 1845. As it turned out, the Rigdonite church had even a shorter life than *The Church of Jesus Christ, the Bride the Lamb's Wife,* though a faction hung on at Buffalo after the central organization was dead. Later Hinkle sought to re-establish his church in Mercer County, Illinois, and Decatur County, Iowa, but he did not meet with much encouragement, and his children joined the Reorganization." (Morgan, Dale L., *A Bibliography of the Churches of the Dispersion,* nd, pp. 108-109)

On page 123 of the same publication, Morgan reviews the only known bibliographic contribution of George M. Hinckle's church, a magazine called *The Ensign.* Published at Buffalo, Scott County, Iowa, "one full volume of *The Ensign* was published, made up of

12 numbers issued monthly from July 1844 to June 1845. Each issue was composed of sixteen pages with cumulative pagination, a total for the volume of 192 pages. The first number was dated July 15, but thereafter *The Ensign* was dated only by month. Initially the publishers were George M. Hinkle and William E. McLellin, with McLellin as editor. The paper was to be 'devoted to the dissemination of the religious principles and views of *The Church of Jesus Christ, the Bride the Lamb's Wife.*' In August, Isaiah Matteson was named printer. With the October number, after a dispute with McLellin, Hinkle became editor and sole publisher, McLellin's farewell address appearing in this issue. In November F.A.C. Foreman became co-publisher with Hinkle, though he was not a member of the church. During Hinkle's absences, which were frequent, Foreman served as editor; and when the suspension *The Ensign* was announced in June 1845, notice was given by Hinkle that he had sold to Foreman his interest in the printing establishment.

"During the year it was published, The Ensign printed much material of value concerning the history and doctrine of Hinkle's church...and it printed many sidelights on contemporary Mormon history, especially the emergence of Sidney Rigdon's church. One interesting development was the intention formulated as early as June 1844, and announced in the issue of October, to publish a hymn book. This was never done because of the rapid progress of negotiations for a merger of Hinkle's church with Rigdon's, and the prior appearance of a hymn book by Rigdon himself; this latter hymnal was advertised for sale in The Ensign for May 1845..."

See also Church of Jesus Christ of the Children of Zion *and* Samuel James, George M. Hinckle.

OLIVER H. OLNEY

On March 17, 1842, Oliver H. Olney was removed from fellowship in the LDS Church on charges of having set himself up as a prophet. An editorial comment in the Times and Seasons, Volume 3, Number 11, for April 1, 1842, reads: "Mr. Olney has also been tried by the high council and disfellowshipped because he would not have his writings tested by the word of God; evidently proving that he loves darkness rather than light because his deeds are evil."

Olney claimed to have been set apart by the "ancient of days" as a prophet and been charged with setting up a new dispensation. Squaw Grove, Illinois, was to be the new gathering place.

Two pamphlets were published by Olney, one called *Spiritual*

Wifery at Nauvoo Exposed which was done in St. Louis in 1845. The other was published March 3, 1843, at Hancock County, Illinois, entitled *The Absurdities of Mormonism Portrayed.* This pamphlet touches on many of the practices and doctrines of the LDS Church with which Olney disagreed. He also makes reference to his writings, including his revelations, which were taken from him, presumably by the high council which tried his case of membership in the church. Good evidence of polygamy at Nauvoo is brought out, including information that it had its earliest beginnings in Kirtland. He discusses a brief history of the LDS Church and the persecutions it was forced to bear, the temple, John C. Bennett, and the inequalities he felt existed in the church.

Whether Oliver Olney was successful in gathering converts or not is unknown.

CHURCH OF JESUS CHRIST OF LATTER DAY SAINTS
(Francis Gladden Bishop)

Francis Gladden Bishop had been excommunicated from the LDS Church as early as 1835, then restored to full fellowship, only to be excommunicated again in 1842 at Nauvoo on charges of having received and taught revelations which were not consistent with the teachings of the church. Little is known of Bishop's life from that time, until 1851 when he published a "Proclamation," possibly from Kirtland, although no place of publication is noted.

That he was in the Voree, Wisconsin area for some time circa 1848, is attested to by comments made by James J. Strang in his *Gospel Herald.* Strang seems to indicate that Bishop had published earlier than the 1851 proclamation, but no details have been discovered.

Strang comments: "Gladden Bishop was one of the early members of the church, and one of the first Seventy. He assumes that Joseph had only the Aaronic priesthood, but that he has the Melchisedec, received by his ordination under the hand of Jesus Christ; that he is David, the King that shall reign over the united nation of Israel restored, and the Lord of the whole earth..." (*Gospel Herald,* May 30, 1850, Voree, Wisconsin)

Dale L. Morgan comments in his bibliography on the various publications of Bishop and those of his followers including William Swett, who left the church in Utah in 1854 to join with Bishop's followers, and also Joel Shearer who at times presided over the group during Bishop's absence.

Bishop apparently intended to travel to Utah in 1852 as a missionary, but never consumated his desire. He was still able to gain a few followers even at a distance. In 1853, Brigham Young denounced him from the pulpit in the old tabernacle in Salt Lake City, Utah.

Bishop established his headquarters at Little Sioux, Iowa, where his followers gathered. Sometime before 1878, Bishop died, and what few followers were left of his group joined with the RLDS Church.

TRUE CHURCH OF JESUS CHRIST OF LATTER DAY SAINTS
(Law, Foster, Higbee)

In the spring of 1844, a new church was founded at Nauvoo, whose leaders had been prominent in the LDS Church. William Law, one time second counselor in the First Presidency, joined with Wilson Law, Robert D. and Charles A. Foster, Francis M. and Chauncey L. Higbee, and Charles Ivins in opposing the practice of plural marriage which was rumored to be taking place in secret among a select group of the LDS Church's higher officials.

Secret meetings were held to discuss how to dispose of the Prophet Joseph Smith, and William Law was chosen as the new prophet.

The group succeeded in publishing a prospectus for the *Nauvoo Expositor* in May of 1844, and in printing the first and only issue of the paper on June 7, 1844.

Joseph Smith, the Mayor of Nauvoo and his city council declared the paper a public nuisance and the press was ordered destroyed. Unfortunately, this action seems only to have set off an explosive chain of events in the region which eventually led to the assassination of Joseph Smith and his brother Hyrum at Carthage Jail on June 27, 1844.

Thomas C. Sharp's *Warsaw Signal,* published weekly in nearby Warsaw, Illinois, was the unofficial voice of the anti-Mormon sentiments in Hancock and surrounding counties.

Just five days after the *Nauvoo Expositor* made its appearance, the *Warsaw Signal* of June 12, 1844, contained both a column of praise for the *Expositor* and a brief summary of its contents, a letter from C. A. Foster describing the destruction of the press, and a commentary, probably written by Sharp, which called for the surrounding communities to unite in violence against Nauvoo.

Quoting in part: "We have received the first number of this long looked for paper...the first number contains a long exposition of the views of the new church, or dissenters. They still adhere to the doctrines originally taught by Joe, 'which is contained in the Old and New Testament, the Book of Mormon, and Doctrine and Covenants, as verily true.' They speak of Joe as the embodiment of every abomination, and state the reasons why they have not heretofore exposed him—which is, that they had hoped that gentle reproof in private would produce reform."

In commenting on the letter from Foster, 'We received the above communicaton by the hands of Charles A. Foster, about ½ past 11 o'clock today. We have only to state, that it is sufficient! War and extermination is inevitable! Citizens ARISE, ONE and ALL!!! Can you stand by, and suffer such INFERNAL DEVILS! to rob men of their property and rights, without avenging them. We have no time for comment, every man will make his own. LET IT BE MADE WITH POWDER AND BALL!!!"

After Joseph's death, the group disintegrated, with its members scattering to various places around the country.

The single issue of the *Expositor* has been reprinted several times. The first in the 1890s by the Temple Lot group, during the court proceedings with the RLDS Church over the ownership of the temple property. This was before the era of photolithographic printing processes, and the type was set by hand. Nevertheless, it is a faithful reproduction. Another reprint was done by Robert L. Maley of the Book of Mormon Foundation, date unknown. Maley's plates were used by David C. Martin in printing yet another edition in the early 1970s.

PART 2—1844-1982

At the Prophet Joseph Smith's death, the church became seriously fragmented over the question of leadership and successorship. Many proposals and claims were presented to members of the church. Some followed one, some followed others. Many groups which have survived to the present day maintain that, for one reason or another, they are the legal successor to the church of 1844, or a fragment of that church which has continued without interruption.

I have not singled out any one church as the "divine" continuation of the original church, but will present the claims of each to the best of my understanding.

In the text that follows, references to *LDS Church* or *Mormon Church* will specifically refer to that portion of the church who followed Brigham Young to Utah.

THE CHURCH OF JESUS CHRIST OF LATTER-DAY SAINTS
(Mormon)

At the Prophet's death there were many who came forth with proposals for the continuation of the church leadership. Sidney Rigdon, James J. Strang and others each had a claim for leadership. Most of the members of the church in the Nauvoo, Illinois and surrounding areas chose to follow Brigham Young, President of the Quorum of the Twelve Apostles—whose leadership claims were based on Doctrine and Covenants, section 107.

At a meeting held in Nauvoo on August 8, 1844, a unanimous vote of the members of the church who were present chose the Quorum of Twelve as the leading body of the church. Many have claimed that they saw Brigham Young transfigured into the likeness of Joseph Smith during his speech before that assembly. (Roberts, *Comprehensive History of the Church,* Volume 2, pp. 418-419)

The church made its way to Utah in a history making exodus that actually extended over a period of many years. From its home base in Salt Lake City, the church has sent missionaries the world over and established itself firmly in almost 100 countries, with thousands of congregations and more than 4.5 million members—which number is continually growing.

Popularly known by the nickname *Mormon Church,* its doctrine and other literature is published to the world by several privately owned companies in addition to the church's own publishing house. A concentrated public relations effort and extensive tours by the renowned Mormon Tabernacle Choir have gained respect for the church from people of all walks of life.

Temples, wherein members of the church perform ordinances of eternal salvation for dead ancestors and themselves, have been and are being built around the world.

Doctrine

Articles of Faith

In 1842, Joseph Smith wrote a brief history of the church and a basic summary of its beliefs for John Wentworth, publisher of the *Chicago Democrat.* This letter, commonly referred to in church circles as the *Wentworth Letter* was printed in its entirety in the *Times and Seasons,* Volume 3, Number 9, March 1, 1842, at Nauvoo, Illinois. It was therein that what is now known as the *Articles of Faith* in the Pearl of Great Price, first appeared. Quoting:

We believe in God the Eternal Father, and in his son Jesus Christ, and in the Holy Ghost.

We believe that men will be punished for their own sins and not for Adam's transgressions.

We believe that through the atonement of Christ all mankind may be saved by obedience to the laws and ordinances of the Gospel.

We believe that these ordinances are 1st, Faith in the Lord Jesus Christ; 2d, Repentance; 3d, Baptism by immersion for the remission of sins; 4th, Laying on of hands for the gift of the Holy Ghost.

We believe that a man must be called of God by prophecy, and by laying on of hands by those who are in authority to preach the gospel and administer in the ordinances thereof.

We believe in the same organization that existed in the primitive church, viz: apostles, prophets, pastors, teachers, evangelists, etc.

We believe in the gift of tongues, prophecy, revelation, visions, healing, interpretation of tongues, etc.

We believe the bible to be the word of God as far as it is translated correctly; we also believe the Book of Mormon to be the word of God.

We believe all that God has revealed, all that he does now reveal, and we believe that he will yet reveal many great and important things pertaining to the kingdom of God.

We believe in the literal gathering of Israel and in the restoration of the Ten Tribes. That Zion will be built upon this continent (ie American continent). That Christ will reign personally upon the earth, and that the earth will be renewed and receive its paradasaic glory.

We claim the privilege of worshipping Almighty God according to the dictates of our conscience, and allow all men the same privilege let them worship how, where, or what they may.

We believe in being subject to kings, presidents, rulers, and magistrates, in obeying, honoring and sustaining the law.

We believe in being honest, true, chaste, benevolent, virtuous, and in doing good to all men; indeed we may say that we follow the admonition of Paul, we believe all things, we hope all things, we have endured many things and hope to be able to endure all things. If there is anything virtuous, lovely, or of good report or praiseworthy we seek after these things.

Godhead

The church teaches that there are three distinct and individual beings which compose the godhead: God, Jesus Christ and the Holy Ghost. The first two are viewed as beings like man, with flesh and bone, the third a personage of spirit. The church also teaches that man may at some future time in his eternal progression become a god—also that God was once a man. A very enlightening explanation of the church's doctrine on this subject can be found in Volume 6 of the *Journal of Discourses,* beginning on page 1 and continuing through page 11. This discourse was given by Joseph Smith, Jr. in Nauvoo, Illinois on April 6, 1844, during a conference of the church.

Plan of Salvation

Teaching that all mankind existed as literal spirit children of our Father in Heaven in the pre-existence, man came to this earth having a veil drawn across his mind so previous memory became hidden in order that he might gain a body of flesh and bone and learn to choose between good and evil for himself. After death, man's body is placed in the grave and his spirit goes to the spirit world where he will reside either in paradise or prison, depending on how he lived on earth and whether or not he accepted the gospel of Jesus Christ. If he did not, he will have another chance in the spirit prison to learn and accept or reject the gospel. At the time of the resurrection, all mankind will have their spirits and bodies eternally and inseparably reunited, whereupon they will be judged and placed in one of several kingdoms. The most righteous will reside in the Celestial Kingdom, along with all three members of the Godhead. Next is the Terrestrial kingdom, where only Jesus and the Holy Ghost will share their presence. The least of the kingdoms is the Telestial. Only the Holy Ghost will present himself to those living here. The followers of Satan will be cast into outer darkness.

Because it is believed the various ordinances of the gospel must be performed for an individual while he resides on this earth, and many people passed on before being baptized, etc., the church has established temples wherein the living may be baptized on behalf of those who have died. Men are also vicariously ordained to the priesthood, and families are *sealed* in an eternal family unit.

Next to missionary work, this vicarious temple work is considered one of the most important tasks of a church member.

Tithing

Taught as a direct commandment from God, the law of tithing dictates that each member of the church contribute one-tenth of his gross annual income. Tithing monies are used by the church for its operations. Unless a member is a full tithe payer, he is not admitted into the temples of the church. (See Doctrine and Covenants, sections 119, 120)

Word of Wisdom

Originally revealed to Joseph Smith, Jr. in 1833, the Word of Wisdom was for many years considered only as healthful advice. Since the church's move to Utah the words given in the health law have been made binding as a commandment from God by the church leadership.

Members of the church are taught to abstain from smoking tobacco, drinking coffee, tea and liquors and to partake only of the healthful things of the creations of God. The Word of Wisdom may be found in the Doctrine and Covenants, Section 89. As with tithing, only those members fully living this law are admitted within the sacred confines of the temple.

Church Government

Within the church are two priesthoods, to which only male members may be ordained. The lesser, or Aaronic Priesthood, is generally conferred upon the younger male members of the church. Since it is considered a training stage for leadership, the Aaronic Priesthood offices, ranging from Deacon, Teacher to Priest, allow certain responsibilities and assignments to be given to these young men. The Priest, usually conferred upon a 16 year old, has the most responsibility, which includes blessing the Sacrament of Lord's Supper, performing baptisms, and the authority to ordain (under the supervision of the bishop) other young men to offices in the Aaronic Priesthood.

The Melchizedek Priesthood is the higher priesthood in the church. Its offices include Elder, Seventy and High Priest. The missionaries sent by the church are usually Elders. Most other church leaders hold the office of High Priest. Section 20 of the Doctrine and Covenants goes into detail concerning the priesthood responsibilities and church organization.

The church is divided into ecclesiastical units called stakes, which are composed of several small units called wards. In some of the less developed areas, the smaller units are called branches. A stake is usually comprised of 6 to 8 wards.

The ward is presided over by a Bishop and two counselors, who hold the office of High Priest. The stake is led by a Stake President and two counselors, also High Priests. Under the immediate direction of the Stake Presidency is the High Council, comprised of twelve High Priests. These men act as representatives of the Stake Presidency in supervising the affairs of the stake. They also take part in church trials dealing with the membership of an individual in the church.

The church as a whole is a highly centralized organization, with offices in Salt Lake City, Utah, gathering historical, financial and membership records from all of the small divisions. The President of the Church is also Prophet, Seer and Revelator and he alone is able to dictate the conscience of heaven to the members of the church. He is usually assisted by two counselors.

The next quorum of leadership in the church is the Twelve Apostles. All of these men are sustained by members of the church as Prophets, Seers and Revelators—under the supervision of the First President.

Next is the First Quorum of Seventy. These men have the direct responsibility of overseeing the missionary work of the church. This body, along with the First Presidency and Twelve Apostles constitute the General Authorities of the church. The office of Patriarch to the Church was recently discontinued, although since the beginning of the church the office was considered of major importance.

Several auxilliary organizations assist members of the church in both temporal and spiritual matters of importance. The Sunday School provides a place for members of the church to learn about the gospel and church history. The Primary provides similar opportunities for younger members of the church. The Relief Society organization works specifically with the women in the church. Various learning opportunities are provided in fields of spirituality, culture and homemaking. The Relief Society is always prepared to come to the aid of those members of the church in need, whether it be in the event of the death of a loved one, illness, birth of a child or even economic problems.

Publications

Hundreds of publications explaining the doctrine and practices of the church are readily available to the English-reading public, and in many other languages. The Church itself publishes scores of missionary tracts, books, etc. Lesson manuals and teaching aids of various sorts are also part of the material officially prepared by the church.

The church publishes three magazines for its members in English—which are generally combined into one in other languages. These magazines are *The Friend* for young people, *The New Era* for the youth, and the official voice of the church is *The Ensign.*

Scriptures used by the church are known as the *four standard works* and include the Holy Bible (King James Version), The Book of Mormon, the Doctrine and Covenants (a compilation of various revelations and instructions by Joseph Smith, Jr. and some of his successors), and the Pearl of Great Price (which contains the Book of Moses, Book of Abraham, Articles of Faith, and a few excerpts from the writings of Joseph Smith.) All four books are published by the church, and as with each succeeding entry in this volume, scripture references are taken from the particular editions published by the church about which the individual report is being presented.

CHURCH OF JESUS CHRIST OF THE CHILDREN OF ZION
(Sidney Rigdon)

A close associate and counselor to Joseph Smith, Jr. since March, 1832, Sidney Rigdon was well known to most members of the church. He had firm grounds on which he based his claim that the church should appoint him as guardian after the death of the prophet. He was the First Counselor in the First Presidency; the only living member of that body at the time. No precedent in leadership succession in the church had been established, so Rigdon's claim, by virtue of his position, was relatively valid. But as the historical record has shown, few members of the church accepted him as their leader. Brigham Young excommunicated Rigdon in September, 1844.

Undeterred by this confusion and rejection by many members of the church, Rigdon continued in his claims to the leadership of the church and was eventually successful in gathering about him a sizeable membership, including many who had been faithful to the Prophet Joseph.

Proceeding to organize the *Church of Christ,* Sidney Rigdon called Ebenezer Robinson and Samuel James as his counselors. On October 15, 1844, the church began publishing the *Latter Day Saints' Messenger and Advocate* at Pittsburgh, Pennsylvania. This had previously been a publication of the church in the 1830s at Kirtland, Ohio. A gathering place was established at Greencastle, Pennsylvania and subsequently the church, its press and most members relocated to that place.

Originally the church had used the name *Church of Jesus Christ of Latter Day Saints* but the April 1845 conference altered the name to *Church of Christ* which had been the original name of the church established by Joseph Smith. At the same time, the church paper became the *Messenger and Advocate of the Church of Christ.*

The March 15, 1845 issue of the church paper carried the following statement of policy clearly stating the church's position:

Whereas, the connection which has heretofore existed between ourselves and the people calling themselves the Church of Jesus Christ of Latter Day Saints renders it necessary that we publish to the world a succinct statement of facts relating to the position we now sustain to God and our fellow men; and

Whereas, in consequence of the rejection by that people, of what we undoubtedly deem to be the order of the church and kingdom of God, and the introduction of doctrines and practices clearly inimical to the law of God, and altogether subversive of the laws of the land, abrogating the marriage contract, and substituting under the professed sanction of heaven, a system of extreme licentiousness, uprooting every legal restraint, and eminently calculated in its very nature to produce the entire destruction of every virtuous tie, and pouring contempt upon every holy principle contained in the revelations of God to his creature man, and must inevitably entail upon that people abject wretchedness and woe, subjecting them to the righteous condemnation of every virtuous intelligence, whether in heaven or on earth; and

Whereas, the better to conceal the justly odious system of polygamy, duplicity, hypocrisy, and falsehood are inculcated as virtues, the most sacred obligations constantly violated, and families and individuals plunged into irrevocable ruin and despair; therefore

Resolved, that we hold no fellowship with the people calling themselves the Church of Jesus Christ of Latter Day Saints, and can have no communion with them, unless they repent and obey the principles of righteousness and truth.

Resolved, that we maintain the truth and the truth only, at all hazards, renouncing at once and forever, the unsanctifying dogma that it is sometimes lawful to lie.

Resolved, that we maintain and do earnestly contend for the faith which was once, and is again, delivered to the saints, contained in the Bible, Book of Mormon and Book of Covenants.

Resolved, that we feel it a solemn and imperative obligation we owe to God and our fellow men to disseminate to the extent of our ability, correct information regarding certain pernicious doctrines and practices which are secretly taught by the leaders and many members of the society called the Church of Jesus Christ of Latter Day Saints; verily believing them demoralizing and destructive, combining all the worst features of barbarism, and containing all the elements of the wildest anarchy, and would if unchecked by the power of truth, ultimately extinguish the species. (*Messenger and Advocate,* Volume 1, page 176)

A complete church organization was effected with a Quorum of Twelve Apostles, patriarch, seventies, high council, bishopric, etc. A stake established at Pittsburgh was presided over by a duly constituted Stake Presidency.

In addition to what was contained in the books of holy writ previously mentioned, Rigdon added to the canon of latter day scripture many messages which he presented to the world as direct revelation from God.

Rigdon's group began to disintegrate in the fall of 1846 during a conference at which Rigdon apparently began teaching doctrines that many members could not agree with. By the new year, the church was virtually extinct, although a few scattered branches and individuals remained faithful to the cause.

Rigdon moved to Friendship, New York with his family. In the 1850s he began corresponding with Stephen Post, at one time a Strangite faithful. This correspondence continued for several years, during which time Post became convinced of Rigdon's claims as a prophet.

Early in 1861, a former member of Rigdon's first church, Joseph Newton, also began correspondence. Newton started preaching and baptizing in the Philadelphia, Pennsylvania area. Although Rigdon seems to have discouraged Newton's efforts, enough people had gathered that Sidney Rigdon was moved upon to visit in the spring of 1863. (See *BYU Studies,* Volume 21, Number 1, Winter, 1981, p. 55). At that time Rigdon organized the *Church of Jesus Christ of the Children of Zion.* The next year, Rigdon counseled Post to move the church to Iowa.

Rigdon never made the move, but his largest congregation was settled in Attica, Iowa. Post and Newton were made counselors to Rigdon and a new Quorum of Twelve Apostles was established.

Several years passed, during which time Rigdon ran the church by mail. However, in 1869 Joseph Newton and John A. Forgeus, president of the Twelve, were both excommunicated. In 1875 the main body of the church moved to Canada.

Sidney Rigdon died in 1876 at Friendship, New York. He remained faithful to his testimony of the truthfulness of the Book of Mormon, but never reconciled with any of the other church leaders from Joseph Smith's time. For several years after his death, many followers remained faithful to the cause, but without Rigdon's leadership, the group was doomed.

Publications

Rigdon's first group published two volumes of the *Messenger and Advocate,* two broadsides expressing their views, and a hymnal which was printed in Pittsburgh in 1845.

The later group published three known pamphlets. In 1863 at Philadelphia, *An Appeal to the Latter Day Saints* by Joseph H. Newton, William Richards and William Stanley. This 72 page book discussed their views of the gospel and true priesthood authority. Their concluding remark: "If Sidney Rigdon does not convert the Lamanites, restore the tribes of Jacob, bring Salvation to Zion, and purify the Saints, so they can see the face of the Lord; and if, under his administration, the blind do not see, the lame walk, the dumb speak, the heavens shake, and the arm of the Lord be revealed in power, in convincing the nations: then, indeed the books of revelation we have are a tissue of falsehoods, and all our religion vain; Joseph Smith, a base falsifier, an imp of Satan, instead of a prophet of the living God."

Another publication was *Zion's Messenger* by Stephen Post and William Hamilton; and *A Treatise on the Melchisedek Priesthood and the Callings of God* by Stephen Post.

JOHN E. PAGE

Some sources indicate that John E. Page led an independent group of followers as early as 1844 or 1845.

John E. Page became a member of the Twelve Apostles under Joseph Smith, Jr. in 1838 and was disfellowshipped by Brigham Young on February 9, 1846. In June of the same year, Page was formally excommunicated.

An entry in Volume 1, pp. 92-96 of the *Latter-day Saint Biographical Encyclopedia* (1901, Salt Lake City), indicates that Page's actions as a member of the Twelve in the eastern United States in late 1843 and early 1844 had met with disapproval on more than one occasion. It was also noted that upon learning of the death of Joseph Smith, Page advertised in a Pennsylvania newspaper that he would preach for anyone who would sustain his family.

After his disfellowshipment at Nauvoo, it is reported that Page encouraged many members of the church to follow James J. Strang and to gather to Voree, Wisconsin.

A one volume history of the Mormon Church, published in 1976 indicated that "William Marks...attached himself in 1855 to another group headed by former apostle John E. Page." (Allen and Leonard, *The Story of the Latter-day Saints,* Salt Lake City:Deseret Book Company, 1976, p. 241.)

At a conference of the *Hedrickites* in November of 1862, John E. Page formally associated with that group and on May 17, 1863, ordained several members of that church to the office of Apostle. The following July 18, Page and others ordained Granville Hedrick to the office of President of the High Priesthood and President of the Church. (See *Outline History of the Church of Christ-Temple Lot,* p. 102 and *The Story of the Church,* RLDS Church, pp. 434-435.)

Page remained a member of the Church of Christ until his death. However, Inez Smith Davis records "his wife states that Elder Page expressed disappointment with that affiliation on his deathbed..." (Davis, Inez Smith, *The Story of the Church,* Independence, Missouri: Herald Publishing House, 1959, p. 434)

It is possible that while Page may have never organized a church of his own he did gather about him those who felt unable to follow any of the various leaders claiming to be the true prophet at that time.

CHURCH OF JESUS CHRIST OF LATTER DAY SAINTS (STRANGITE)

Having been a member of the LDS Church for just a few short months, James Jesse Strang was one of the most prominent and successful leaders to emerge from the turmoil which surrounded the church after the death of the Prophet.

A resident of Wisconsin, Strang had joined the church early in 1844. Shortly after the Prophet's death, he produced a letter, purporting to have been written on June 18, 1844 by Joseph Smith, appointing Strang as his successor and commanding the Twelve Apostles to proclaim Voree, Wisconsin as the gathering place. (See Roberts, *Comprehensive History of the Church,* Volume 2, page 429.) In part, this letter states: "And now behold my servant James J. Strang hath come to thee from far for truth when he knew it not, and hath not rejected it, but had faith in thee, the Shepherd and Stone of Israel, and to him shall the gathering of the people be, for he shall plant a stake of Zion in Wisconsin, and I will establish it; and there shall my people have peace and rest, and shall not be moved, for it shall be established on the prairie on White River, in the lands of Racine and Walworth; and behold my servants James and Aaron [Smith] shall plant it, for I have given them wisdom..." (In a letter from James J. Strang to Mrs. Cory, September 26, 1854.)

The letter continues for several paragraphs, in the language of revelation from God, which is what the writer states it is, and talks about gathering the Saints, etc. The closing paragraph states: "And now I command my servants, the Apostles and Priests and Elders of the church of the Saints, that they communicate and proclaim this my word to all the Saints of God in all the world, that they may be gathered unto and round my city of Voree, and be saved from their enemies, for I will have a people to serve me." And all this above the signature of Joseph Smith. The authenticity of this letter has been established to the satisfaction of the Strangite faithful.

If this letter was in fact written under inspiration and revelation from God, then Strang had a very strong position in his favor in light of LDS Doctrine and Covenants, Section 43:4, which states: "But verily, verily I say unto you, that none else shall be appointed unto this gift [that of receiving revelations and God's word for the church] except it be through him [Joseph Smith] for if it be taken from him, he shall not have power except to appoint another in his stead." (See also Book of Commandments-1833 45:4, RLDS D & C 43:2a.)

With this strong argument backing his claim, Strang persuaded many prominent church leaders and members to follow him, including John E. Page, William Smith, William Marks (former Nauvoo Stake President) and several members of the Smith family.

On June 27, 1844 at 5:30 p.m., an angel of the Lord appeared to Strang and ordained him as the successor to Joseph Smith. The reader will note the date and time as that of the death of Joseph Smith, Jr. Of all the early claimants to the leadership of the church, Strang is alone in claiming divine ordination.

Strang first led his people to Voree (Burlington), Wisconsin, but by 1850 most of his followers had settled on Beaver Island in the northern end of Lake Michigan. There they established a thriving community, a kingdom of God.

In 1850 Strang was crowned King in an elaborately staged ceremony, and effected a complicated church government system which is no longer followed due to the present situation of the church and its smallness of numbers. This complex church organizaton is explained in great detail in *The Book of the Law of the Lord.*

For several years prior to his death, Strang's following rivaled that of Brigham Young!

On June 16, 1856, two men attacked Strang and inflicted a mortal wound. Anti-Mormon sentiments were aroused in the area, and after Strang's demise about 2000 of his followers were evicted from Beaver Island by force—many left the church never to return. His death and the circumstances surrounding it were simply too much for a people who had suffered persecution of every type for so many years.

Unfortunately, Strang did not appoint a successor before he died. In fact, several church properties are being held in trust to this date in expectation and hope that God will appoint a successor to Strang. The church is currently administered by a Presiding High Priest.

Without a leader, the church membership dwindled while the apostles exerted every effort to find a leader. Joseph Smith, III was approached in 1863; James' son Charles was approached in 1882—but the church was unsuccessful on both counts.

Lorenzo Dow Hickey became the leader of the church, and in 1897 ordained Wingfield Watson as his successor and Presiding High Priest. (letter to the author from Bruce Flanders, March 29, 1975.) Watson had lived on Beaver Island, known Strang and been a faithful member of the church for most of his life. He was a dynamic leader and prolific author. Watson died in 1923. Vernon Swift heads the church today, a position to which he was ordained at a conference in 1955.

Another important event rocked the conference in that same year, and the outcome was a split in the church. Theron Drew led part of the church away from the main body, filed a lawsuit against the church for property and was judged successful. His position will be presented later.

The church presently has several hundred members settled in Wisconsin, Michigan, Colorado and New Mexico.

Doctrine

The Sabbath

Saturday, the seventh day, is regarded as the true day of rest and worship. It is believed that early Christians met on the first day of the week also (Sunday), in order to avoid the pagan festivals of the era. When the Roman emperor Constantine declared himself

Pope, he ordered Sunday to be the day of worship for all, at the same time making Christianity (Catholicism) the national religion. (See *Book of the Law of the Lord,* 1948, pp. 22-23)

In a letter from Brother Flanders, March 12, 1973, he explains: "It is known that Joseph Smith kept the Sabbath on the seventh day and held meetings on the first day as well for the benefit of those who lived by Christian traditions. It would seem that keeping the Sabbath was dropped after the exodus from Nauvoo."

Temples

Strang's letter of appointment spoke of an edifice being built at Voree. It has been indicated to me that such a structure was started but never finished due to the circumstances of Strang's death. Perhaps at some future date a temple will be constructed.

Eucharist

Known as *sacrament* or *communion* in some churches, the eucharist commemorates the sacrifice of Jesus Christ. Although not a deity, he was called of God to perform the sacrifice and receive the keys of the resurrection. Having led a perfectly righteous and pure life, and by performing this great and infinite sacrifice, he became exalted by his Father and became a God and the Father of the world to come. (See *Book of the Law of the Lord,* 1948, pp. 147-158.)

As to the nature of the eucharistic symbols, I quote from pages 145-146 from *The Book of the Law of the Lord:*

"Wine is to be preferred for the blood of the sacrifice, and bread of wheat for the flesh; but the expressed juice of any edible fruit whatever is lawful, and bread of any grain. No article of commerce should be used for wine, on account of the practice of adulterating so perfectly that the fraud cannot be detected...

"Jesus Christ was the real sacrifice, of which the bread and wine are the symbols. By consecration, and not by any change in their physical nature, structure or identity, they become the body and blood of Christ, that by eating them we may truly feast upon him as a sacrifice and live."

Sacrifice

This one doctrine, above all others, sets the Strangite Church apart from most other followers of Joseph Smith.

From the *Book of the Law of the Lord,* pages 106-107:

"Thou shalt offer upon the altar of the Lord thy God, and before his Priests, sacrifices for sin offerings, and for trespass offerings, and for memorials, and for peace offerings, and for thank offerings.

"Thy offerings shall be of the firstlings of thy flocks, and of the choice of thy fields, and of the chief of all holy things.

"Of thy flock shalt thou offer the firstling of male or female, without deformity or blemish, of such as divide the hoof and chew the cud; and of fowls, shalt thou offer all singing birds; and of fishes, all that have scales and fins; and of shell fish, such as have two shells, and move about from place to place: these shall be holy unto the Lord thy God, and shall be offered upon the altar.

"Of the choice of thy fields, that which is good for food without change or addition, and whatsoever is used for bread for man, that is holy unto the Lord thy God, and shall be offered unto him as an offering, and lifted up to the Priest; but it shall not be offered on the altar.

"And whatsoever other thing ye offer, it shall be accompanied with one of these, and thus thy gift shall be sanctified. But if it be not accompanied with one of these, thou shalt redeem it at the Priest's valuation, and it and the price thereof shall be the Lord's."

The doctrine is not currently practiced. It is generally conceded that the Prophet would need to be a functioning office in order to have sufficient priesthood for this holy ordinance. The day of sacrifice is observed with feasting.

Other Beliefs

The Book of the Law of the Lord explains to great length and detail the various doctrines of the church, many of which are very similar to the Mormon Church, previously discussed. However, without a properly designated Prophet, many of the ordinances of the church can be held only as theoretical.

The following summary of church doctrine is taken from a letter from Bruce Flanders, March 31, 1972:

We believe in the ordinance of baptism for the dead, but we do not practice it since it is to be carried out under the direction of a prophet, an office which we do not now claim in the church.

We believe that this religion is a revealed religion, that is, it was revealed in the beginning and continues to be revealed constantly to those who seek its mysteries. As far as revelation concerning the direction of the church or further laws governing the people, there have been no such since the days of the prophet Strang.

This is not to say that we do not feel all has been given, but we understand that the period which we are now passing through is an interim between the gentile dispensation and the dispensation to the House of Israel which must come in before the Savior comes again.

We follow the law of tithing (one-tenth of one's gain) as closely as possible. Due to the scattered condition of our people, it is not 100% in effect, but in the active branches such as this one in

Voree (Burlington), it is nearly unanimously adhered to.

The law of consecration and stewardship like many other laws which are a part of the Kingdom function will be made effective when the kingdom is again established within the dominion.

We teach that marriage for time and eternity is available to those who are members in good standing and who desire such a bond. Otherwise, marriage is for life and only a careless person or one not truly converted would deny themselves such a blessing.

Polygamy was instituted under the prophet James as an extension of the law of inheritance. It can only be practiced by a very righteous people. Certainly today's immoral attitude would tend to destroy the meaning of such a practice, and too great an emphasis would be placed on the physical conditions involved.

There were few plural marriages during the latter part of the prophet Strang's ministry. I do not know how many. To my knowledge, there were no plural marriages contracted after the prophet's death. The Church has not taken direct action against the practice, but by common consent, the practice was given up.

Voree is the one gathering place that was set aside as a place of refuge for the people, and the promises which were made at its selection are still in full effect 126 years later. (Letter in author's file.)

Publications

Dale L. Morgan published a complete bibliography in the early 1950s listing and describing every known publication printed by the Church or those associated with it. It offers excellent source material, so I will offer but brief comments here.

Although the church does not print its own editions, the King James Version of the Bible, the Book of Mormon and the Doctrine and Covenants are standard scriptures, along with The Book of the Law of the Lord, which has been referred to often in this report. This volume of some 330 pages (1948 edition) consists of an inspired translation of some of the most important parts of the Law given to Moses, and a very few additional commandments, with notes and references. The original of this book was considered the most important of the books, many of which now make up the Bible, and thus was kept in the Ark of the Covenant. This book was translated from an authorized copy of that book, made upon metallic plates before the Babylonian captivity. Book of Mormon believers know this record as the *Brass Plates of Laban.*

This testimony is printed in the front of the book:

"Be it known unto all nations, kindred, tongues and people, to whom this Book of the Law of the Lord shall come, that James

J. Strang has the plates of the ancient Book of the Law of the Lord given to Moses, from which he translated this law and has shown them to us. We examined them with our eyes, and handled them with our hands. The engravings are beautiful antique workmanship, bearing a striking resemblance to the ancient oriental languages; and those from which the laws of this book were translated are eighteen in number, about seven inches and three-eights wide by nine inches long, occasionally embellished with beautiful pictures.

"And we testify unto you all that the everlasting kingdom of God is established, in which this law shall be kept, till it brings in rest and everlasting righteousness to all the faithful.

"Samuel Graham, Albert N. Hosmer, Samuel P. Bacon, Ebenezar Page, Phineas Wright, Warren Post, Jehial Savage."

The book was first published in 1851, with an enlarged edition published in 1855. A reprint was done by the church in 1948.

Having set up a printing facility at Saint James (city on Beaver Island) the church set about publishing a paper, books and various other publications. All publishing operations ceased when the island was evacuated in 1856 after Strang's death.

After the church members regrouped and began to rebuild their lives, homes and church, others took up the cause and throughout the years a number of publications have been issued, including a book of Strang's revelations, published in 1939. More recently Wingfield Watson's series called *The Prophetic Controversy* has been reprinted, along with some new books of more recent authorship.

The church has been publishing a quarterly entitled *The Gospel Herald* which comments on doctrine, news of the church, etc. This publication began in the late 1960s.

CHURCH OF JESUS CHRIST OF LATTER DAY SAINTS (Lyman Wight)

A member of the Twelve Apostles under Joseph Smith, Jr., Lyman Wight was called upon to serve various assignments and missions.

Shortly before Smith's death, plans were being made to move some colonies of the church west. Texas, a newly formed republic, had been considered as a possible place for the Saints to find refuge. The plan, however, was tabled when the Mormons tried to have Joseph Smith elected President of the United States.

A special company had been formed in order to secure lumber for the temple at Nauvoo, but it was in fact the beginnings of the proposed Texas colony. Lyman Wight and Bishop George Miller had been appointed to head this company. After Joseph's death, Wight attempted to convince Brigham Young to let him go ahead with the plan to lead a colony to Texas. The two men were in disagreement and Wight, having been given a divine commission from the Prophet Joseph, felt he must go ahead with the plan and led a group of about 150 people to a place near Austin, Texas.

Several natural disasters caused the colony to move about in order to obtain suitable land for farming. Finally in 1847 a place near Fredricksburg, Texas on the Pedernales river was located. Here a community named Zodiac was founded.

In 1848 George Miller joined Wight after a quarrel with Brigham Young. However, by the summer of 1849, Miller had become convinced that James J. Strang was the rightful successor to Smith and left the colony to join with Strang in Wisconsin-Michigan.

On January 1, 1849, the colony formally organized the church with Lyman Wight as President, although he never thought of himself as the successor to Joseph Smith.

The upper floor of the storehouse was finished on February 17 and it was dedicated as a temple of the Lord. Anointings, feet washing and possibly other Nauvoo era temple ordinances were introduced. Earlier this same month, on the 12th, Brigham Young had formally excommunicated Wight from the Mormon Church.

In the fall of 1849, Lyman Wight joined forces with William Smith's church organization at Covington, Kentucky. In a revelation received by Smith, Wight was chosen a member of the First Presidency of that church, and admonished to continue with his mission of establishing a colony in Texas. A conference of the church at Zodiac voted to accept William Smith as the head of the church in November. It was agreed that this arrangement was only temporary—until "young Joseph" was able to claim his position as the successor to his father. After the demise of Smith's organization Wight's group merely continued as they had previous to the merger. (See *Lyman Wight Colony in Texas,* J. Marvin Hunter, pp. 16-18.)

The colony was forced to move in 1851 due to severe flooding, and moved again in 1853 when they settled near Bandera, Texas.

In 1858, Wight set out on a mission to the Indians and appears to have been planning to go into Mexico and possibly further south. Wight died suddenly on March 30, 1858 near San Antonio, Texas. He was buried at the old colony of Zodiac. Most of his followers united with the Reorganized LDS Church.

Doctrine

Lyman Wight and his followers practiced the same basic church organization and doctrines as had been followed in Nauvoo. No new scriptural works were introduced. The group did attempt to live the law of consecration, as had been attempted in Missouri in the early 1830s. It would appear that this group was quite successful in their goal and lived a community way of life quite peacefully.

Publications

The only known publication of Lyman Wight is a pamphlet entitled *An Address by Way of an Abridged Account and Journal of My Life from February 1844 up to April 1848, With an Appeal to the Latter Day Saints, Scattered Abroad in the Earth.* In this way Wight replied to the various accusations which had been made against him by Brigham Young and the Twelve since he left Nauvoo. He also appealed to the reader to come and join him and his people in Texas.

In a letter written to James J. Strang in July 1855, Wight stated, "I consider my mission and calling the same as Peter's was after the death of Christ who taught him in his life time and left without a successor."

CHURCH OF CHRIST (Aaron Smith)

Aaron Smith, James J. Strang's brother-in-law and a member of Strang's first presidency, led a short lived split from the group in July of 1846. John C. Bennett, former Nauvoo Mayor, was given considerable prominence in Strang's church organization. A council had been called to try Bennett on the charge of immorality, and Strang sided with Bennett, embittering Smith.

This group attempted a periodical, *The New Era and Herald of Zion's Watchmen*, from which I quote:

"Our motto—truth vindicated and primitive Mormonism revived. No absolute sovereign but God the Father. No King in time but Jesus Christ. No Pontiff, Premier or General in Chief. No secret combinations or oath bound societies. No resistance to the laws or constitution of the United States. The foundation of our faith—Bible, Book of Mormon, Book of Doctrine and Covenants." (Volume 1, Number 1, January 1847.)

Smith eventually joined with the RLDS Church and later went with H. H. Deam.

INDIAN MORMON

Quoting from an article which appeared November 17, 1846, in the Cincinnati, Ohio *Commercial*:

"We mentioned, a few days since, that a big Indian Mormon had visited our city with his wife, and proclaimed himself 'the Lord Jesus Christ'!, established apostleship, and proceeded to organize a church of followers, numbering in male and female, some sixty persons. Having finished his mission he went back to Louisville. After arriving there he wrote back to his brethren here, that he thought the Lord's work was not fully completed. Money was sent him to bear his expenses up, and he accordingly arrived in our city last week. We understand that his first act was to dispense blessings to his fold, individually, but whether he sells them or not, we are yet ignorant. The following is a form of the blessing, the first part being written so as to be read on the back of the paper, and is read backwards. The whole is written with an iron pen, (a sort of keel) on white paper: 'Pledge of confidence Indian natural fluest and Lucella Bhuba, his Delaware wife: Accept this blessing in the name of the Son, Jesus Christ, Mary the Mother, God the Father our Father, our Lord. Amen. It will preserve yours, yourself, your dead, your family through this life into celestial kingdom, your name is written in the Lamb's book of Life. Amen.'

"The above is an exact copy, and strange to say, is kept very secret; and it is highly prized by the new sect now numbering not over thirty."

No further information is available.

CHURCH OF CHRIST (McLellin/Whitmer)

One of the most colorful characters of early LDS Church history was William E. McLellin. He joined the church shortly after its organization, and later was called as one of the original members of the Twelve Apostles.

As church history records, the Missouri problems of the church created many difficulties in 1838 and a number of prominent church leaders were removed from the body. McLellin was among these excommunicants.

In the mid-1840s McLellin was associated at different times with George M. Hinckle, William Law and later Sidney Rigdon. In January of 1847, a conference was called by McLellin to be held at Kirtland, Ohio where it was announced that a new church had been organized to be led by David Whitmer.

McLellin reminded church members that Whitmer had been publicly designated by Joseph Smith as his successor at a conference of the church in 1834. He records, quoting Joseph Smith: "Now, brethren, there has been an anxiety in the minds of many to know who, if I should be taken, would be the one to lead the church in my stead. I want now to put that matter to rest. Joseph then called David Whitmer forward and said, This is the Man. He then with others laid his hands upon him, and ordained him to his station." (*Ensign of Liberty,* Volume 1, Number 1, Kirtland, Ohio, March 1847, page 6)

Martin Harris was one who supported this move, and the church was organized under the name of the *Church of Christ.* A periodical, *The Ensign of Liberty* was published beginning March, 1847 at Kirtland. Seven issues were published, but towards the end at lengthy delays. Issue number seven was published more than one year after issue number six.

David Whitmer was living in Missouri at the time and it appears that he never made the trip to Kirtland or formally accepted the position being offered by McLellin.

The church gradually dissolved and a number of years later, David Whitmer and some faithful followers succeeded in organizing a mildly successful church. A later entry will discuss this group.

McLellin eventually moved to Independence, Missouri and joined with the Hedrickites in the 1860s, but soon left them and remained unchurched until his death.

GEORGE MILLER

George Miller, a Bishop in the church under Joseph Smith, began the westward trek with Brigham Young, but became disillusioned at Winter Quarters in 1847 and led a small group of followers south toward Texas. They made their way to Lyman Wight's colony and joined with them.

On the trek south, Miller preached the gospel to the Indians and became so successful that other ministers petitioned the government authorities to ban his preaching. Regular church meetings were conducted by Miller's group.

After a short sojourn with Wight, Miller joined with James J. Strang in 1849, after claiming to be the recipient of divine manifestations.

SAMUEL JAMES/GEORGE M. HINCKLE

George M. Hinckle had attempted a church organization early in the 1840s, but later joined forces with Sidney Rigdon. When Rigdon's group began to fall apart in 1847, Hinckle and Samuel James (a member of Rigdon's first presidency) attempted to establish a church of their own.

Remarks made by William McLellin in the *Ensign of Liberty* in the December 1847 issue, on page 35: "On the 6th of October [1847], we attended a little meeting, called a general conference of the Hinkleites, in Mercer Co., Illinois. Here we saw and heard queer things. Samuel James, S. Rigdon's left hand man, professes, and told it publicly, that while he was operating with Rigdon in the fall of 1845, while in Philadelphia, three personages in the garb and appearance of women, whom he believed to be angels appeared to him, and contrary to his wishes placed Rigdon's crown upon his head. He told me that in 1846, he received a commandment from God to organize a first presidency for the whole church, himself as Seer, of course—and that it was the privilege of G. M. Hinkle and James Blakeslee to be his counselors."

In the May 1848 issue of the same paper, page 90, McLellin added: "...Samuel James, and George M. Hinkle, during '47, found their way from the death-groans of Rigdonism in the [Cumberland] valley, to the fertile plains of Illinois, and there tried to resurrect and again rear up the fallen kingdom; but a late letter from a valued friend in that region [says] 'There is nothing more of James and his man George—their ism has breathed its last."

CONGREGATION OF JEHOVAH'S PRESBYTERY OF ZION
(Charles B. Thompson)

Having learned of Mormonism, Charles Blancher Thompson traveled from New York to Kirtland, Ohio, in February 1835 to be baptized. He served for several years as a missionary in New York and in 1843 he joined the Saints in Nauvoo, but became dissatisfied in 1846 and joined with James J. Strang.

By the fall of 1847 he was in St. Louis, Missouri and in January, 1848 he published a leaflet in which he announced that he had been commanded by God to "organize schools of Preparation, for the Order of the Priesthood of Regeneration and Restitution." He claimed that the LDS Church had been rejected by God at the death of Joseph Smith in 1844, and that no more church organizations were to be created until Zion had been redeemed. Thompson had been given the necessary authority to organize subsidiary groups to aid in the work of redemption. He also stated that he was "Ephraim born again among the Gentiles, and Baneemy, Patriarch of Zion, Patriarch and Apostle of the Free and Accepted Order of Baneemy and Fraternity of the Sons of Zion."

Dale Morgan has left an interesting narrative: "Beyond any of his contemporaries save Joseph Morris, the Utah prophet of the next decade, Thompson had a taste and talent for metaphysics, and for his church he worked out a complex doctrine and structure, with interesting Masonic overtones. No effort can be made here to expound his doctrine system, but the duty laid upon Thompson to act as Chief Teacher in the 'Schools of Preparation' had as its corollary the principle of gathering. The place chosen was Monona County, in western Iowa, where the new settlement was given the name Preparation. The church organization itself was called Jehovah's Presbytery of Zion. Among other things, the Presbytery was an experimental communism, with Thompson in full control of the community resources, and this had a great deal to do with the explosion which came in October, 1858, the leader being chased for miles across the open prairie before he outpaced his followers.

"A litigation ensued which lasted till 1867, when the one-time members of his church won out over Thompson in the Iowa Supreme Court. Meanwhile he had returned to St. Louis. Presumably at this period and for some time after he supported himself at his trade as a tailor. At a later date not yet fixed he moved to Philadelphia. City directories place him there by 1879 and it was Philadelphia which saw Thompson's final creative effort in the field of religion.

"This last phase of Thompson's career is mainly recorded in a little manuscript book preserved in the Reorganized Church library, into which are copied some of Thompson's covenants, with the names of those who subscribed to them—a pathetic little following of half a dozen persons. Although two baptisms are recorded as early as October, 1883, these may not have been performed by church authority, and the ms record is more properly concerned with the period July, 1885-July 1889. Thompson managed to get out a periodical *Cypiz Herald and IABBA's Evangel,* and a dispute arose about the paper. His principal convert wanted the papers given away and Thompson wanted to sell them; the convert would not permit Thompson the use of his hall to preach in unless he yielded, so as a note in Thompson's own handwriting attests, 'I took the papers away with his consent to another place.' One last note read, 'Date of Brother Thompson leaving July 14th 1889.'

"Although Thompson cut himself off from these converts, he may have continued his struggle for a following. The Philadelphia directories list 'C. Blancher Thompson (Rev.)' down to 1892. Whether he died in that year or removed to some other city, I have not established." (Morgan, *Bibliography...*, pages 114-115.)

Publications

Thompson wrote prolifically and in addition to the leaflet published in 1848 at St. Louis, a periodical *Zion's Harbinger and Baneemy's Organ* made its appearance in January 1849 and ran for 5 volumes, but with somewhat sporadic publication towards the end, spanning a period of 6 years. A number of other periodicals were either announced or attempted, but none ever became very well established.

Several other publications were released which explained various points of doctrine, but the most significant was *The Laws and Covenants of Israel; Written to Ephraim, from Jehovah, the Mighty God of Jacob. Also, Ephraim and Baneemy's Proclamations.* This book of 208 pages of revelations and other documents was published at the church printing house in Preparation, Iowa in 1857.

I assume that the scriptures used by the LDS Church at the time of Joseph Smith's death were used by Thompson in his organization.

CHURCH OF JESUS CHRIST OF LATTER DAY SAINTS
(William Smith)

William Smith, the last surviving adult male member of the Smith family, was ordained Patriarch to the Church shortly after the death of his brother Joseph. He was also a member of the Twelve Apostles. As history records, he and Brigham Young were unable to see eye to eye, which led to Smith's demotion from patriarch over the church to simply a patriarch in the church. This, along with other disagreements led to Smith's publishing of a declaration in October 1845 wherein he compared Brigham Young to Pontius Pilate—accusing him of usurpation of authority, anarchy, and spiritual wickedness. He claimed that, "I heard my brother Joseph declare before his death, that Brigham Young was a man, whose passions, if unrestrained, were calculated to make him the most licentious man in the world, and should the time ever come, said he, that this man should lead the church, he would certainly lead it to destruction."

William maintained that his apostolic authority, given him by his brother Joseph, was as valid as any other of the apostles, including Brigham Young, and went on to urge the Saints to "stop paying tithing, cease gathering, locate themselves in the large branches of the church and remain there for a season, not letting themselves be led astray by false hopes and promises, to California or elsewhere."

Brigham Young wasted no time in excommunicating Smith from the church on October 19, 1845.

Smith teamed with James J. Strang for a season, but conditions were not much better there than they had been previously with Young. In 1847 a broadside pronounced William Smith as the Patriarch and Prophet of the Most High God, President of the Church. Smith stated that he excommunicated the Twelve Apostles and called the saints to gather "in the Land of Palestine, Lee County,

Illinois." Aaron Hook, another former Strangite follower, co-signed the document with Smith.

A revelation received by Smith on August 28, 1847, commanded him to do the work God had appointed him to do, and called Aaron Hook as his counselor.

A periodical called *Zion's Standard* was attempted at Palestine Grove, Illinois in 1848, but little seems to have come of it. The following year Isaac Sheen of Covington, Kentucky began publishing the *Aaronic Herald.* The first issue was published February 1, 1849 and became the official church paper, although Sheen was not yet a church member.

The following May, with the release of Volume 1, Number 3, the name was changed to *Melchisedek and Aaronic Herald.* This issue contains a revelation appointing William as prophet and Aaron Hook and Selah Lane as counselors. It also provided for the appointment of twelve apostles. Later issues contain further revelations, minutes of conferences and special attention is given to a committee of five elders who were appointed to go to Texas and seek a place of refuge. Volume 1, Number 5, dated August 1849, includes the very important explanation that since the oldest sons of both Hyrum and Joseph were minors, it was William's right to act in their stead and on their behalf. It is interesting to note that both Joseph F. Smith and Joseph Smith, III were being considered in the lineal priesthood context.

The final number of the church paper, April 1850, contains a new revelation directing the church to move to Texas. It also contained the minutes of a conference held at Covington. Isaac Sheen had replaced Selah Lane as one of Smith's counselors.

A few weeks later, the church at Covington broke apart, over the question of polygamy. Isaac Sheen was cut off from the church and later stated that, "[William] offered me his wife on the same terms that he claimed a partnership with other men's wives." Sheen later joined the Reorganization and began publishing the *True Latter Day Saints' Herald* in 1860.

Smith's group teamed up with Lyman Wight for a short time in Texas and the final publication of Smith's church was released in 1851, titled an *Epistle of the Twelve.* An interesting feature is that in addition to William being named as the First President, Prophet, Seer, Revelator, Translator and Patriarch over the Whole Church, and Lyman Wight and Aaron Hook listed as his counselors, Joseph Wood is presented as "God's Spokesman for, and Counsellor to the said William Smith, President of the Quorum of the Twelve Apostles and the whole ministry; also, a Prophet, Seer, Revelator, and Translator; holding the keys of the ministry of this latter day dispensation, equally and jointly with the said William Smith." His sudden rise to prominence is completely unexplained.

Shortly thereafter the church disintegrated and William became, as what some have recorded, a passive member of the RLDS Church.

CHURCH OF CHRIST (James Colin Brewster)

In 1836, when only ten years old, James C. Brewster announced himself to be in communication with the Angel Moroni and proceeded to write a Book of Moroni, but was quickly stopped by the church authorities in Kirtland. Pronouncing it as the work of the devil, the church authorities disfellowshipped the boy. Undeterred the boy began writing another work in December, 1838. The work was published at Springfield, Illinois in 1842 under the title *The Words of Righteousness to All Men, Written from One of the Books of Esaras [sic], Which Was Written by the Five Ready Writers, In Forty Days, Which was Spoken of by Esaras [sic], in His Second Book, Fourteenth Chapter of the Apocrypha, Being One of the Books Which Was Lost and Has Now Come Forth, by the Gift of God, In the Last Days.*

Thus the first publication, leading to the organization of Brewster's church in 1848, was launched. Three other publications were issued, one being a rebuttal to an article which had appeared in the *Times and Seasons* at Nauvoo, another being an additional part of the books of Esdras. The third, appearing just before Brewster organized his church, was an *Address* in which he quotes and discusses some of the prophecies of Esdras and how they related to the current events of the LDS Church and for the establishment of his own church.

A periodical, *The Olive Branch,* was launched in August, 1848, at Kirtland, Ohio. The last issue was published in January, 1852—in the midst of Volume 4.

Hazen Aldrich, formerly a member of the First Council of Seventy of the LDS Church, joined with Brewster early in 1848. A church was organized with Aldrich as President and James C. Brewster and Jackson Goodale as counselors. A complete organization, with Twelve Apostles, Seventies, Priests, Teachers and Deacons was also established.

A colony, under the direction of Brewster and Goodale, moved west to the gathering place, which had been previously designated by Brewster. Aldrich remained at church headquarters in Kirtland and continued with the publication of the church paper.

Brewster claimed that the original church, organized by Joseph

Smith, Jr. had gradually departed from the truth and by 1842 had become so full of error that a reorganization had to be effected. Divine communication played a very important role in the church.

The people who went west made a settlement on the Rio Grande River and named it Colonia. Some of the followers became disaffected and went further west to the valley of the Colorado and Gila Rivers and attempted their own settlement, but neither was successful.

Strife set in and by August, 1851, Aldrich announced from Kirtland that Brewster had "misconstrued the writings of Esdras to his own liking." Brewster retaliated with a revelation charging Aldrich with usurping authority. Goodale was found guilty of transgression and lost his leadershp position. The church came to an end and Brewster made his way to California where he lectured the rest of his life on spiritualism.

LORENZO D. OATMAN

Lorenzo D. Oatman, who resided near Fulton, Illinois, set himself up as a prophet sometime in 1848 and later joined with James C. Brewster (about 1850) and followed him west. Becoming dissatisfied with Brewster, he continued west and ended up in California. Tragedy struck the family on the way when Apaches massacred all but three of the children. Two of these children were girls, and one survived captivity among the Mojave Indians.

AUSTIN COWLES

On June 23, 1849, a general assembly of James C. Brewster's church opened in Kirtland, Ohio, presided over by Hazen Aldrich. Aldrich announced that no one would be allowed to have a voice in the matters of the church unless they believed and followed implicitly the *Writings of Esdras* and the revelations received by Brewster.

A vote was called to accept two of Brewster's revelations before the assembly was officially organized and a group of believers, led by Austin Cowles, protested that the assembly must be organized before any official business was conducted.

The Cowles group withdrew, forming a separate organization with Austin Cowles as chairmain and I. H. Bishop as secretary.

A conference of the Brewster church in Springfield, Illinois, on September 29, 1849, formally excommunicated Cowles and his followers.

No further details are available.

INCREASE M. VAN DUSEN

At one time a faithful member of the Mormon Church—having been led through the endowment by Brigham Young in Nauvoo—Increase M. Van Dusen and his wife followed James J. Strang soon after his church organization began gathering momentum. They did not stay long, for conference minutes of that church indicate that members were being removed for believing in Van Dusen's revelations.

In 1847-1848, Van Dusen and his wife Maria published a number of pamphlets in opposition to the Mormon Church under the leadership of Brigham Young. One of these publications exposed the temples ceremonies. His writings include *A Dialogue Between Adam and Eve, Mormonism Exposed* and *The Mormon Endowment.*

In *The Mormon Endowment* Van Dusen has some harsh comments on the "spiritual wife system." He says: "The substance of the Spiritual Wife doctrine (as it is called) is, we are told at this temple ceremony, of which we have been speaking, is the commencement of the law of God, and we are no more under obligation to the laws of the land. All of our former ties of marriage as performed by the ministers and justices, etc., are now all cut asunder, and we are all thrown loose upon the world, as if never married. It is now the woman's privilege to choose whom she sees fit; and it is the man's privilege to one, two, four, eight, twenty, etc., according to his standing in the church, and the favor he has with the women; and the leader, Brigham Young. And, as an inducement for the women to choose the leaders, they say the one who stands the highest in authority in this church, will receive the highest degree of honor and glory in heaven, (which is to be on earth) and of course, this is an inducement for a woman who is of an aspiring disposition to take the leader, Brigham Young, the man who led ten or twelve thousand of us through those Temple mysteries, and bound us all by a solemn oath at the expense of life, never to reveal it, even to a Mormon. And as an inducement to those who have not been let into this secret, to follow them to California, he says to them when they get there, he will reveal it to them in a tent in the wilderness, on which the glory of the Lord rested.

"...for the benefit of the peculiarity of the Mormons in all the world who are under this man's influence, for we are satisfied from a personal acquaintance of four years, that if his principles are carried out, it will prove the people's ruin."

Whether Van Dusen formally organized his followers or not is unknown.

SAMUEL C. BROWN

"For all that is known of Brown's faction we are indebted to some remarks by Strang in the Gospel Herald, May 30, 1850. Strang says that Brown 'went to Hyrum Smith to be appointed on a mission, and he sent him to work in the quarry at Nauvoo three months getting out stone for the Temple. Afterwards he asked for another mission, and as he seemed to think himself uncommonly well qualified to teach, Hyrum appointed him (in mere irony) to preach to the Twelve, the High Priests, and the authorities of Nauvoo. He attempted to perform his mission immediately, but the Saints hardened their hearts and would not hear him. Bishop George Miller even whipped him out of his garden with a bean pole. Since their death he has discovered that Hyrum Smith was the duly appointed successor of Joseph by the revelation of June 19, 1841, in pursuance of the law of succession in the D & C, and that he is Hyrum's successor by virtue of his appointment to teach the authorities. The seat of his future empire is not determined, but he issues a paper occasionally from the press of Philadelphia and Baltimore.' [circa 1849-1850]

"Bibliographically, Brown is a very elusive character, for it is also known, from the contemporary Times and Seasons, that in 1842-1843, he published a paper at Baltimore called the *Mormon Expositor.* This was unauthorized and gave offense to the local branch, who made official complaint about the paper to Nauvoo. But no files are known." (Morgan, *Bibliography...*, page 180.)

ELIJAH SCHWACKHAMMER

"The sum total of information concerning this entry comes from some remarks on the factions in Strang's Gospel Herald, May 30, 1850: 'Elijah Schwackhammer heard the gospel preached in New York by Bro. [George J.] Adams, and offered to be baptized face downwards. George however did not think that would produce the likeness of a proper resurrection, and declined. By some means he got baptized, and S. Rigdon ordained him an Apostle of his pretended kingdom. By some transformation, which we are too blind to trace out, this priesthood has made him the great expected one of the nations. He has commenced the publication of a paper in Philadelphia, and preaches from house to house, as well as in a hall. His paper exhibits the usual talent of the better class of schismatics, and excites the usual interest wherever known. It wants only some men of energy to make it blaze out as well as any of the rest of the same sort. Elijah has had the gift of speaking in what he calls the tongues of insects, but has lost it.' Evidently Schwackhammer soon gave up his effort to build a church of his own, for when George J. Adams began publishing *The Sword of Truth* in the sixties, Schwackhammer contributed occasional letters from New Jersey which have not the slightest intimation that he laid claim to any special calling." [circa 1849-1850] (Morgan, *Bibliography...*, p. 130)

THE BRIDE, THE LAMB'S WIFE or CHURCH OF JESUS CHRIST OF LATTER DAY SAINTS (Jacob Syfritt)

Jacob Syfritt was baptized into the Philadelphia branch of the LDS Church on June 15, 1840. Nine months later he was ordained a bishop and continued in that calling until he left the city in 1843. An early record of the branch notes that Syfritt and his wife Jane were excommunicated from the church at Nauvoo, but no date is given.

Syfritt associated with the Strangite group for a while, but in 1848 became affiliated with William Smith. However, a few months later, he claimed to have received a revelation telling him that William Smith had fallen into transgression and that he was to succeed as the head of the church.

Two publications, one a 22 page pamphlet containing several of Syfritt's revelations and the other a broadside containing a revelation are all that Syfritt is known to have published. The second was listed as a revelation having been received in November of 1850.

No further information concerning Syfritt's church or activities has come to light.

ARNOLD POTTER

Arnold Potter "came to Utah in 1848, returned east and brought his wife to the valley in 1849, settling in Mill Creek, Salt Lake County. Mr. Potter was one of the colonizers of San Bernardino, California, and was so dedicated to the principles of the church that he was called on a mission to Australia where he labored diligently for some time. Here he became very ill and when he recovered he claimed he had received revelations from the Lord saying he was the chosen one to lead the church. Many manuscripts were written by him concerning his beliefs. He was called home from his mission and disfellowshipped. His wife left him and from then on nothing is known of his activities until an account of his death was published in a newspaper in Council Bluffs, saying that he had made his way to a little town called St. Mary's, twelve miles south of Council Bluffs, where he had a number of followers.

"Mr. Potter was a brilliant man, calm and serene in manner.

In later life he had a long white beard, always dressed in white robes, while his followers were clothed in black robes. He died April 2, 1872, and was buried in Council Bluffs." (Carter, *Denominations...*, page 32)

In 1870, the second edition of a 16 page booklet containing Potter's revelations was published at Council Bluffs, Iowa.

MOSES R. NORRIS

In April, 1851, the first number of a periodical, *Ensign to the Nations,* made its appearance at Kirtland, Ohio, with Moses R. Norris as the publisher. It is the only number known to have been published, but it contains some very interesting comments by Norris.

He indicates that "The object is to comfort and console the scattered lambs of Christ's flock, and call them to Christ's body—the Church—..."

Later he comments on a meeting that was scheduled to have been held in the Kirtland Temple the following June. Whether such a meeting ever materialized has not been determined.

I am of the opinion that this man is the same, who in 1837, was removed from the LDS Church for supporting the revelations of James C. Brewster, although no indication is given in Norris's paper of that previous connection.

CHURCH OF JESUS CHRIST (Alpheus Cutler)

Alpheus Cutler was baptized into the LDS Church on January 20, 1833, by David W. Patten in western New York state. He moved with the church through its many hardships and upon settling in Nauvoo, was called to the High Council of the Stake in October 1839.

When the saints left Nauvoo, Cutler was appointed captain of one of the pioneer companies, but before going west he performed some missionary work among the Indians in Kansas. A number of his company stayed in Iowa to whom he returned in 1852. These families continued holding church meetings with Cutler as their leader.

In the spring of 1852 the settlers moved about thirty miles to the southeast of Big Grove on Silver Creek, and named the place Manti. Here they remained for a number of years.

Cutler claimed to be the recipient of a revelation from Joseph Smith in which it was said that when Cutler saw "two half moons with their backs together" it would signify to him that the time was come for him to reorganize the church. This sign was seen in 1853.

According to the beliefs of the church, Joseph Smith had appointed and ordained seven men as leaders of the kingdom.

These men were given the power, by seniority of their ordination, to reorganize the church after it was rejected. This is the doctrine of the *Council of Seven High Priest Apostles* as taught by several of the Mormon fundamentalist church organizations. The rejection came about when the saints were forced from Nauvoo before the temple was actually completed and when the Prophet Joseph sealed his testimony with his blood. Cutler was the seventh member of this council and had waited until all the others had either died or followed another leader, thus unable to fulfill their calling.

And so, on September 19, 1853, the church was reorganized at Manti, Iowa—a settlement of about 30 families—and all members were required to be baptized again because this church was not simply a continuation of the rejected church, but a reorganization. Cutler was the only one who was not rebaptized as he felt that it would sever the tie of authority between himself and Joseph Smith.

Plans were made to move the entire church to Minnesota, but the death of Father Cutler on August 10, 1864 at 80 years of age caused considerable sadness and a short delay but the first group of pioneers was underway within a month. Another group followed in January of 1865. Church headquarters and a settlement was established at Clitherall, Minnesota, with the first families arriving on July 31, 1865. The highest membership of the church was in 1859 when church rolls recorded 183 members. The formal organization of the RLDS Church in 1860 caused many to leave Cutler and join with Joseph Smith, III.

The church attempted to live the law of Enoch, or all things in common.

On June 30, 1867, Chancey Whiting was accepted and ordained as President of the Melchizedek Priesthood—having served as Cutler's Second Counselor, he was the only remaining member of the First Presidency of the church. Cutler's son, Thaddeus, had been First Counselor but several years previous he had left the church and was temporarily replaced by Charles Sperry, in hopes that Thaddeus would return to the church. He never did.

An official church corporation was established on March 10, 1873, with Chancey Whiting and Lyman Murdock as Trustees in Trust for the Church of Jesus Christ. The church continued to decline in membership as those who had become dissatisfied for some reason or another left and joined with other restoration churches.

Whiting passed away in June, 1902, and was succeeded by his son, Isaac M. Whiting, who had been his First Counselor. The community had deteriorated for many years, but through Whiting's leadership, reluctant though it was at first, the church members rallied to the cause and built a new church building in 1912 and tried to reestablish their united order.

Upon Isaac's death in 1922, his First Counselor, Emery Fletcher, became the President of the High Priesthood and the Church. Fletcher called Erle Whiting as his first counselor. A second counselor was not chosen until 1950 when Clyde Fletcher was ordained to that office.

In October 1928, President Emery Fletcher went to Independence, Missouri with his family to erect another church building, which has been maintained to date as the headquarters of the church. First Counselor Erle Whiting moved his family there in 1929.

The long distance and difficulties in communication at the time caused a schism in the church when Emery Fletcher died in 1953. The Minnesota congregation ordained Clyde Fletcher as the President of the Church. The Missouri congregation could not accept this, as the succession of the presidency to the first counselor had been well established. During the conference of the church in Missouri on April 10, 1955, Erle Whiting was ordained President of the Church, with Rupert J. Fletcher as first counselor and Julian Whiting as second counselor. On September 21, 1958, Rupert J. Fletcher became president of the church, a position he held until his own demise in November of 1974. Julian Whiting, who had served as Fletcher's first counselor became president of the church on July 6, 1975.

The Minnesota church will be discussed later in this volume, and although never legally incorporated as a separate entity, they did continue on their own—divided over the question of succession. Since the separation, the church in Missouri took upon them the name *True Church of Jesus Christ* to distinguish themselves from the Minnesota congregation. Since the two groups have essentially become reconciled the prefix *True* has been dropped.

The church does not actively proselytize for new members, believing that God will lead those who are faithful to the church. The Independence congregation has approximately 30 members and the Minnesota group has 2 members, who are not actively conducting church services there.

Doctrine

The Temple

A very important part of the practices and beliefs of the church is that of the temple. The meeting houses have the upper floor set apart for temple ordinances with a baptismal font set in the floor of the chapel, which is the ground floor.

A letter from Julian E. Whiting, president of the church, states:

"We believe a pattern was given for a temple, with a baptismal font below, a first floor for public assembly, and rooms above for the ordinances of the Holy Priesthood, and we try to build our churches to that pattern. We assuredly believe in the secret ordinances of the Melchesidek Priesthood (secret only to those who fail to take the oath and covenant pertaining to that Priesthood) and the vital importance to the Work of the Lord of these most holy ordinances."

Baptism for the Dead is believed but not presently practiced as the church feels the need for further instruction in that matter and other matters pertaining to temple work. Celestial marriage and sealing are not accepted as a priesthood ordinance.

It is my opinion that the temple ordinances practiced by the church are probably very similar to that which was done in Nauvoo after the death of Joseph Smith, Jr.

Godhead

The godhead consists of three separate and distinct personages, God and Christ having bodies of flesh and bone and the Holy Ghost having an entity of spirit.

In the words of the late Rupert J. Fletcher: "The fact that Jesus Christ received and retained a body of his own shows that he was not the Father who had laid aside his immortal body to come here and become a mortal, for he did not go back into eternity and pick up the other body. If it had been the Father who came here posing as the Christ and grew up as a little child, who would have looked after the affairs of the universe while he was in that innocent child-like state?"

Tithing

The "tenth" law of tithing is not accepted as a part of the true gospel. "...it does not fit in with the plan of Zion. And I do not believe that Joseph ever received it because it conflicts with the plan given in the first one hundred and five sections of the Book of Doctrine and Covenants and also the other scriptures..." (Fletcher, Rupert J., *Alpheus Cutler and the Church of Jesus Christ,* Independence, Missouri, 1974.)

The law of consecration is the ultimate way of life.

Exaltation

There are three degrees of glory to which all people will be assigned after the final judgment. The Celestial glory being the highest and to be inherited by the "kings and priests after the Holy Order of the Son of God," the Terrestrial being inherited by those who fall short of the Celestial, and finally the Telestial glory where those who did not repent and receive the gospel on the earth or did not receive a testimony of Jesus when he preached to them in the spirit world, will be assigned.

Scripture

Quoting from a personal letter from Daisy W. Fletcher, late wife of the late President Rupert J. Fletcher, "We have never been able to publish our own books so purchase the Inspired Version of the Bible from the RLDS branch of the church and use the Book of Mormon and the Doctrine and Covenants published by both the Utah branch and the RLDS. Some prefer one and some the other. We would like to have the Lectures on Faith published in the front of the book as it was at first but since they are no longer available we use the small pamphlet forms as we can get them. I might add that we do not accept the revelations given after 1844, or the martyrdom, and not all that are supposedly given before that date, including section 132." (letter to the author, November 30, 1974.)

Built in the late 1920s, the headquarters building on South Cottage Street in Independence, Missouri is used today for church services. The second story is set aside for the sacred ordinances of the Melchizedek priesthood and is not open to the public.

Publications

Along with a few pamphlets which have been issued, two books have been published. One *Alpheus Cutler and the Church of Jesus Christ* was published in 1974. This volume relates the history and beliefs of the church to great extent. Another book is a small musicless hymnal published in 1942 for the church by Deseret News Press in Salt Lake City, Utah.

REORGANIZED CHURCH OF JESUS CHRIST OF LATTER DAY SAINTS

Although not officially re-organized until April 6, 1860 when Joseph Smith, III was accepted and ordained as President of the Church at a conference in Amboy, Illinois, the actual movement toward that end began in the early 1850s, under the able leadership of men such as Jason W. Briggs and Zenos H. Gurley, Sr.

These men had led congregations of believers in James J. Strang's group for a number of years. Briggs left that affiliation in part because of Strang's involvement with polygamy and joined with William Smith's group, but shortly thereafter became disaffected with the goals of that organization and William Smith's advocation of polygamy.

Encouraged by his sincere belief that a descendant of Joseph Smith, Jr. should head the church as its prophet, Briggs began writing to others of his belief and other spiritual experiences which had been made manifest to him.

Joined by others who felt as he, the first conference of what became known as the *New Organization of the Church of Jesus Christ of Latter Day Saints* was convened in June 1852. In the succeeding years, several attempts were made to convince Joseph Smith, III, to step forward and claim his rightful position at the head of the church—but for various reasons he was reluctant to do so. Finally, in response to what he called "a power not my own" he consented to act in accordance with the blessing and designation of his father. This blessing, referred to by the Reorganized Church as one of the strongest bases for their claim to legal succession of the church, was known only second hand until its remarkable discovery in early spring 1981. Officially authenticated, the text follows:

"A blessing, given to Joseph Smith, 3rd, by his father, Joseph Smith, Jun., on Jan. 17, 1844.

"Blessed of the Lord is my son Joseph, who is called the third, for the Lord knows the integrity of his heart, and loves him, because of his faith, and righteous desires. And, for this cause, has the Lord raised him up; that the promises made to the fathers might be fulfilled, even that the anointing of the progenitor shall be upon the head of my son, and his seed after him, from generation to generation. For he shall be my successor to the Presidency of the High Priesthood; a Seer, and a Revelator, and a Prophet, unto the Church; which appointment belongeth to him by blessing, and also by right.

"Verily, thus saith the Lord: if he abides in me, his days shall be lengthened upon the earth, but, if he abides not in me, I, the Lord, will receive him, in an instant, unto myself. When he is grown, he shall be a strength to his brethren, and a comfort to his mother. Angels will minister unto him, and he will be wafted as on eagle's wings, and be as wise as serpents, even a multiplicity of blessings shall be his. Amen." (See *Saints' Herald,* Volume 128, Number 8, April 15, 1981, Independence, Missouri.)

This blessing, and its fulfillment, are in accordance with the latter day scriptures, wherein it has been stated by the Lord: "...none else shall be appointed unto this gift, except it be through him [Joseph Smith, Jr.]..." (RLDS *Doctrine and Covenants*, 43:2a; see also Utah Doctrine and Covenants, section 43.)

All succeeding presidents of the RLDS Church have been appointed in a similar fashion. The current president, Wallace B. Smith, a grandson of Joseph Smith, III, succeeded his own father in 1978. However, the prophet does not necessarily have to be a direct descendant. The point at issue is the *method* of the appointment of a successor.

Since 1860, the church has strived to live the commandments given to the original church, and missionaries have been sent to all parts of the world. Total membership today is about one-quarter of a million, making the RLDS Church second largest of the restoration churches.

After headquartering the church in various places in Illinois, a new community, Lamoni, Iowa, was selected and from about 1880 to 1921, the church was able to set a firm foundation for the future growth which was to come.

Graceland College was established at Lamoni in 1895. It continues today to provide four year college degrees to church members and other students enrolled therein. Herald Publishing House was also established at Lamoni. Now headquartered in Independence, Missouri, it continues to publish to the needs of the church.

After the church finally established is formal headquarters in Independence in the early 1900s, a magnificent domed structure, "The Auditorium" was erected in which conferences and many offices of the church are maintained.

The name of the church has remained the same, with the exception of the adoption of an official nickname in the mid-1970s—*Saints' Church.* However, according to the February 15, 1980 *Saints' Herald,* the name of the church in most areas outside the English-speaking world is the *Restored Church of Jesus Christ.*

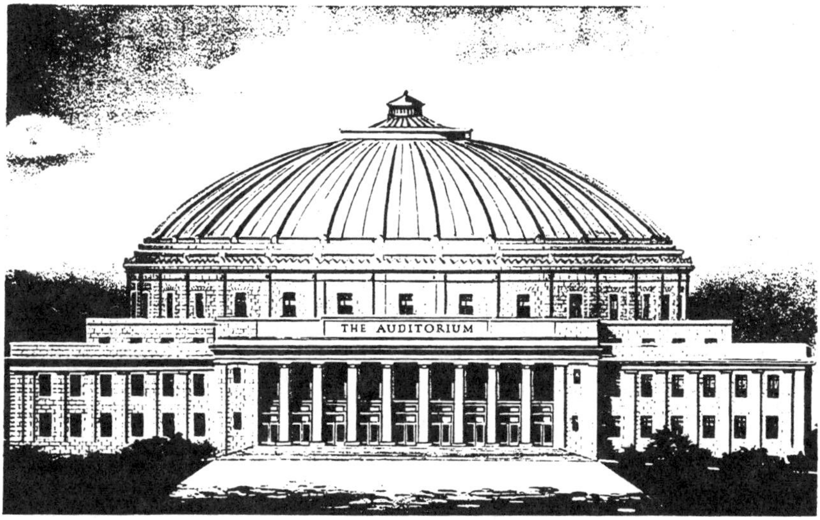

This architect's drawing of the then in progress Auditorium, was published as a supplement to the *Saints' Herald* on May 8, 1929.

Doctrine

Statement of Faith and Belief

We believe in God the eternal Father, source and center of all love and life and truth, who is almighty, infinite, and unchanging, in whom and through whom all things exist and have their being.

We believe in Jesus Christ, the Only Begotten Son of God, who is from everlasting to everlasting; through whom all things were made, who is God in the flesh, being incarnate by the Holy Spirit for man's salvation; who was crucified, died and rose again; who is mediator between God and man, and the judge of both the living and the dead, whose dominion has no end.

We believe in the Holy Spirit, the living presence of the Father and the Son, who in power, intelligence, and love works in the minds and hearts of men to free them from sin, uniting them with God as his sons, and with each other as brethren. The Spirit bears record of the Father and of the Son, which Father, Son, and Holy Ghost are one God.

We believe that the Holy Spirit empowers men committed to Christ with gifts of worship and ministry. Such gifts, in their richness and diversity, are divided severally as God wills, edifying the body of Christ, empowering men to encounter victoriously the circumstances of their discipleship, and confirming the new creation into which men are called as sons of God.

We believe that the Holy Spirit creates, quickens, and renews in men such graces as love, joy, peace, mercy, gentleness, meekness, forbearance, temperance, purity of heart, brotherly kindness, patience in tribulation, and faithfulness before God in seeking to build up his kingdom.

We believe that man is endowed with freedom and created to know God, to love and serve him, and enjoy his fellowship. In following the dictates of pride and in declaring his independence from God, man loses the power to fulfill the purpose of his creation and becomes the servant of sin, whereby he is divided within himself and estranged from God, and his fellows. This condition, experienced by our ancestors who first came to a knowledge of good and evil, is shared by all who are granted the gift of accountability.

We believe that man cannot be saved in the kingdom of God except by the grace of the Lord Jesus Christ, who loves us while we are yet in our sins, and who gave his life to reconcile us unto God. Through this atonement of the Lord Jesus Christ and by the gift of the Holy Spirit, men receive power to choose God and to commit their lives to him; thus are they turned from rebellion, healed from sin, renewed in spirit, and transformed after the image of God in righteousness and holiness.

We believe that all men are called to have faith in God and to follow Jesus Christ as Lord, worshipping the Father in his name. In this life those who hear the gospel and repent should commit their lives to Christ in baptism by immersion in water and the laying on of hands. Through living by these principles they participate in God's promise of forgiveness, reconciliation, and eternal life.

We believe that the church was established by Jesus Christ. In its larger sense it encompasses those both living and dead, who, moved by the Spirit of God, acknowledge Jesus as Lord. In its corporate sense, it is the community of those who have covenanted with Christ. As the body of Christ through which the Word of God is tangibly expressed among men, the church seeks to discern the will of God and to surrender itself to him in worship and service. It is enlightenend, sustained, and renewed by the Holy Spirit. It is to bring the good news of God's love to all people, reconciling them to God through faith in Jesus Christ. The church administers the ordinances through which the covenant is established, cares for all within its fellowship, ministers to the needy, wages war on evil, and strives for the kingdom of God.

We believe that all men are called to be stewards under God. They are accountable to him, in the measure of their perception of the divine purpose in creation and redemption, for managing all gifts and resources given their care. In the exercise of stewardship, men embody the divine will and grow in spiritual maturity through developing native powers and skills achieving dominion over the physical order and perfecting human relationships in the Spirit of Christ.

We believe that the kingdom of God sustains men as the stable and enduring reality of history, signifying the total Lordship of God over all human life and endeavor. The kingdom is always at hand in judgment and promise, confronting all men with the joyful proclamation of God's rule and laying claim upon them as they acknowledge the new Creation in Christ. The full revelation of the kingdom awaits the final victory over evil, when the will of God shall prevail and his rule shall extend over all human relations to establish the dominion of peace, justice, and truth. To this end the church proclaims the gospel of the kingdom both as present reality and future hope in the midst of a faithless world.

We believe that Zion is the means by which the prophetic church participates in the world to embody the divine intent for all personal and social relations. Zion is the implementation of those principles, processes, and relationships which give concrete expression to the power of the kingdom of God in the world. It affirms the concern of the gospel with the structures of our common life together and promotes the expression of God's reconciling love in the world, thus bringing forth the divine life in human society. The church is called to gather her covenant people into signal communities where they live out the will of God in the total life of society. While this concrete expression of the kingdom of God must have a central point of beginning it reaches out to every part of the world where the prophetic church is in mission.

We believe that all are called according to the gifts of God unto them to accept the commission and cost of discipleship. Some are chosen through the spirit of wisdom and revelation and ordained by those who are in authority in the church to serve in specialized ministries. These include ministry to persons, families, and community, as well as preaching, teaching, administering the ordinances, and directing the affairs of the church. The authority of every member of the body in this respective calling emerges out of divine endowment to him and his faithfulness in servanthood with Christ.

We believe that the ordinances witness the continuing life of Christ in the church, providing the experiences in which God and man meet in the sealing of covenant. In the ordinances God uses common things, even the nature of man, to express the transcendent and sacramental meaning of creation. God thereby provides the continuing means of investing his grace in human life for its renewal and redemption.

We believe that God reveals himself to man. He enters into the minds of men through the Holy Spirit to disclose himself to them and to open their understanding to the inner meaning of his revelation in history and in the physical order. Revelation centers in Jesus Christ, the incarnate word, who is the ultimate disclosure of truth and the standard by which all other claims to truth are measured.

We believe that the Scriptures witness to God's redemptive action in history and to man's response to that action. When studied through the light of the Holy Spirit they illumine men's minds and hearts and empower them to understand in greater depth the revelation in Christ. Such disclosure is experienced in the hearts of men rather than in the words by which the revelation is interpreted and communicated. The Scriptures are open because God's redemptive work is eternal, and our discernment of it is never complete.

We believe in the resurrection. This principle encompasses the divine purpose to conserve and renew life. It guarantees that righteousness will prevail and that, by the power of God, men move from death into life. In resurrection God quickens and transforms the soul, i.e. the body and spirit, bringing man into fellowship with his Son.

We believe in eternal judgment. It is the wisdom of God bringing the whole creation under divine judgment for good. This judgment is exercised through men as they are quickened by the Holy Spirit to comprehend the eternal implications of divine truth. Through the judgment of God the eternal destiny of men is determined according to divine wisdom and love and according to their response to God's call to them. The principle of eternal judgment acknowledges that Christ is the judge of all human aspiration and achievement and that he summons men to express truth in decision until all things are reconciled under God.

We believe that the inner meaning and end toward which all history moves is revealed in Christ. He is at work in the midst of history, reconciling all things unto God in order, beauty, and peace. This reconciliation brings to fulfillment the kingdom of God upon earth. Christ's presence guarantees the victory of righteousness and peace over the injustice, suffering, and sin of our world. The tension between our assurance that the victory has been won in Christ and our continuing experience in this world where God's sovereignty is largely hidden is resolved in the conviction that Christ will come again. The affirmation of his coming redeems us from futility and declares the seriousness of all life under the unfailing and ultimate sovereignty of God. (*Exploring the Faith,* Independence, Missouri: Herald House, 1970, pp. 10-15.)

Priesthood and Church Organization

There are two major divisions in the priesthood, Aaronic and Melchizedek.

The Aaronic priesthood is comprised of the offices of *Deacon*—to which office those called have the responsibility of the physical well-being of the members of the church; *Teacher*—men who are ordained to be concerned with the specific needs of individual members, to assist and strengthen them; and *Priest*—whose major responsibility is to take religious instruction into the homes of members. Priests are also empowered with the authority to administer Communion, baptism, ordinations and marriages.

The primary officer of the Melchizedek priesthood is the elder, who oversees the administration of the congregations of the church and ministers to the various spiritual and temporal needs of the congregations. The elder performs the ordinances of the gospel. The Seventy are elders with special missionary assignments, and High Priests are the administrators of the larger ecclesiastical units of the church.

The church is divided into large administrative regions which are comprised of several stakes or districts. Stakes are organized in areas where there are higher concentrations of members. Districts are established in areas with a smaller church membership.

The general leadership of the church is vested in the First Presidency—the Prophet-President and two counselors. The Twelve Apostles have the immediate responsibility of the missionary work of the church, and also fulfill many of the administrative needs of the church.

The Presiding Bishopric oversees the area of temporal needs of the church.

The stakes are presided over by Stake Presidencies, the districts by District Presidencies. There is usually a stake bishopric which functions in a similar fashion as the Presiding Bishopric, but on a smaller local scale.

The Presiding Patriarch, at the World Church level, oversees and assists the other brethren who are called as local patriarchs. One of the patriarch's function is that of giving "patriarchal blessings" to those worthy members who desire such spiritual guidance. The patriarchs are not encumbered with administrative responsibilities, and thus are able to minister to other spiritual needs of those in their jurisdiction. The term "Patriarch-Evangelist" is commonly used.

Tithing

Members of the church are asked to contribute one-tenth of their annual increase to the Lord. The law of tithing, as taught by the church, allows members to fulfill their basic needs in order to sustain an adequate standard of living, then contribute one-tenth of the excess to the church. This provides an equitable method for all to give of their resources, while making allowances for families of all economic situations and size. The primary objective of tithing is the development of stewardship, rather than the monetary aspect.

Members are also encouraged to contribute of their resources to their local congregations, as conditions permit.

Zion

Perhaps the major doctrinal belief which has been receiving the most attention in recent years is that of Zion, its meaning and the responsibilities of the individual members pertaining thereto.

Early in the history of the restoration, Jackson County, Missouri—and more specifically the city of Independence, was designated by the Lord as "the land which I have appointed and consecrated for the gathering of the saints: wherefore this is the land of promise, and the place for the city of Zion..." (RLDS *Doctrine and Covenants,* section 57:1a-g; Utah D & C, section 57:1-3.)

"The Reorganized Church continues to take very seriously its Zionic stewardship of *religiously social reform.* This is essential to our mission of individual redemption." (Bradley, John W., *Zion and Authority,* np, nd, p. 8.)

Word of Wisdom

This sound advice, given of the Lord to Joseph Smith, Jr. in

1833, admonishes members of the church and gives them instruction pertaining to their individual health and eating practices. The RLDS Church still observes the word of wisdom as it was originally given: "not by commandment or constraint." Even so, most members observe the instructions given. (RLDS *Doctrine and Covenants,* section 86.)

The Temple

The RLDS Church believes that the temple, which will be built in Independence at some future time which the Lord has not yet revealed, will be for the strengthening and instruction of the members of the church in the ways of the Lord, and to further the building up of the kingdom of God here on earth. There is no provision for secret ordinances.

In recent years, revelations pertaining to the temple have been received by the prophet of the church:

"The time has come for a start to be made toward building my temple in the Center Place. It shall stand on a portion of the plot of ground set apart for this purpose many years ago by my servant Joseph Smith, Jr. The shape and character of the building is to conform to ministries which will be carried out within its walls. These functions I will reveal through my servant the prophet and his counselors from time to time, as need for more specific direction arises." (RLDS D & C, section 149:6a.)

"It is also to be noted that the full and complete use of the temple is yet to be revealed but that there is no provision for secret ordinances now or ever, although there will be provision for instructional opportunities which will of necessity be restricted to the particular category concerned, viz, high priests, patriarchs, bishops, seventies, elders, Aaronic priesthood, and so forth. (RLDS D & C, section 149A:6.)

Publications

The RLDS Church has used the Inspired Version of the Holy Bible since its first printing in 1867 as the accepted standard of holy writ, along with the Book of Mormon and Doctrine and Covenants. The church publishes its own editions of these scriptures.

The Book of Mormon is basically the same as all other editions published by the various restoration churches with the exception that chapter and verse designations differ throughout the several editions currently being published. One must remember that the book was not divided into verses until long after the dispersion of the church.

The Auditorium, as it appears today. Situated on temple hill in Independence, it can be seen for miles around.

The Doctrine and Covenants differs widely from the book of the same title published by the Mormon Church, in the matter of compilation. The RLDS Church uses virtually all the sections which were included in the book of the same title published during the lifetime of Joseph Smith, Jr. Additional sections, received by his successors in the prophetic office, and approved by the conferences of the church, have been added and continue to be added from time to time.

The Saints' Herald is the official church magazine, currently being published twice monthly. It is the oldest, continuous publication of any of the restoration churches, being published since 1860.

Herald House, the church publishing firm, produces hundreds of other items, in addition to the scriptures: books, official church literature, lesson materials for the church, etc. Since they do sell directly to the public and have a catalog of their materials readily available, further enumeration is deemed unnecessary.

GEORGE HICKENLOOPER

A possible church organization may have been led by George

Hickenlooper beginning circa 1854. A dissenter from Charles B. Thompson's *Jehovah's Presbytery of Zion*, he published a tract explaining his beliefs.

"All that is known about this 'lost' pamphlet is derived from Thompson's own periodical, Zion's Harbinger and Baneemy's Organ. As a convert, Hickenlooper had begun contributing letters and articles to the Harbinger early in 1853, at which time he was identified as the 'Late Clerk of the St. Louis Conference of the Church of Jesus Christ of Latter Day Saints.'

"Some of these contributions would seem to have been published separately as Harbinger Extras; among the more interesting was a communication by Hickenlooper to his uncle in Utah, dated November 15, 1853, upholding 'Baneemy.' But by October, 1854, Thompson was making some strictures on Hickenlooper, who it seems had gone to Utah. Hickenlooper's hostile attitude, he says, was first made manifest in a denunciatory letter to Thomas A. Lyne, and 'we next find him before the public with a written lecture on our faith and doctrine, and denouncing C. B. Thompson as a great imposter; charging him with...tyranny and despotism...' This is the June, 1854, Harbinger; Hickenlooper may merely have published something in a Kanesville paper. The pamphlet here entered under an unknown title is, however, specifically referred to by Thompson in April, 1855 (Harbinger of October, 1854), when he mentions the receipt from Hickenlooper about seven weeks since of a letter and pamphlet." (Morgan, *Bibliography...*, p. 157.)

HENRY HARRISON DEAM

H. H. Deam was an apostle in the "New Organization" and was working with Jason W. Briggs, Zenos H. Gurley and others in persuading Joseph Smith, III, to accept the presidency of the church.

Deam and others advocated rebaptism as a test for fellowship, but Briggs and Gurley rejected this proposal. A perfect organization of the First Presidency was also advocated by Deam.

On October 6, 1854, Deam was removed from the Council of Twelve while he was away holding a conference of his own, at which he was sustained as the president of the church with Aaron Smith, (the former Strangite) as the first of two counselors.

What became of this organization is not known. (See *RLDS History of the Church,* Volume 3, pp. 229-230.)

WILLIAM MARKS

Joining with the Latter Day Saints early in the 1830s, William Marks rose through the ranks of the church and on October 5, 1839, when a stake was organized at Nauvoo, Marks was chosen as the stake president. He served in that position until the October church conference of 1844, just four months after the Prophet Joseph's death, at which Brigham Young removed him from the office and subsequently had Marks excommunicated from the church.

Some sources indicate that Marks attempted a church organization of his own, while others have him wandering from church to church seeking his place among them.

By the April 6, 1860 conference of the Reorganized Church, during which Joseph Smith, III, was ordained President of the Church, Marks appears to be firmly attached to that group, and remains so until his death in 1872. He stood in the circle of priesthood holders who ordained Young Joseph to his high calling.

THE CHURCH OF CHRIST (Temple Lot)

At the death of Joseph Smith, when the church became divided into many groups, several local branches tried to continue on in their local capacities with local leadership as they had done before the martyrdom, rather than following any one of the various leaders claiming successorship.

A group of Saints in Illinois—Half Moon Prairie, Bloomington and Crow Creek branches of the church among them—were a few of these local branches.

In the fall of 1857, these Illinois Saints sent two representatives—Granville Hedrick and Jedediah Owens—to meet with another group of Saints in Wisconsin. These Wisconsin Saints consisted mainly of dissatisfied followers of James J. Strang and William Smith. Some years before they had formed what had become known as the *New Organization of the Church of Jesus Christ of Latter Day Saints* and introduced, formally, the doctrine of lineal priesthood succession, wherein a call was made for Joseph Smith, III to step forward and assume his position as the leader of the church. The Illinois saints could not accept this action and finally in 1863, Granville Hedrick was ordained President of the High Priesthood under the hands of John E. Page. It is interesting to note that in a few years this group of saints became convinced, through scriptural evidence, that no such office office should exist in the church and it was dropped as was the office of High Priest. Hedrick then became the Presiding Elder, as Joseph Smith had been when the church was first organized in 1830. Later, it was decided that the leadership of the church rested only with the Twelve Apostles, who direct the affairs of the church today.

The church also returned to its original name, as established on April 6, 1830, *The Church of Christ.*

In 1864 Granville Hedrick received a revelation calling the church to return to Independence, Missouri. By 1867, they had reestablished themselves in that city and two years later purchased the first lots of what had been designated as the *temple lot* by Joseph Smith in 1831.

Through the years the church has suffered more than its fair share of controversy and conflict from within, but has been able to maintain stability and withstand the test of time.

The Church of Christ maintains that they are not "a faction, but a remnant of the Church of 1830, bearing the same name, teaching the same doctrine, believing the same truths, practicing the same virtues, holding the revelations as originally given and enjoying the same spirit." (from *A Brief History of the Church of Christ,* nd) The church claims about 3000 members.

The headquarters building of The Church of Christ stands on a portion of the original temple lot. The stone monument at the left marks the spot where the church began constructing the temple, but has been unable to complete.

Doctrine

Articles of Faith and Practice

We believe in God the Eternal Father, who only is Supreme; Creator of the universe; Ruler and Judge of all; unchangeable and without respect of persons.

We believe in Jesus Christ, the Only Begotten Son of God, the manifestation of God in flesh, who lived, suffered, and died for all mankind; whom we own as our only Leader, Witness and Commander.

We believe in the Holy Ghost, the Spirit of Truth, the Comforter, which searcheth the deep things of God, brings to our mind things which are past, reveals things to come, and is the medium by which we receive the revelation of Jesus Christ.

We believe that men will be punished for their own sins and not for Adam's transgression, and that as a consequence of the atonement of Christ "all little children are alive in Christ, and also all they that are without the law. For the power of redemption cometh on all they that have no law; wherefore, he that is not condemned, or he that is under no condemnation, can not repent; and unto such, baptism availeth nothing." (Moroni 8:25,26)

We believe that through the atonement of Christ all men may be saved by obedience to the laws and ordinances of the Gospel; viz: Faith in God and in the Lord Jesus Christ; Repentance and Baptism by immersion for the remission of sins; Laying on of hands for: (a) Ordination; (b) Blessing of Children; (c) Confirmation and the Gift of the Holy Ghost; (d) Healing of the Sick.

We believe in the literal second coming and millennial reign of Jesus Christ; in the resurrection of the Dead, and in Eternal Judgment; that men will be rewarded or punished according to the good or evil they may have done.

We believe in the powers and gifts of the everlasting Gospel; viz: the word of wisdom; the word of knowledge; the gift of faith; the gift of healing; working of miracles; prophecy; discerning of spirits; divers kinds of tongues; interpretation of tongues.

We believe the fruits of the spirit to be love, joy, peace, long suffering, gentleness, goodness, faith, meekness and temperance.

We believe that in the Bible is contained the word of God, that the Book of Mormon is an added witness for Christ, and that these contain the "fullness of the gospel."

We believe in the principle of continuous revelation; that the canon of scripture is not full, that God inspires men in every age and among all people, and that He speaks when, where and through whom He may choose.

We believe that where there are six or more regularly baptized members, one of whom is an elder, there the Church exists with full power of church extension when acting in harmony with the law of God.

We believe that a man must be called of God by revelation, and ordained by those having authority, to enable him to preach the gospel and administer the ordinances thereof.

We believe in the same church organization as existed in the time of Christ and His Apostles. The highest office in the church is that of an apostle, of whom there are twelve, who constitute special witnesses for Jesus Christ. They have the missionary supervision and the general watchcare of all of the churches.

The primary function of the general church, of which each local church is a component part, is missionary and the building up and extension of the Kingdom of God in all the world.

We believe that local churches should govern their own affairs, and that general church officers may, with propriety, give counsel and assistance. Local congregations are subject to the Articles of Faith and Practice and must be governed thereby.

We believe the Church of Christ comprehends the true brotherhood of man where each esteems his brother as himself and wherein the divine command to "love your neighbor as yourself" is demonstrated by the prevalence of social equality.

We believe that all men are stewards under God and answerable to Him not only for the distribution of accumulated wealth, but for the manner in which such wealth is secured. The primary purpose of stewardship is not the increase of church revenue or the mere contribution of money by those who have to those who have not, but to bring men to a realization of the common fatherhood of God, and the universal brotherhood of man in all the affairs and expressions of life, and to maintain such social adjustment that each may enjoy the bounty and gifts of God, and be free to exercise his talents and ability to enrich the life of all.

We believe that men should labor for their own support and that of their dependents. Ministers of the gospel are not absolved from this responsibility, but when chosen or appointed by the church to devote their entire time to missionary work, their families are to be provided for out of the general church funds. The admonition of Christ that the ministry should not provide purse or scrip for their journey, but go trusting in God and the people is applicable.

We believe that the temporal affairs of the general church are to be adminstered by the general bishopric under the direction of the general conferences of the church and under the supervision of the Council of Twelve. The temporal affairs of the local churches shall be administered by local bishops under the supervision and direction of the local congregations.

We believe that marriage is ordained of God and that the law of God provides for but one companion in wedlock for either man or woman. In case of a breach of this covenant by adultery, the innocent one may remarry.

We are opposed to war. Men are not justified in taking up arms against their fellows except as a last resort in defense of their lives and to preserve their liberty.

We believe in the literal gathering of Israel, and in the restoration of the ten lost tribes.

We believe a temple will be built in this generation in Independence, Missouri, wherein Christ will reveal himself and endow his servants whom he chooses with power to preach the gospel in all the world to every kindred, tongue, and people, that the promise of God to Israel may be fulfilled.

We believe that a New Jerusalem shall be built upon this land "unto the remant of the seed of Joseph." (Ether 6:6-8; III Nephi 10:1-4); "which city shall be built, beginning at the Temple Lot." (Doctrine and Covenants 83:1)

We believe that ministry and membership should abstain from the use of tobacco, intoxicating liquors and narcotics, and should not affiliate with any society which administers oaths or covenants in conflict with the law of God, or which interferes with their duties as freemen and citizens. (From a tract by the same title published by the church.)

Priesthood and Church Organization

As previously indicated, the church has no High Priests or a first presidency. The church is directed by the Twelve Apostles, about which the Articles of Faith and Practice are very explicit in their duties. They function as the highest priesthood authority on the earth. The temporal affairs of the church are directed by a council of bishops, and the local congregations are directed by presiding elders. The seventy, or Evangelists, are Elders with the additional missionary calling.

Other priesthood offices consist of priests, who are commissioned to teach and baptize, but may not bestow the gift of the Holy Ghost. The teacher, as the name implies, is called to instruct the membership of the church. The office of deacon is also included in the priesthood organization.

All members of the priesthood are called "as was Aaron" and ordained by the laying on of hands.

A prophet is but a functional office, and as stated in the Articles of Faith and Practice, the Lord may speak through anyone he chooses at any particular time, regardless of his priesthood or position in the church.

Tithing

Quoting from a report of the Twelve Apostles in 1931:

"An epistle to the Church of Christ concerning tithing from the Quorum of Twelve—Whereas, it has come to our attention that there is a widespread misunderstanding among the membership of the Church of Christ with regard to the question of paying tithes,

"Therefore, we submit for your guidance this epistle praying that by this means your minds might be illuminated and your desires quickened to assist in the great work of the Church in these last days. For that purpose we, the Twelve, call attention to the following provisions of the gospel:

"1. The principle of tithing was instituted of God as an equitable means of financing the work of the Lord's vineyard, in promoting missionary work and caring for the poor.

"2. This principle provides that a tithe of one tenth part should be paid unto those that have been appointed by the Church to receive the tithes and offerings, by all members of the Church on all properties free of indebtedness; to be followed by a tithe of one tenth part of their net earnings; it is further provided that man's living expenses should not be deducted until he has honored the Lord with the first fruit of his labors.

"3. That inasmuch as missionary is primarily the work of the General Church, and that tithes is for the purpose of promoting this phase of its work that the same should not be used to financing local activities. Local churches should meet their expenses with funds raised by other means than tithing."

The Temple

Foremost in the minds of the Saints as they returned to Independence was the redemption of Zion, purchasing back the temple lot property and building the temple.

Property which had been dedicated by Joseph Smith, Jr. was purchased a few short years after returning to Jackson County, and although challenged for title to the property in the 1890s, the Church of Christ was upheld by the courts as it had clear title by purchase to the land. In 1929 original stone markers, placed under the direction of the Prophet Joseph in 1831, were excavated which prove the location of the consecrated temple lot.

Construction on a temple was started in 1929, but a few years later ceased due to lack of necessary funds. In the 1960s the

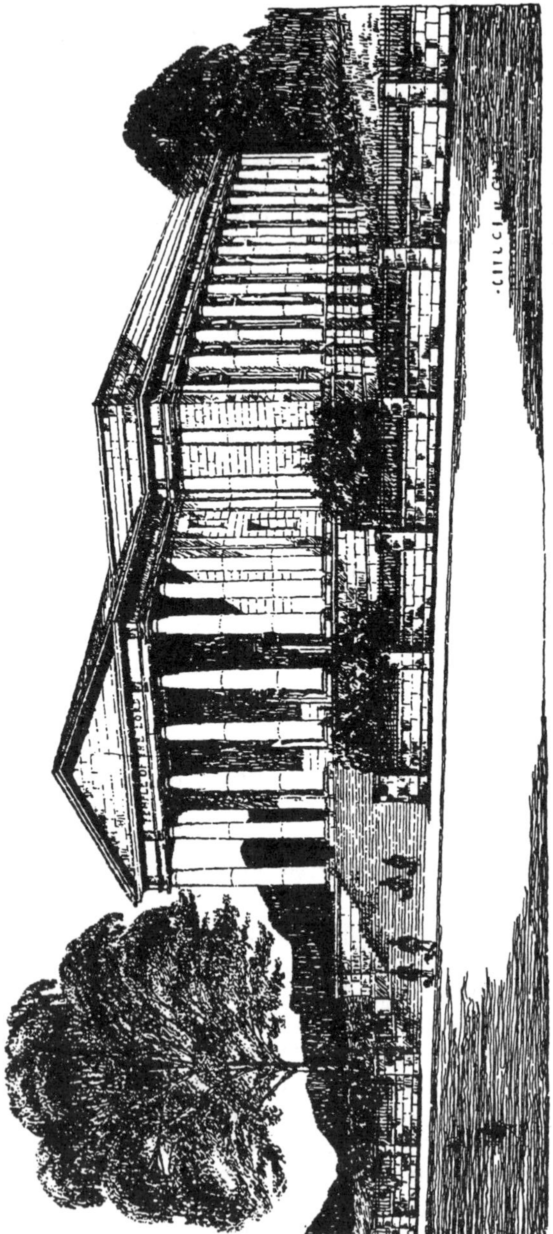

This architect's drawing of the proposed temple was published in *Zion's Advocate*, in November 1930.

excavation was filled and in 1967 a marker was erected in memory of a dream which has yet to be fulfilled.

The church maintains that but one temple is to be built. The purpose of the temple is to be like unto that of the Kirtland Temple. Eternal Marriage, Baptism for the Dead and other such practices are not found in the scriptures and therefore have no place in the doctrines of the church.

Scriptures

The King James Version of the Holy Bible is the accepted work of scripture in the church, but other versions, particularly the Inspired Version, are allowed to be used by individuals for study and reference.

The church uses the 1908 Authorized Version of the Book of Mormon, printed by the RLDS Church by special arrangement for the church.

A third book of scripture used is the Book of Commandments. Over the years a great deal of controversy between the differences in the Book of Commandments and the Doctrine and Covenants has arisen. Many of the revelations first published in 1833 appear in a much changed version in 1835 when the Doctrine and Covenants was first issued. In the early part of this century, Apostle Daniel MacGregor headed a committee whose assignment was to prepare a new edition of the Book of Commandments so that it would be readily available to the church. The first printing was in 1926.

Publications

In addition to the Book of Mormon and a Concordance to the same published by the RLDS Church, the Church of Christ publishes the Book of Commandments, a one volume history of the church and a score of pamphlets expounding its doctrines, beliefs and practices. In 1975 the major accomplishment of publishing its own hymnal was realized.

Periodicals have also found their place in the Church of Christ. In the mid-1860s, a monthly, *The Truth Teller,* appeared. Volume 1 began in July of 1864 and continued for one year. It was published in Illinois. Volume 2, Number 1 was delayed until June of 1868—presumably interrupted while the Saints were relocating in Independence. It was later replaced by *The Searchlight,* which was published in 1896, after many years of no church paper. It continued until March, 1900. The following May a new paper, *The Evening and the Morning Star* made its debut. It was to be the church paper for 16 years. After a gap of no paper for six years, the present paper, *Zion's Advocate* made its appearance on May 15, 1922.

CHURCH OF CHRIST (Zadoc Brooks)

Zadoc Brooks and his followers had control of the temple at Kirtland, Ohio, for a few years in the 1850s, until the demise of the church and the incorporation of its remaining members into the Reorganized Church shortly after its official organization in 1860.

The only substantial contribution Brooks and his followers made to the historical record, was the publishing of their own Book of Mormon.

"This is one of the more curious editions of the Book of Mormon. The copyright on the book having expired, and public attention being focused on Utah in consequence of the Utah Expedition, the James O. Wright firm in New York late in 1858 undertook to place on the market a commercial edition, with an introduction which set forth both Mormon and non-Mormon versions of its origin. The printing was a reasonably faithful one, and the Utah Church at least was pleased. Commercially the book may not have been a success, for when they were approached by the Brooks faction, the publishers sold or leased the plates for a new printing with different front matter. (Or perhaps sold the remainder of their own edition in sheets.) Sabin's note on the book adequately covers the ground saying: This second issue, known as the *Huntley* or *Brooks-Huntley* edition, was made some time between 1859 and 1861 for a group of Mormons at Kirtland, Ohio, who were followers of Elder Zadoc Brooks and opposed to polygamy. It is said that four thousand copies were printed, the cost of which was paid by Elder Russell Huntley, a prosperous member of the church. The alteration consisted in the cancellation of the original advertisement and introduction, and the substitution of new ones, signed at the end, *Written by Z. Brooks, Elder in the Church of Christ.* The advertisement was changed to read: *The present edition...is an accurate reprint of the third American edition, originally published at Nauvoo, eighteen years ago, under the official sanction of the leaders of the Church of Jesus Christ. The apostacy of the great body of the church, through the influence of false teachers, who privily brought into the church Damnable Heresies...together with the fact that they have for a long time supressed the Book, on account of its pointed condemnation of their practices, has appeared to the Publisher as a sufficient reason for reissuing it; so that the many firm believers in the Book that are scattered throughout the land...may have an opportunity to avail themselves of its precious truths...the real weapon with which to put down Polygamy and its *kindred institutions,* etc. The new introduction is called 'a mere synopsis of the evidences of the divinity of the Book,' and contains six pages only, numbered v-x, followed directly by xiii, there being no pp. xi-xii as in the first issue.

"It was from this edition, after the downfall of the Brooks faction, that the early needs of the Reorganized Church were satisfied. Curiously, Brooks has lived on in Mormon memory almost solely by reason of the introduction he wrote for this issue of the Book of Mormon; long after he had abandoned Mormonism for Campbell-ism, the Bickertonite Church of Jesus Christ began printing his introduction as a separate tract on the Book of Mormon, and more recently still incorporated it into their own edition of the book." (Morgan, *Bibliography...,* pp. 175-176.)

CHURCH OF JESUS CHRIST OF LATTER DAY SAINTS
(Walter Murray Gibson)

Probably the most dynamic and ambitious of any church leader the restoration movement has yet seen, Walter M. Gibson joined the Mormon Church on January 15, 1860, and served a mission to New York. Upon his return to Utah, he was called on a mission to Japan. Perhaps foreseeing future events, he had his commission written on parchment and signed by Brigham Young. It is reported that he later covered this document with ribbons and seals to add to its official appearance.

Gibson left for Japan in 1861, but never made it past the Hawaiian Islands, where he hoped the church would move its headquarters. Using his official document to impress the natives, Gibson quickly took charge of the Mormon settlement on Lanai and adopted the official title of "Chief President of the Islands of the Seas and of the Hawaiian Islands for the Church of Jesus Christ of Latter Day Saints." Things came easily for Gibson as all the Elders of the Church were in Utah, and the natives generally had not yet had enough experience to realize, at first, what was happening.

A conference was called at Wailuku in October, 1861, and many of the Saints came to meet Gibson. Funds were raised by selling offices in the priesthood to the natives—the price varying with the level of the office.

In time Gibson began wearing a white robe and created about himself such an atmosphere of authority that all who wished audience with him were required to present themselves by entering the room on their hands and knees.

A plot of ground on Lanai was chosen and some records and a Book of Mormon were deposited in a hollowed rock which Gibson said was sacred and would one day be the cornerstone of a great temple. Lanai was designated as the Land of Zion.

A large settlement was built, and members of the church were encouraged to leave their homes and congregate on Lanai.

Finally, some of the members of the church realized that what was happening was not in accordance with their understanding of the gospel and the church procedures. Word was sent to Salt Lake City about the situation.

In 1864, Ezra T. Benson, Lorenzo Snow, Joseph F. Smith, Alma L. Smith, and W. W. Cluff went to Hawaii to inquire into the situation. Their discoveries led to Gibson's excommunication from the church. His followers were given the choice of staying with Gibson or returning to their homes and re-establishing the branches of the church. Joseph F. Smith stayed and took charge of the church in Hawaii.

Gibson remained in Hawaii and became known as the "Shepherd Saint of Lanai." He became the Prime Minister of Hawaii in 1882, a position he filled very ably until a revolt in 1887 which forced his resignation and flight to the United States. He died in San Francisco, California on January 21, 1888.

CHURCH OF JESUS CHRIST OF LATTER DAY SAINTS or CHURCH OF THE FIRST BORN

(Joseph Morris)

Joseph Morris was converted to the Mormon Church in England and came to Utah in the fall of 1853. He was called to assist in the settlement of the Sanpete Valley in southern Utah.

By the following spring, the bishop had asked him to leave the settlement because some of his teachings were felt to be out of harmony with the teachings of the church. He returned to Salt Lake City, but by 1857 had moved to Provo. Morris claimed that it was at this time he received his first revelation, wherein it was made known to him that he was to be the prophet.

The good saints in Provo prompty rejected him for these claims and Morris made his way to the South Weber area and settled at Kingston's Fort, having already been excommunicated from the Mormon Church for his claim to the prophetic calling.

Here in South Weber Morris began teaching and continued to receive revelations. He succeeded in gathering a sizeable following. On April 6, 1861, he organized his church. By 1862 he had amassed more than 500 believers.

In his revelations, Morris had been told that Brigham Young was teaching false doctrine and leading the saints astray. In addition,

Morris had been appointed as the President of the Church with Brigham Young being called as the First Counselor. When Young refused to step down, Morris was commanded to organize the church again.

Several times Morris had revealed the time of the Second Coming of Christ, but was disappointed each time. He had been able to furnish an explanation out of these awkward situations, but finally Morris revealed that the day to end all days would come on May 30, 1862. A great celebration ensued, and Morris announced that he was Moses reincarnate. Christ did not come and many members became disillusioned with the church and attempted to leave.

One man, William Jones, left the church and requested the release of his wife and children and the return of his property. It is recorded that Jones' wife did not want to leave and Morris ordered the retention of Jones' property for her support. But, being persistent, Jones finally ambushed a wagon heading to the fort and sent the driver away on foot. Morris was infuriated and ordered the arrest of Jones and two of his associates.

A writ demanding the release of Jones and his fellow prisoners was issued by Chief Justice J. F. McKinney of the Supreme Court of the Territory of Utah. The writ was burned by a Morrisite faithful.

Three weeks later the Judge issued a writ for the arrest of five of the leaders of the church. Deputies Theodore McKean and Robert T. Burton were placed in command of 250 militiamen by the Acting Governor and proceeded to the fort to serve the writ.

On June 13, 1862, McKean and Burton led their men to the fort, and when the guns and cannon were in position, delivered the ultimatum to Morris, which was refused. A battle lasting several days followed, during which many people in the fort were killed. Finally Morris surrendered, but as he was being led away, requested to speak a few words of farewell to his people. Climbing a platform he raised his hands and shouted: "All who are willing to follow me through life and death, come on." As the Morrisites dashed for their rifles, the militia opened fire. When it had ended Morris and one of his counselors was dead and the other mortally wounded. Two women, who had tried to protect Morris were also dead.

The remaining members scattered throughout the west. Some went to Nevada and California—there following the leadership of the Dove family; others went north to Soda Springs, Idaho and Montana—mostly following the leadership of George Williams. These and other groups will be discussed later.

Doctrine

In five short years, between 1857 and 1862, Morris received several hundred revelations. Most of the doctrines of the church were identical with those of the Mormon Church. Polygamy was practiced. The law of consecration was carried out and a unique doctrine, that of reincarnation, was introduced.

The Priesthood had a variation from that of the Mormon Church in that there were three orders: the lesser or Aaronic, the Melchizedek and the High Priesthood of the Prophetic Order. The members of the Melchizedek order were the ministers of the church and the celestial second-born sons. The members of the High Priesthood of the Prophetic Order were the first-born sons. Morris was the president of the highest order and presumably designated all other positions in the priesthood. (See Anderson, C. LeRoy, *For Christ Will Come Tomorrow,* Logan, Utah: USU Press, 1982.)

THE PROPHET CAINAN (George Williams)

George Williams was one of the new leaders that attempted to gain control of Joseph Morris' church and followers after the war at South Weber in the fall of 1862.

Claiming to be witness to marvelous visions and revelations, Williams asserted that he had been ordained by Elias and Enoch to take the place of Joseph Morris and lead the church. Boldly preaching the doctrine of reincarnation, he alledged that in his first state he was Cainan, one of the seven angels. In his second reincarnation he lived as Melchizedek the great king of Salem.

He launched a heavy correspondence campaign and eventually became accepted by most of the Morrisites who had settled in Soda Springs, Idaho. Over the next few years, Williams seems to have been able to gather a number of Morris' followers, and eventually missionaries were sent to various parts of the world. Although apparently unsuccessful, a mission to the Middle East was also undertaken.

A holy city was established at Deer Lodge, Montana, where Williams taught that the Kingdom of God would be established.

Williams died on April 25, 1882, leaving instructions that a successor should be elected one year from that time. With most of Williams' followers gathered at that city, the church continued under a number of leaders from that time until the 1950s when the last leader, George Johnson, passed away.

The church building they built still stands as the sole reminder of Joseph Morris and his church.

THE CHURCH OF JESUS CHRIST (William Bickerton)

Claiming direct ministerial authority and direction from God, the church under William Bickerton was officially organized in July, 1862 at Green Oak, Pennsylvania. Although church headquarters are maintained at Monongahela, Pennsylvania, the church has spread across the United States and in many other countries. A church auditorium was dedicated in 1971 at Greensburg, Pennsylvania, and more recently, the church's printing operations have been established in Bridgewater, Michigan.

Going back now in history, the reader will recall that after the Prophet Joseph's death, the church was in turmoil with a number of people claiming authority to lead the church. Sidney Rigdon, who had been Joseph's First Counselor in the Presidency of the Church, laid claim to the leadership by virtue of that fact, and also that he had been called, by the Lord, an equal with Joseph Smith. However, being rejected by Brigham Young and many of the Saints gathered in Nauvoo, he led a group of faithful away from that area, and they eventually settled in Pennsylvania and the surrounding area. William Bickerton joined this group in 1845 and was ordained to the priesthood—which authority can be traced directly to May 15, 1829, when Joseph Smith, Jr. and Oliver Cowdery received their authority from an angel.

Due to the irregularity and other problems in Rigdon's group, Bickerton was essentially left without a church within a few years, and for a short time associated with the Mormon Church at West Elizabeth, Pennsylvania. However, upon hearing of the public announcements of polygamy, Adam-God, and other strange doctrines in Utah circa 1852, William Bickerton knew that he had been deceived and left the association with the Utah Church.

It was after this time that Brother Bickerton became prepared by the Lord to accept the calling of leadership and carry forth the message of the true gospel of Christ. The Lord called Bickerton with a marvelous vision, and the work commenced. Many branches and conferences were organized even before the formal organization of the church in 1862.

Throughout the church history, many members and leaders of the church have been participants in divine communications from the Lord. Prior to Bickerton's formal appointment and ordination to the office of President and Prophet of the Church (which occurred in October 1861) Charles Brown gave a revelation in tongues which was interpreted by another brother present. This revelation indicated that these faithful were God's chosen people.

At the time of Bickerton's ordination in 1861, Charles Brown and George Barnes were sustained as his counselors. Barnes received a revelation which told of the truthfulness of their cause. It might be noted here that later, Barnes withdrew from the church and joined with the Mormon Church and died in full fellowship with that group.

Bickerton served as church president until 1880 when some difficulties arose concerning, in part, the church's colony in St. John's, Kansas, where Bickerton resided. William Cadman became president of the church at this time and served until his death in 1905. Upon resolution of the previous difficulty, Bickerton was reinstated as a member and elder in 1902.

A number of men have served in the position of president of the church since that time, being elected annually at the church conferences.

The Church of Jesus Christ has over 6000 members and has done extensive missionary work in several foreign countries, namely Italy, Ghana and Nigeria in Africa, India, Canada, Mexico and South America, besides the on-going work throughout the United States.

Doctrine

The Faith and Doctrine of the Church of Jesus Christ

1st. We believe in God, the Eternal Father; and his Son Jesus Christ; and in the Holy Spirit; these three are the great matchless power that rules all things visible and invisible, for it is of him and through him that we receive all things both for this life and that which is to come.

2nd. We believe God, the Father, to be a personage of glory and that the Son is the express image of the Father, and that he was with the Father before the foundation of the World; and that in the fullness of time he came from the bosom of the Father and was born of the Virgin Mary according to the Scriptures, became man, suffered and died for the sins of the whole world, and on the third day he rose again and brought about the resurrection (according to the scriptures), and ascended up on high to sit at the right hand of God. Principalities and powers being subject to him, who is the image of the invisible God, the first born of every creature; for by him were all things created that are in Heaven and that are in Earth, visible and invisible, whether they be Thrones or Dominions, Principalities or Powers; all things are created by him and for him; and he is before all things; and Christ is the Head of the Body, the Church, the Beginning, the first born from the dead; that in all things he might have the pre-eminence; for it pleased the father that in him should all fullness dwell. See Colossians first chapter. We believe also, that he will come again the second time to Judge both the living and the dead according to the scriptures.

We believe the Holy Ghost to be: A. The mind of the Father and of the Son; B. The unseen power and glory which emanates from God and can, at his will, manifest itself in various forms; C. The Witness of God; D. The Gift of God. It is pure and holy, just and good, omnipresent, full of light and knowledge, and a discerner of thoughts and intents of mankind.

3rd. We believe in the Church or Kingdom as set up by the Savior to be sufficient for life and salvation for all people.

4th. We believe that the New Testament Scriptures contain a true description of that Church or Kingdom as established by our Savior at Jerusalem, and that no principle or doctrine inconsistent therewith ought to be practiced or respected, or any principle or doctrine consistent therewith rejected.

5th. We believe The Church of Jesus Christ in this age (in order to be worthy of the name), must be molded substantially and minutely after the pattern left us by Christ. The Scriptures bear witness that its officers consist of Apostles, Prophets, Evangelists, Pastors and Teachers, (all inspired), for the work of the Ministry, for the perfecting of the Saints, for the edifying of the body of Christ, till we all come into the unity of the faith, unto the measure of the stature of the fulness of Christ.

6th. We believe that mankind will be punished only for their own actual transgressions, and not for the sins of our first parents, as is clearly implied by the Savior in representing little children to be heirs of the Kingdom. "Suffer little children to come unto me, and forbid them not, for of such is the Kingdom of Heaven."

7th. We believe that Divine inspiration is an indispensable qualification for preaching the Gospel. General information about the world is advantageous to man when properly used. Theological education is good only when spiritually correct; such instruction, however, is not absolutely requisite to teach the Word of God. Furthermore, formal schooling or practical training which fosters the belief that inspiration and the Gifts of the Holy Spirit are unnecessary in the Ministry of Christ's gospel is erroneous and harmful. (See 2 Timothy 3rd chapter.) Moreover, we believe in preaching the Gospel without purse or scrip according to the Savior's instructions: "Freely ye have received, freely give." (Matthew 10:8) The language is of supreme importance as containing the full force of both Christ's authority and example.

8th. We believe that all men must obey the Gospel before they can be saved.

9th. We believe the first principle of action required in the Gospel is belief in the Lord Jesus Christ, the once crucified and now risen Redeemer. The second is repentance, which signifies nothing more or less than feeling a Godly sorrow for our sins with a fixed determination to sin no more. The third is Baptism by immersion in water in the name of the Father, and of the Son, and of the Holy Ghost, for the remission of sins. The fourth is the laying-on-of-hands in the name of Jesus Christ for the Baptism of the Holy Ghost.

10th. We believe in being buried with Christ by Baptism, and planted together in the likeness of his death, and raised in the likeness of his resurrection; and that we should walk in newness of life. Let not sin, therefore, reign in your mortal body; being then made free from sin, ye became the servants of righteousness: therefore, yield ye yourselves unto God, as those that are alive from the dead.

11th. We believe in the promises of the Savior as they are written in Mark 16:15-18. "These signs shall follow them that believe; in my name shall they cast out Devils; they shall speak with new tongues; they shall take up serpents; and if they drink any deadly thing, it shall not hurt them. They shall lay hands on the sick, and they shall recover."

12th. We believe in partaking of the Lord's Supper every first day of the week; the Bread as his Body, and the wine as his Blood, in commemoration of his death and his suffering.

13th. We believe in the washing of feet as an ordinance instituted by our Lord and Savior, to be observed in the Church. We further believe it to be our duty to attend to that ordinance at least once within each three months.

14th. We believe in saluting the Brethren with a holy kiss.

15th. We believe in the Resurrection of Jesus Christ as recorded in the Scriptures, which was a victory over the power of death, and a reintroduction of the principle of continuous or eternal existence; that this principle of continuous existence was not only attained for himself but for all Adam's race; the wicked as well as the righteous, by which the former will be accountable for their conduct during this life and receive due punishment. Also, that the latter may be duly rewarded for their righteousness or good conduct. We also believe that the righteous that lived previous to the days of Jesus Christ expected their resurrection through, and as a direct result of Christ's resurrection; also, that there was a general resurrection of the righteous that lived before the days of Christ (in the flesh) immediately following Christ's resurrection. The Scriptures inform us, "That many of the Saints which were dead arose and appeared unto many." A few moments of reflection by a person acquainted in a reasonable degree with the principles of God's divine justice will force him to conclude, that God could not grant this great privilege of the resurrection to some (at that time) and deny it to others, who were equally worthy and expectant, and deprive them of the enjoyment of the benefits of Christ's resurrection, until a period still beyond our day when Christ will come again. We believe, also, in a future resurrection of those that die after Christ, according to the Scriptures.

16th. We believe in observing all things whatsoever the Lord has commanded us, and on these conditions he has promised to be with us always, even to the end of the world.

17th. We believe there has been a gross and widespread apostasy among men from the true order and doctrine of the early Church as set up by the Savior. Few Scriptural subjects are treated of more extensively in the Sacred Word, and to make anything like a comprehensive statement of the matter would be an extensive task. We refer the reader to several very pointed passages on the subject. (Isa. 24:5-6; Acts 20:29-30; 2 Thes. 2nd chap.; 1 Tim. 4th chap.; 2 Tim. 3rd and 4th chaps.; 2 Peter 2nd chap.; Book of Mormon: 4 Nephi 1:24-49.)

18th. We believe that this apostasy from the true Gospel was so widespread, complete and general, that man himself was utterly unable to provide a remedy, and we recognize all efforts at reformation as utter failures to reproduce even a faint resemblance of the duties and privileges of the ancient Saints or the older and excellence of the ancient church as established by the Savior. We will further state that we know of no Scripture that in the least degree intimates that a reformation of the Gospel and Church of Christ ever would take place from the aforesaid Apostate condition. The Scriptures, however, do foretell a restoration of the Gospel of Jesus Christ in the latter ages of time, in the hour of God's Judgments. "And I saw another Angel fly in the midst of heaven, having the everlasting Gospel to preach unto them that dwell on the earth, and to every nation, and kindred, and tongue, and people, saying with a loud voice, fear God, and give glory to him; for the hour of his judgment is come: and worship him that made Heaven and Earth, and the Sea and the Fountains of water." We should all remember that in the time of John, there is no doubt of the true Gospel then existing, and that he saw in visions occurrences of future times. It necessarily follows then, that this Scripture foretells the restoration of the Gospel by an Angel, calling back mankind from erroneous religion to the worship of the true God, and announcing the hour of God's judgments, reminding people that worship, a God without body, parts or passions of the necessity of contrasting him, with that God, who is the author of this vast creation. The next Angel that John mentions declares that Babylon is fallen and thereby clearly locating the period of these occurrences.

19th. We believe that the fullness of the Gospel shall soon be taken from the Gentiles because of their iniquity; and they will be punished for their disobedience. Moreover, God will remember his covenants to the House of Israel and bring them to a knowledge of the fullness of the Gospel.

a. We believe in the restoration of Israel as it is spoken of by the Prophets; and that God will use man as his instrument for its accomplishment in this age, as he did in ages past. We believe also, that in order to bring about these events, God must and will reveal his will to man as he did in days of old.

b. We believe that God will employ this church for that purpose. "Hear the Word of the Lord, O ye nations, and declare it in the Isles afar off, and say, He that scattereth Israel will gather him and keep him as a shepherd doth his flock." "Behold, I will send for many fishers, saith the Lord, and they shall fish them; and after I will send for many hunters, and they shall hunt them from every mountain, and from every hill, and out of the holes of the rocks."

c. We believe also, that blindness in part is happened unto Israel, until the fullness of the Gentiles be come in; and so all Israel shall be saved; as it is written, "There shall come out of Zion the Deliverer, and shall turn away ungodliness from Jacob."

d. We believe that the aborigines, or Indians, upon this hemisphere, are a part of Israel, descendants of Ephraim and Manasseh, the Sons of Joseph, and that this land of America is theirs by an original God-given right. Also, that it is the land referred to by Jacob, as a land given of god to Jacob, and of Jacob to Joseph. Also, that it is the land referred to by Moses when blessing the children of Israel before his departure from them, and the land of Joseph. It is the land referred to by Ezekiel and Isaiah. In short, it is the land of restored Israel, where the "little stone of Daniel" will smite the image at the feet and bring about the wonderful results by him described.

20th. We believe the Word of God, wherein he says, "He will write unto Ephraim the great things of his law and they should be counted as a strange thing." We also believe that the Book of Mormon is that strange thing, or the great things of God's law to Ephraim; also, that it contains a true record of the Gospel of Christ, as given to the tribe of Joseph, by Christ in person after his resurrection, whom he recognized as the sheep of whom he spake, that had to hear his voice, and become one fold and have one shepherd.

21st. We believe that the Book of Mormon is the book spoken of by the Prophet Isaiah, and also the book that Ezekiel refers to in his book, as the stick of Joseph in the hand of Ephraim.

22nd. We would just state, that the Book of Mormon has been shamefully misrepresented, and we desire every lover of truth to read it for themselves, as they cannot afford to rely on common report concerning any matter connected with their soul's salvation. We hereby assure all men that it teaches nothing contrary to purity and sound doctrine, and is a history of the dealings of God with the Aborigines of this land. It also contains a vast amount of prophetic matter of unlimited importance bearing upon the future. It is impossible for lovers of truth and virtue who are reasonably free from prejudice, to carefully peruse its contents without experiencing delight and satisfaction; or for persons who are soaked in greed, hypocrisy and sensuality, to read this book without being maddened by its stinging reproaches of their character and conduct. It affords cold comfort for polygamists or bigamists. Jacob, a former Prophet of the Lord of this land writes as follows: "Therefore, I the Lord will not suffer that this people shall do like unto them of old." (Meaning David and Solomon with their many wives.) "Therefore, my brethren, hear me, and hearken to the Word of the Lord; for there shall not any man among you have, save it be one wife; and concubines he shall have none; for I the Lord delighteth in the chastity of women, and whoredoms are an abomination before me: Thus saith the Lord of Hosts." This is not the only instance by any means where polygamy is condemned in the Book of Mormon. The Almighty commanded Lehi, when he brought him to this land, positively against the practice of polygamy. Old King Noah was condemned by Abinadi for the same abomination. Therefore, we believe that a man shall have only one wife and a woman but one husband, and base our faith especially upon the Book of Mormon in this particular.

23rd. We believe in the fulfillment and ultimate establishment of the Kingdom of God on the earth while men are still in the flesh. We refer to this period of time as "The Peaceful Reign," which shall precede the "Millennium," or "Thousand Years" with Christ.

24th. We believe in continuous divine revelation (such revelations are consistent with the Holy Scriptures.) The Lord reveals himself through the Holy Ghost in dreams, visions, signs, gifts, and His word.God speaks when, where and through whomever he chooses.

25th. We believe in the second coming of Christ; that he shall appear in glory at the end of the world to wed his Bride (the church) to gather unto himself all the righteous to dwell with him for a thousand years (the Millennium), and then for all eternity.

26th. We believe that marriage between man and woman is a holy institution. "Therefore shall a man leave his father and his mother, and shall cleave unto his wife; and they twain shall be one flesh." We believe that a man shall have one wife and a wife but one husband; except when death takes one of the parties, in which case the survivor is at liberty to remarry." (*Faith and Doctrines of The Church of Jesus Christ*, Monongahela, Pennsylvania: the Church, 1969.)

The church dedicated this building in 1971 at Greensburg, Pennsylvania. The Auditorium serves as the meeting house for the local branch of the church as well as the site of the conferences of the whole church. *(From Restoration Reporter, November 1972.)*

Feet Washing

This ordinance is performed at least once in three months. In most branches, the brothers assemble together towards the front of the auditorium, the sisters towards a section in the rear of the same. The Deacons and Deaconesses prepare the pails of water and the pans. The brothers (sisters do the same) will do as Jesus commanded, gird himself with a towel and bow down before his brother and wash his feet. By way of a more detailed explanation; in a kneeling position, the brother bows; he places the foot of the brother in the pan and with his hand applying the water; he offers a prayer to God, asking that God watch over him and bless his brother and his family, etc. There is no written prayer; it comes from the heart.

Feet washing is practiced as it was a command of Jesus. The humility displayed by washing one another's feet as Jesus said was meant to do just that—to keep us humble. (Calabrese, Joseph, *Questions and Answers,* Monongahela, Pennsylvania: The Church of Jesus Christ, 1977, pp. 37-38.)

Priesthood and Church Government

The church is directed by the Quorum of Twelve Apostles, three of whom are elected annually by the general conference of the church to serve as President, First and Second Counselors. Originally this Quorum of Three was separate from the Twelve, but since that would make fifteen apostles and did not seem in accordance with the scriptures, the church councils, after considerable prayer, fasting and discussion, felt it in the best interest of the church to reform this practice. So today, there are Twelve Apostles in the church, who direct its affairs, three of whom are elected to preside as the administrative decision making body in the church. No one person is specifically designated as prophet. (See Faith and Doctrine, article 24.)

There is also a Quorum of 70 Evangelists, with a President, Vice-President and Secretary.

Other officers in the church are Elders—who provide the leadership for local branches, Teachers, Deacons, and Deaconesses.

There is only one order of priesthood in the church and that is the priesthood which is after the order of the Son of God. The Apostles, Evangelists and Elders are the only priesthood offices in that order. Teachers, Deacons and Deaconesses are considered assistants to that order. (See Calabrese, *Questions and Answers,* pp. 27-30)

Finances

The church has not made tithing a law or doctrine which is to be adhered to by members. All financial needs are met by freewill offerings.

The church headquarters is located at Sixth and Lincoln Streets in Monongahela, Pennsylvania. (From *Scriptural Lessons*, published by the church, 1949.)

Publications

The church accepts the King James Version of the Bible and the Book of Mormon as scriptural standards. All other revelations received by the church must be tested by the principles set forth in those two books.

The church publishes its own edition of the Book of Mormon, and has been doing so in English since 1934. An edition in the Italian language is also published.

Many pamphlets, church history, hymnal, sermons and other matters of interest in making the gospel message known, along with lesson materials, are published by the church.

The monthly church paper, *The Gospel News,* has been in publication since 1945.

CHURCH OF THE MESSIAH (George J. Adams)

George J. Adams joined the Mormon Church in 1840, but was excommunicated in 1845 and later joined with James J. Strang. He became one of Strang's counselors and staged the elaborate coronation ceremony at which Strang was crowned King of the Kingdom of God. However, in 1856, he was removed from that affiliation on the charge of immorality.

He made his public reemergence in 1860 with the publishing of a pamphlet *Lecture on the Destiny and Mission of America, and the True Origin of the Indians.* Dale Morgan states: "...Mormonism with the Mormonism excised." (Morgan, *Bibliography...*, p. 177.)

Adams organized the Church of the Messiah in January, 1861, at Springfield, Massachussetts, and the official church organ, *The Sword of Truth,* began publication on September 15, 1862, being published at South Lebanon, Maine, where Adams had moved a few months prior. The paper continued until at least 1865.

During the summer of 1865, Adams set sail for Palestine, in accordance with commandments received by way of revelation. Upon his arrival he sent directives to his followers in Maine telling him to join him in Jaffa. On August 11, 1866, 156 people set sail for the Holy Land. They took with them all types of tools, seed and other necessities for colonizing the area near Jaffa.

Unfortunately the colony failed. Not being able to obtain what they had expected and crop failure contributed to the dissolution of the colony. By 1870 Adams returned to the United States, having left Jaffa two years previous.

George J. Adams died on May 11, 1880 in Philadelphia, Pennsylvania. (See Holmes, Reed M., *The Forerunners,* Independence, Missouri: Herald House, 1981.)

WILLIAM DAVIES

William Davies joined the Morrisite group in 1861, moved to Kingston's Fort, consecrated his properties and joined the Morrisite army. After the war in 1862, Davies was one of the group of pioneers who forged their way to Soda Springs. He at first accepted the leadership of George Williams, moved to Deer Lodge, Montana and was for a short time in charge of the settlement there.

On January 24, 1866, Davies received a vision in which he learned that he was to usher in the millennium. He claimed that since that time he was in direct communication with God and received various instructions.

One of these instructions directed Davies to establish the Kingdom of God at Walla Walla, Washington. A colony was established near there in 1867. Land was purchased and some forty followers attempted to reestablish Morris's law of consecration. A press was purchased and various publications were issued proclaiming their doctrines and practices.

Believing in the imminent coming of Jesus Christ, Davis proclaimed that he was Michael the Archangel (from a previous incarnation), and when his son Arthur was born on February 11, 1868, the child was proclaimed to be Jesus Christ reincarnate. A second son was born September 28, 1869, whom Davies named "Our Father," which meant God the Eternal Father of Spirits.

Ten years later, Davies' wife, the mother of deity, died. Later, in the winter of 1880, a diptheria epidemic claimed the lives of both of the boys.

This doomed the colony. Members demanded a redistribtution of the consecrated goods, which was done to some degree. Some of the members filed suit against Davies in October 1880. The court awarded the plaintiffs $3200 of the community property. Since Davies had no money, the land was sold at a sherriff's auction for just enough to pay court costs and the plaintiff's judgments.

A few faithful followers remained, and in September 1881, Davies remarried.

As late as 1892 Davies was reported as residing in San Francisco. (See Anderson, *For Christ Will Come Tomorrow.)*

CHURCH OF ZION (William S. Godbe)

In late 1868, William S. Godbe, Elias L. T. Harrison and others began receiving spiritual manifestations and revelations directing them in their efforts opposing many of the current trends in the Mormon Church at the time and in part the tremendous power wielded by Brigham Young.

Their major opposition was Brigham Young's recently organized Zion's Cooperative Mercantile Institute,' which all Mormon merchants were to join, and to which all faithful Mormons were to bring all of their business. Godbe and his followers believed in the open society of free enterprise.

ZCMI and its principles were designed to create what Brigham Young foresaw as a temporal and self-sufficient "Zion" which was supposed to benefit the church membership as a whole.

Godbe wanted to industrialize the state, bring cultural refinement to the valley and create an open society which would become a vital part of the United States. The doctrines, including plural marriage, were to remain basically the same as in the Mormon church's then accepted theological outline.

Almost as fast as it began, the Church of Zion declined and within a few short years of its organization in Salt Lake City had ceased to exist.

GEORGE BARNES

"In 1873, George Barnes, who was the second counselor in the presidency of the Bickertonites, denied that God had revealed many of the revelations the leaders claimed to have received. Members residing in Rock Run, Pennsylvania, followed Barnes. Eventually Mr. Barnes joined the Utah Church where he died in full fellowship." (Carter, *Denominations...*, p. 28)

BARNET MOSES GILES

In 1875, Barnet Moses Giles published a pamphlet entitled *The Pure Testimony to the Church of Jesus Christ of Latter Day Saints and unto all nations of the World.*

He testified that the Bible, Book of Mormon and Doctrine and Covenants were inspired books and contained the true gospel of Jesus Christ. He further indicated that Joseph Smith was a true prophet of God who had all the priesthood power and authority.

Giles claimed that the church had been rejected in 1844 at the death of Joseph Smith and at the same time all authority which the church had ever had was taken away.

He claimed the Church of Jesus Christ of Latter Day Saints was wrong because Brigham Young was not a true prophet. A true prophet, according to Giles, was the son of the previous prophet. Therefore, Joseph Smith, III, was the legal president and prophet of the church.

Giles said that the church had apostatized because they had not yet built a temple—and since there was no temple, the Mormon Church was practicing polygamy illegally.

He also said the RLDS Church was in error because they had not yet built a temple. Joseph Smith, III had been rejected as a prophet because he was not obeying all the laws of God. According to Giles when the sons of the prophet are rejected, the priesthood and leadership of the church belonged to a "literal Israelite." Giles was this very person, the "One Mighty and Strong" to set the house of God in order.

In a letter to Joseph Smtih, III Giles asked him to come forth, build a temple, and assume his rightful place as the prophet of the church. Giles said that the Lord wanted the Saints to unite and had called upon them to set the wheels of unification in motion. The letter was signed, "Barnet Moses Giles, a literal descendant of Israel, Prophet, Seer and Revelator of the Church of Jesus Christ of Latter-day Saints."

Whether Giles had a formal organization of followers or not is unknown at this writing.

CHURCH OF CHRIST (David Whitmer)

In the late 1840s a movement began which advocated David Whitmer [one of the Book of Mormon witnesses] as the rightful president and prophet of the church. This movement failed to obtain Whitmer's support and shortly disintegrated.

However in 1875-76, David Whitmer is recorded as performing baptisms and forming a church organization of sorts. A return to "original" Mormonism was advocated.

His famous work *Address to All Believers in Christ* was published at Richmond, Missouri in 1887. It is in this book that he refers to his religious ventures. Whitmer died in 1888.

Missionaries were sent out to preach the gospel, but just how widely they traveled is not known. Various publications crop up from time to time in the bibliographical record, written by members of Whitmer's church.

Beginning in 1889, a monthly called *The Return* began publication. Ebenezer Robinson was the editor. It appeared regularly until Robinson's death when it was suspended. Internal problems in the church created some difficulties when the magazine recommenced, but eventually these were worked out and it continued until 1896 when additional internal strife caused a cessation.

Two years later Volume 6, Number 5 (May 1898) made its appearance in Denver, Colorado. It continued until the fall of 1900. In the final issue a new publication, *The Messenger of Truth*, was announced. It was published at Independence, Missouri from October 1900 through April 1901.

The church was quite active in publishing. A hymnal for the church was released c. 1890—a sizeable volume of 218 pages. In 1899 an edition of the Book of Mormon under the name *The Nephite Record* was published and in 1903 the Book of Commandments was reprinted "verbatim."

Some sources indicate the church to have ceased to exist by 1905, although John J. Snyder (who had led the church since Whitmer's demise) remained quite active until 1925 publishing various tracts, etc. which promoted the Whitmerite faith.

In 1925, Snyder and the remaining members of the church united with the Church of Christ (Temple Lot). *Zion's Advocate* remarks:

"...it gives us peculiar satisfaction to receive the application for membership of Bro. J. J. Snyder and others of the Whitmerite group of latter day believers." The article quotes Snyder: "So we will labor with these brethren, looking forward to the time when God will establish the church in its purity, when all the elders will be teaching the same things in the doctrine of Christ." (*Zion's Advocate,* Volume 2, Number 6, Independence, Missouri:Church of Christ, July 15, 1925, p. 2)

CHURCH OF THE FIRST BORN (George S. Dove)

Pulled together from the Morrisite remnants who had gone to Nevada and California, George S. Dove and his associates began forming a more fully organized church sometime between 1874 and 1877.

George Williams had corresponded with them for a number of years, but seemed unable to win the loyalty of many of the faithful.

George Dove's father James had been a Morrisite apostle. These men and the other Morrisites had attempted to maintain the church since the exodus from South Weber in 1862. In 1864, with at least half of the original Morriste apostles, John Livingstone was elected to lead the church and ordained to receive revelations for its guidance. However, most of these men were at the same time receiving and attempting to follow instructions from George Williams. In December 1865, James and George Dove left San Francisco for New York as missionaries for Williams. The mission was a failure and this could have contributed to the Doves' loss of faith in Williams. Shortly after this mission the Doves and others withdrew their support from Williams and for a number of years searched for leadership.

In 1873 George S. Dove began receiving spiritual communications and visions. The Spirit of the Lord later directed him and those who accepted his leadership to organize the Church of the First Born.

In 1885 the Dove's attempted to win over the followers of the deceased Williams, but received a mixed reception at the colony in Montana.

A monumental work containing the revelations of Joseph Morris was published by the Doves at San Francisco in 1886.

Convinced that South Weber, Utah was to be the gathering place, the Doves returned to Utah in 1885. James maintained residence until about 1891, with George seemingly dividing his time between Utah and San Francisco. There never seems to have been a large enough following for George to accomplish his plans.

With his death the cause was lost.

Doctrine

The Doves published their Articles of Faith in 1887, which listed many doctrines and principles common to Mormonism, but with some important differences.

"Among these were the rejection of the principle of a literal resurrection after one life on earth in favor of a belief in reincarnation. It was believed that persons could not become perfected in one lifetime upon the earth, but that several sojourns would be required in different bodies and places before the eternal spirit would be prepared to dwell with the angels of heaven.

"The Doves taught that reincarnation was not only available to the righteous but was open to all. The Church of the First Born believed in rewards and punishments, but not in an endless hell. Sinners were given a second chance. 'After we have cast off this mortal, the deeds done in the body come to memory, and if our deeds have been evil, we at once feel convicted, and fully realizing our condition, we are anxious to come in mortality to try again.'

"Another unique belief concerned the Godhead. God and Jesus Christ constituted the Godhead. 'The Holy Ghosts, spoken of in the scriptures, are the angels of God who are sent to...be ministering spirits of the heirs of salvation upon this earth." (Anderson, C. LeRoy, *For Christ Will Come Tomorrow*, Logan, Utah: USU Press, 1982, p. 194.)

THE PRIESTHOOD GROUPS (Fundamentalists)

Although the Mormon Church's official public sanction of polygamy was repealed with the Manifesto of 1890, many faithful to that doctrine continued on in its practice. These people, who today are generally excommunicated from the Mormon Church, number several thousand and are located in many areas, mainly in the western United States and Mexico. At one time the movement was relatively unified, but has been split into various factions over the years basically concerning the question of leadership and authority. The doctrine of these peoples remain essentially the same throughout, although some factions are more liberal in practice than others.

These faithful believe they have been chosen as a select group to carry on the practice of plural marriage and some other doctrines, namely the Adam-God doctrine and the exclusion of blacks from the priesthood, all of which have been publicly renounced by the LDS Church leadership in Salt Lake City. Some of these people recognize the leaders of the LDS Church while at the same time maintain they hold a higher priesthood authority.

The most significant upheaveal in the fundmentalist groups was circa 1951 when the largest group dealt with an internal power struggle. Joseph W. Musser, the leader, formed a new *council.* LeRoy S. Johnson formed an opposing leading *council.* About half of the believers followed Musser, who was later succeeded by Rulon C. Allred.

Allred, who was gunned down in his Murray, Utah office in 1977, was in turn succeeded by his brother Owen. Before his death Rulon estimated his church membership at about 35,000. (See Taylor, Samuel W., *Rocky Mountain Empire,* New York: MacMillan, 1978, p. 105)

Truth Magazine had been the standard of fundamental Mormonism since 1935 and continued until 1956. Joseph Musser had originally been involved with its publication, but when the 1951 trouble occurred, the other group retained the magazine and for about four years Musser's *new* group published the *Star of Truth.* Both magazines are excellent source material regarding the beliefs and practices of the fundamental Mormons.

In addition to these two large groups, a number of others exist today, as do many self-proclaimed polygamists, such as the late John Singer of Summit County, Utah.

I have heard of a group in Hurricane, Utah; a group in Moab, Utah—who are reportedly carving out a mountain to live in. There are a number of others who do not particularly follow any of the current leadership but are waiting for the *Indian Messiah* to come forth.

The fundamentalists trace their authority to September 27, 1886, when LDS Church President John Taylor was residing in Davis County, Utah. It was on this date that Taylor ordained several men with the authority to carry on the practice of polygamy even after the rest of the members of the church were forbidden to do so. This was in accordance with the teaching of the council of Seven High Priest Apostles.

Joseph W. Musser received this special authority on September 22, 1929, and was instructed that "a year should not pass without children being born under the covenant of plural marriage."

Doctrine

Marriage

Marriages are performed for time and eternity. Temples are the preferable place to perform this ceremony, but not indispensible.

Since the LDS Church considers these people apostate, they are denied access to the temples of the church.

Plural marriage is held as the fullest degree of living the commandments of god, but there are members who do not yet live in this covenant.

Church Organization and Priesthood

Regular church services are held and the officers are Seven Presiding High Priests as outlined in Section 107 of the Utah Doctrine and Covenants.

Work for the dead, as practiced by the LDS Church, is believed but not practiced since there is no accessible temple facility. It is understood that in the future God will send a leader who will set the house in order and at that time the temple will become available for use.

The priesthood is exclusive in that those with negroid blood are ineligible.

God

It is taught that Adam is God the Eternal Father and that we are his literal spiritual and mortal children. Under the supervision of Adam's father Eloheim, and of Christ, Adam created this earth. All men have the opportunity of progressing to the status of a God. Adam-God is the literal father of Jesus Christ.

JAMES BRIGHOUSE

In 1887, James Brighouse published a book in which he claimed the Latter-day Saints were hated by their enemies and driven to the Rocky Mountains because they failed to keep the covenants which were made at the organization of the church on April 6, 1830. He went on to claim that Brigham Young had unrighteously taken the office of prophet, seer and revelator.

Through the doctrine of reincarnation, Brighouse claimed that the Latter-day Saints were the same people who had been led out of Egypt by Moses. Through this same doctrine, Brighouse claimed to be Michael, the Great Prince; the Ancient of Days, the First and the Last, the Alpha and Omega.

He stated that Joseph Smith, Jr. had no need for a successor because while he was living all work assigned to him by God had been completed and no more revelation was necessary.

At another point in the publication, Brighouse additionally claimed to be Adam, Enoch, George Washington and Joseph Smith. The Millennium was to have begun in 1885.

The Battle of Armageddon is supposed to begin in the Salt Lake Valley.

JOHN H. KOYLE

A resident of Spanish Fork, Utah and very active in his duties as a leader in the local LDS Church, John H. Koyle was participant to numerous spiritual manifestations at times in his life. He had several dreams, mostly of a personal nature, which strengthened his faith and testimony of the gospel.

Although throughout most of his life he was persecuted for his beliefs in the Nephite gold mine, he was not actually excommunicated from the Mormon Church until 1948, just a few months before his death. In fact, he served faithfully for many years as a bishop of the church in the Spanish Fork area.

The big event took place in late August 1894, when Koyle was visited by an Angel who took him to a mountain near Salem, Utah—located south of Spanish Fork. Inside the mountain Koyle was shown an ancient Nephite gold mine filled with rich ore, gold coins and sacred records engraved on metal plates—richer than any gold mine ever to be discovered, it was to be called the Relief Mine because it would not yield its richest treasures until a time of great worldwide crisis, when all peoples and economies would need relief of an extraordinary nature.

The ancient entrances to the mine had long since caved in, but Koyle was not to dig them out. The angel would give directions from time to time on how to proceed.

This messenger was believed to have been Moroni.

Koyle devoted 55 years of his life digging a shaft through the mountain and erecting a mill—which stands today. In order to finance the operations of mining, the mine was incorporated and shares of stock were sold—and at one time became so popular that the LDS Church leaders publicly preached against it.

Testimony meetings were held on Thursday evenings, but since Koyle's death very little has been done.

There are still many believers and stock can still be purchased for a few dollars. The mine's promoters say one share will be worth thousands when the mine finally gives up its treasure.

After Koyle's death and until his own demise a few years ago, Norman C. Pierce was the most active promoter of the mine and the world events relating to its treasure.

The mine has not yet produced any ore of significant value, and the late Pierce's many revised predictions have yet to be fulfilled. For example, he predicted, in the third revision of his schedule, that the New Jerusalem would be built and the Millennium would begin in 1978.

NATHANIEL BALDWIN

"In 1903 a group of men under the leadership of Nathaniel Baldwin organized a cult for the purpose of preaching the gospel to the Indians. They believed in the Book of Mormon statements that the Lamanites would become a white and delightsome people, and hoped through their teachings, to bring about a realization of the statement. They had quite a following and located in southeast Salt Lake County, Utah. The group also practiced polygamy." (Carter, *Denominations...*, p. 34.)

SAMUEL EASTMAN

In the spring of 1904, Samuel Eastman of Salt Lake City, Utah, claimed to have received a heavenly message informing him that the LDS Church was out of order and that he was to prepare it for the coming of the One Mighty and Strong. He received a special priesthood authority, conferred upon him by a heavenly power.

Gathering about him a small group of followers, the doctrine he was preaching was deemed false by the LDS Church authorities and Eastman was excommunicated from the church in November 1905. This group was active for about 30 years until Eastman's death.

Doctrine

Fundamental Articles of Our Faith

We believe and maintain that under our present republican form of government in the United States of America, church and state should be kept separate in their spheres. The state should not dominate the church, nor encroach upon its functions, and nor should the church assume to dominate the state or interfere with its functions.

The Constitution of the State of Utah, after expressing gratitude to Almighty God for life and liberty, proceeds to recognize and establish the following: "All men have the inherent and inalienable right to enjoy and defend their lives and liberty; to acquire, possess and protect their property and to worship according to the dictates of their conscience; to assemble peaceably; protest against wrongs and petition for redress of grievances; to communicate freely their thoughts and opinions, being responsible for the abuse of that right." We believe and maintain that these principles are sacred and constitional, and form a part of our grand political and religious Magna Charta, which no ecclesiastical system or state can destroy or abridge, and that these principles of justice and liberty that have been secured to us through so much bloodshed and terrible suffering, shall be zealously guarded and maintained for every citizen in the land, regardless of creed or race.

The Constitution of the State of Utah further provides: "The rights of conscience shall never be infringed upon; the State shall make no law respecting the establishment of religion, or prohibiting the free exercise thereof." We hold and maintain that this injunction is binding upon religious systems, as well as it is upon the state, and provides the way for every individual, from the humblest to the greatest, to enjoy the freedom of his conscience without persecution from any source whatever. We hold and maintain that it has largely been churches and religious systems themselves that have violated these God-given principles, and brought upon their fellow beings unjust suffering and persecution.

We believe and maintain that all citizens should be instructed in the science of civil government, and in the laws of their country, in order to cast their vote intelligently and take their part in the governmental affairs of the state and nation, and thus help to bring about a more perfect state of society, preparatory to the actual setting up of the literal kingdom of God.

We believe and maintain that it is the duty of all citizens to each day pray to Almighty God that wisdom and sound understanding be given to our rulers, lawmakers, and judges to guide the nation that justice and righteousness might flow to all.

We believe and maintain that the literal kingdom of God, as foretold by the Jewish prophets, is now nigh at the door, and will be set upon the continent of America, but until then we believe in "being subject to the power that He, until he reigns whose right it is to reign and puts all enemies under his feet."

We believe in the divine mission of the Prophet Joseph Smith; that he was called upon to open up the dispensation of the fullness of time; bring forth the Book of Mormon; to organize anew the true church of Jesus Christ and restore the everlasting gospel and the holy priesthood, and to send the gospel among all nations, preparatory to the final setting up of the kingdom of God upon this continent.

We believe in the Book of Mormon, the book of Doctrine and Covenants and the Pearl of Great Price brought forth by Joseph Smith, and that they are holy scripture of equal authority with the Bible. These books, including the Bible, are our standard works, binding upon the priesthood as well as upon the people.

We believe and maintain, with St. Paul, the Apostle, that "all scripture is given by inspiration of God, and is profitable for doctrine, for reproof, for correction, for instruction in righteousness, that the man of God may be perfect, furnished unto all good works." (2 Tim. 16-17) We further believe and maintain that the Word of God, spoken by the authorized prophets cannot be broken or come to naught, but must be fulfilled, no matter what men or system may do to blind or to oppose. The sure word of the Lord is paramount to all the views and opinions of men and all true prophets and apostles, and preachers of righteousness will be in harmony therewith.

We believe and maintain that Joseph Smith, as a prophet, was in harmony with the prophets who preceded him; that he honored and respected their writings and prophecies by continually citing them; and that he threw much light upon their prophecies and like them, has to come, besides himself, to usher in the kingdom of God. (D & C sections 85-103, 113)

We believe and maintain that to the church was committed the task of preaching the gospel among all nations; organizing stakes; building of temples; and of gathering converts from among the nations to the stakes of Zion, and of instructing them in all the principles of the Gospel, preparatory to the actual setting up of the kingdom of God.

We believe and maintain that during the years the church has been located in the Rocky Mountains, it has gradually departed from some of its great principles laid down in the beginning, for its proper guidance and government; that the power of the priesthood has, to a certain extent, been exercised in the wrong spirit from what the Master intended, many having exercised it more in the spirit of masters of the flock of Christ, rather than in the spirit of true shepherds, and as a just consequence much of the power, keys and blessings have been withdrawn from the church.

Consequently, we further believe and strictly maintain that the time has arrived for the fulfillment of the word and promises of the Lord given to Joseph Smith; said he, the Lord "would send one to set His House in order," and raise up a servant to redeem Zion, and bring forth two instruments from the seed of David whose mission it is to gather all Israel home to be one united nation, and to prepare the way for the glorious appearance of the Messiah to rule and reign as "King of kings and Lord of Lords."

We further believe and maintain that, in consequence of the church in the Rocky Mountains having departed somewhat from the faith, and lost much of its power and spiritual blessings, the prophecy of Ezekiel in the 34th chapter particularly refers to the church of the latter days, and the state of the priesthood, that an entirely new administration is to be set up, and a true shepherd of the House of David, under Jesus Christ, is to take their place.

We also believe and maintain that the hour has fully come for the 3rd and 4th chapters of the Prophet Malachi to go into fulfillment, also that the 19th chapter of Isaiah and the 66th chapter of Isaiah, and other prophecies of similar import; that great and marvelous events are at our door even "a great and marvelous work and a wonder." Wherefore, repent, repent, humble yourselves before the Lord, for the hour of his judgment has come, and His "Kingdom to be established, no more to be thrown down."

We also believe and maintain that the hour has come for Zion to be redeemed; the New Jerusalem to be founded; the return of the lost ten tribes from the land of the North; the tribe of Judah to regain their national existence, and build up Palestine, and the coming forth of the royal seed of the House of David, and all the sure covenants of the Lord, concerning latter-day Israel, to be fulfilled.

We believe and maintain that in consequence of the church in the Rocky Mountains having departed somewhat from the faith and exercised the power of the priesthood contrary to the spirit and principles that God has laid down for the government of his church, that the time has come for the prophecy of Ezekiel in the 34th chapter, to be fulfilled, wherein it is expressly promised that a shepherd is to be raised up from the house and lineage of David, who is to feed the sheep after God's own way, and gather them together.

We further believe and maintain that this shepherd is the one foretold of by Joseph Smith in Doctrine and Covenants, Section 113, to whom he says: "Rightly belongs the priesthood and the keys of the kingdom, as an ensign, and for the gathering of my people in the last days."

Concerning the organization of the church of Christ, and the principles of the gospel, we cheerfully and readily affirm that we believe and accept in their entirety the thirteen articles of faith as enumerated and written by the Prophet Joseph Smith, and can truly say with him: "We believe all that God has revealed, all that He does now reveal, and that He will yet reveal great and glorious things pertaining to his kingdom" of whose coming the church is but the forerunner.

We believe and maintain that the prophecy of Daniel, the prophet, to the effect that "in the latter days the God of heaven would set up a kingdom that could never be broken up, nor given to another people" has reference to a literal political kingdom, and not a church, and there has been no promise made to the Church of Christ in latter days, that it is never to be broken up or fall away from the faith, for the scriptures prove the contrary.

We believe and maintain that churches, religious systems, and organized societies have a right to lay down just rules and regulations for the government and discipline of their members, and for just and proper causes, excommunicate them from their society or church, but they have no right, either human or divine to infringe upon conscience, suppress freedom of the soul, nor intimidate the mind, nor hinder the humblest soul from believing and worshipping as their conscience leads them.

We believe and maintain that the only power the church has a right to exercise over its members is that of moral suasion and kind entreaty, coupled with the Word of God, the "two edged sword of the spirit."

We further believe and maintain that while we consider it to be our solemn duty to declare the truth, expound the scriptures and unfold the designs and purposes of the Lord, which He has in view towards His children to bring them nigh unto Him, we believe at the same time that it is neither right nor just to assail, attack by slander or by falsehood in the least, any church or religious system. Let them all stand upon their own merits, and let the Holy Scriptures be the determining factor in the controversy as to who is right.

And lastly of all, we believe and declare to all peoples, tongues, and nations that the actual literal kingdom of God, as foretold by so many of the prophets, is now at hand, to be set upon this American Continent, and that the seed of David, to whom God has made special promises and covenants, respecting the kingdom, are due now to appear, and stand at the head of all Israel, organized into a nation, with Christ their King, and all this to fulfill the sure covenants of the Lord, to Latter-day Israel. (Eastman, Samuel, *The Fundamental Articles of Our Faith,* Salt Lake City, Utah, 1915.)

This group also maintained that the church should continue the practice of polygamy as it was a law of God's Holy Priesthood and that the United Order was to be started once again.

JOHN TANNER CLARK

John Tanner Clark (of Salt Lake City?) was excommunicated from the LDS Church on May 18, 1905 for declaring the Manifesto (respecting polygamy) a "covenant with death and an agreement with hell."

Clark advocated the restoration of plural marriage and claimed that he had been fore-ordained to bring forth the "Last Records" and protect the interests of the Lamanites. He also claimed to receive visitations and revelations. On one occasion it is reported that he heard a voice from heaven telling him that he was the most literal descendant of Jesus Christ living on the earth at the time.

THE ISRAELITE HOUSE OF DAVID (Dissen, Organ)

The only information I have been able to discover pertaining to this group is a letter that was printed in the RLDS Church 1906 General Conference Minutes.

"The Israelite House of David
"The New Eve, The Body of Christ

"To Joseph Smith, President of the Reorganized Church of the Latter Day Saints; Greeting: Believing as we do that your church holds faithfully to the scripture which says, 'Prove all things, hold fast that which is good;' and being informed that your doors open to those who contend for the faith once delivered to the Saints, we propose, not as a challenge to debate, for which we find no precedent in scripture, but as a privilege, that we be permitted to come before your people and present the faith as set forth in the Scriptures on the following conditions:

"First, that there be two or more addresses, number and length of time to be agreed upon.

"Second, that one member of your organization represent your claims as against one of us.

"Third, that the people be allowed to judge for themselves, as to who has presented the truth concerning the faith which was once delivered to the Saints, and still on record in the Scriptures.

"We are the more impressed to make this request from the fact that we have been repeatedly asked if we were willing to meet one of your representatives in joint discussion, before the public, that they might judge for themselves, and not be judged for by another.

"Signed by representative members of the House of David.

"Address Charles Dissen or Walter Organ, general delivery, Independence, Missouri, or meet in person.

"April 10, 1906."

"It was moved that the matter be referred to the presidency of the Independence Stake to take action, with the recommendation that if the discussion takes place at Independence, Missouri, the discussion of the same questions take place also before the society of that people at Benton Harbor, Michigan.

"After some discussion the matter was referred to the missionaries in charge of Missouri and Michigan."

HANNAH SORENSON

Just after the turn of the century, circa 1906, Mrs. Hannah Sorenson began conducting meetings in and around Springville, Utah. She gathered a sizeable following of people from that area, most of whom were members of the LDS Church. She was a staunch advocate of vegetarianism and taught the return to natural foods.

As time progressed, the gatherings of the group began to become more religious in nature. By 1910, the little gatherings had become full-fledged testimony meetings, with members claiming to speak in tongues and possessing the gift of interpreting the same. Many of the people made prophecies concerning the future of the LDS Church, claiming that the leaders of that church were in error.

Some of the group frequently ascended one of the mountains east of Springville, which was named "Kolob" where they would fast and conduct prayer meetings. Many attempts were made to cure people of illness by this method.

A few publications appeared, but the group lasted only a few years.

REORGANIZED CHURCH OF JESUS CHRIST (Allen Wright, et al.)

At the 1907 General Conference of The Church of Jesus Christ (Bickerton), a pamphlet concerning the Millennium, which had been written by Allen Wright, a member of the Twelve Apostles of the church, was publicly condemned. A resolution was passed that any officer of the church who believed in the principles set forth in the pamphlet be suspended.

Six of the Twelve refused to sustain the church in this action and were subsequently stripped of their priesthood offices and removed from the church. These men were Allen Wright, Solomon Van Lieu, Thomas Dixon, James Skillen, J. L. Armbrust and William T. Maxwell. Many other officers and members followed them out of the church.

Within a few months this group conducted a conference in Monongahela, Pennsylvania, at which the *Reorganized Church of Jesus Christ* with William T. Maxwell as president, was formally organized.

By 1935 the organization had all but disintegrated, with many of the members returning to the Bickerton following. Some others joined with the RLDS Church and others the Mormon Church. (See Cadman, W. H., *A History of the Church of Jesus Christ,* Monongahela, Pennsylvania: published by the church, 1945, pp. 107-109)

THE PRIESTHOOD COMPANY

This group was an alleged split, circa 1910, from the RLDS Church. Polygamous in teaching and practice, the group is purported to have been located in the Polynesian Islands.

No further details are available.

PRIMITIVE CHURCH OF JESUS CHRIST (James Caldwell)

Contending that The Church of Jesus Christ (Bickerton) had fallen from the truth, and holding that the church must strictly conform with the principles set forth in the Bible and Book of Mormon, James Caldwell and his followers believed that the time had come for the church to be "reorganized." This group did not consider themselves to be a "break-off" but a continuation.

In 1914, the church was organized under the name "Primitive Church of Jesus Christ" although they believed the true name of the church should simply be the Church of Jesus Christ. Pennsylvania state law at the time prohibited two different church organizations from operating under the same name. A few years later this law was modified in order that two churches could have the same name if they were headquartered in different cities. Thereupon this group became known as "The Church of Jesus Christ, with headquarters in Erie, Pennsylvania."

Although some of the information I have obtained is in conflict with other data, it appears that church headquarters eventually moved to Lawrence Park, Pennsylvania.

Mr. Laurence C. Dias has been credited by some as having his own church, but I have ascertained that he was actually James Caldwell's successor. Dias died circa 1964. Since his death the church has gradually disbanded. Many members rejoined the Bickertonites.

This group recognized Joseph Smith, Jr. as a man called of God to bring forth the Book of Mormon and to be a prophet, but that he was gradually led from the truth by the forces of evil.

The church claimed it was first organized on April 6, 1830; reorganized by William Bickerton on July 7, 1862 as The Church of Jesus Christ; and incorporated as the Primitive Church of Jesus Christ on August 31, 1914.

The Bible and Book of Mormon were accepted as the scriptural standards of the church. The first vision of Joseph Smith was rejected and the church shows from the scriptures that the Godhead of the Father, Son and Holy Ghost is one, spiritual being and not three separate and distinct beings.

CHURCH OF THE CHRISTIAN BROTHERHOOD (Richard C. Evans)

A one time member of the First Presidency of the RLDS Church, Richard C. Evans became disenchanted with the Church and led a rather large group away circa 1917. Establishing their headquarters in Toronto, Ontario, Canada, a sustantial building was erected for their meetings.

They used only the Bible as their scriptural standard. After Evans died in 1928 the group disbanded.

Doctrine

Epitome of Faith and Doctrine

We believe in God the Eternal Father, and in His Son Jesus Christ, and in the Holy Ghost.

We believe that men will be punished for their own sins and not for Adam's transgression.

We believe that through the atonement of Christ all men may be saved by obedience to the laws and ordinances of the gospel. We believe that these ordinances are:

1st. Faith in God and in the Lord Jesus Christ.

2nd. Repentance.

3rd. Baptism by immersion for the remission of sins.

4th. Laying on of hands for the gift of the Holy Ghost.

5th.We believe in the resurrection of the body; that the dead in Christ will rise first, and the rest of the dead will not live again until the thousand years are expired.

6th. We believe in the doctrine of Eternal Judgment, which provides that men shall be judged, rewarded, or punished according to the degree of good, or evil, they shall have done.

We believe that a man must be called of God, and ordained by the Laying on of Hands of those who are in authority, to entitle him to preach the Gospel, and administer in the ordinances thereof.

We believe in the same kind of organization that existed in the Primitive Church.

We believe that in the Bible is contained the word of God, we believe that God, by His Spirit, will continue to reveal his word to man until the end of time.

We believe in the power and gifts of the everlasting Gospel, viz: the gift of faith, discerning of spirits, revelation, healing, wisdom, charity, brotherly love, etc.

We believe that marriage is ordained of God; and that the law of God provides for but one companion in wedlock, for either man or woman, except in cases where the contract of marriage is broken by death or transgression.

We believe that in all matters of controversy upon the duty of man toward God, and in reference to preparation and fitness for the world to come, the word of God should be decisive and the end of dispute; and that when God directs, man should obey.

We believe that the religion of Jesus Christ, as taught in the New Testament scriptures, will, if its precepts are accepted and obeyed, make men and women better in the domestic circle, and better citizens of town, country, and state, and consequently better fitted for the change which cometh at death.

We believe that all men should worship God in "Spirit and in truth;" and that such worship does not require a violation of the constitutional law of the land.

We claim the privilege of worshipping Almighty God according to the dictates of our consciences, allow all men the same privilege; let them worship how, where, or what they may.

We believe that Christ was manifest to the world to destroy the work of the Devil, to destroy death, to rescue all from the grave, to enlighten humanity, to save the lost, to redeem the fallen, and finally restore perfect harmony in all God's vast universe.

We believe that the heathen nations and the sinners of the more enlightened portion of the world may hear the gospel in the intermediate state between death and the resurrection, and that the work of punishment, reformation, or salvation will be accomplished is very evident from the scriptures. (From a leaflet published by the church in Toronto, nd)

MOSES GUDMUNDSEN

On April 6, 1918, Moses and Octavius Gudmundsen each filed for homestead land in West Tintic, Utah. Moses was a teacher of violin and an Associate Professor of Music at Brigham Young University in Provo, Utah.

By encouraging friends to follow his example, Gudmundsen was able to establish a settlement of about 60 people. An attempt was made to form a cooperative agricultural community with a communal way of life.

A branch of the LDS Church was established there with Gudmundsen as the branch president. He was later asked to resign due to the fact that some of his teachings were not in harmony with the doctrines of the church. As time went on, several of their own doctrines developed and were adopted. Gudmundsen began claiming revelation from God.

In the fall of 1920, the principle of "wife sacrifice" was revealed, which allowed men who were married to someone other than their "true" mates, to abandon those wives and take a "spiritual" wife.

The colony broke up in April of 1921 and Gudmundsen went to California. However, the following August, he suddenly returned to the remains of his people and announced that the "day of destruction" was upon them. In December, he and another member of the group were convicted of adultery. Gudmundsen was acquitted and returned to California. The colony disintegrated.

THE CHURCH OF CHRIST, THE ORDER OF ZION (John Zahnd)

John Zahnd left the RLDS Church circa 1918 because of an inability to justify many of the prevalent attitudes in the church at that time. He saw the church preaching and teaching many things which they were not practicing.

He felt that the church should be living the united order, that is having all things in common as is referred to in the New Testament. In addition, he was unable to accept the church offices of High Priest and First Presidency because of the lack of any references to them in the Holy Bible.

Recognizing that Joseph Smith, Jr. was indeed a prophet of god, Zahnd maintained that Joseph had no authority to assume the presidency of the church. In his faith, he asserted that the Twelve Apostles (Elders) were to be the leading quorum of the church in accordance with the biblical precedent.

The Church of Christ, The Order of Zion had its first meeting in Kansas City, Missouri, in September 1918. The following October 20 a revelation to Zahnd is recorded:

"Thus saith Jesus Christ, your Lord that thou my servant John has been called and ordained by the hand of my angel to do a work for me. I have watched over thee since thy youth and you have been caused to suffer many things because of trusting in man. It is my will that you should be an Apostle of Light to set in order My Church and my kingdom on earth as restored by the hand of my angel in these, the last days. Many false leaders have imposed themselves upon My people in teaching those ways that are not my ways; My laws have been transgressed and long have I heard the cry of the widow and orphan ascend unto Me because of the ungodly, and I have chosen thee as one mighty and strong in spirit to proclaim my truth upon the earth.

"It is my desire that my servants O. K. Fry, C. C. Coffeen, G. B. Miller, Charles H. Fish, J. E. Davis, John Flanders and Joseph Florey be chosen and ordained into My Holy Priesthood under your hands to counsel and advise you, to be Mine Apostles of light unto the world and to help in establishing My law of things in common that Zion may be established in haste, for great confusion and distrust is coming upon the earth; men are weary in waiting for justice to be performed.

"As has been made known to you in the past by my voice in vision I again affirm unto you that my servant Fred S. Anderson shall be chosen and ordained a Bishop in Zion, and my servant, Ellis Shimmel, shall be ordained a Bishop in Zion to counsel and assist my servant, Fred, in the temporal affairs and to always advise and work in harmony with Mine Apostles.

"It is my will that all these thy brethren shall come forth and take their place as I have called them, and it is My will that they all assemble in nearness to each other that My law and order be established, I have called them, and if any man fail to fill the place that I desire them to occupy they will do so at their own peril.

"My Spirit has led thee in My way and thou shall have My guiding hand to direct you in My law as you may desire and need wisdom from me, thus spake the power and voice of Jesus Christ.

"Note. An Apostle of Light as referred to in the above manifestation is simply referred to as an elder, one especially favored by the Lord to help in establishing Zion, and should not be construed as meaning Apostles in the sense of the Twelve that preside over the church, as they must be chosen by the casting of lots in accordance with the law." (*The Order of Zion,* Volume 1, Number 3, Kansas City, Missouri, 1918.)

In November 1928 we find John Zahnd writing an article in the *Messenger*, Thomas W. Williams' Church of Jesus Christ monthly, wherein he briefly comments on his past, but gives no details. It is surmised that by this time, Zahnd's church was no longer functioning.

Doctrine

Priesthood and Church Organization

Each year the membership of the church elected twelve elders to be the Twelve Apostles at the head of the church. It was provided that if any of the Twelve who had served the previous year were not reelected, they would take their place as a pastor or teacher in the church.

The various offices in the priesthood were Priest, Teacher, Evangelist and Bishop.

Branches of the church could be organized where 12 or more members of age eight or older lived. Each branch was to select one elder as the pastor of their branch.

A general church conference was held each September where the business of the church could be transacted.

This group tried to practice having all things in common.

Publications

Besides the church newspaper, *The Order of Zion,* several booklets expounding the teachings of the church were issued. The Bible and Book of Mormon were accepted as scriptural standards.

THE CHURCH OF JESUS CHRIST (Thomas W. Williams)

Thomas W. Williams was baptized into the RLDS Church in 1875 as a boy not quite nine years old. He was an active member of the church throughout his life and rapidly moved up through the ranks of church leadership and priesthood responsibility. At the 1920 conference of the RLDS Church, Williams was called to the Apostleship in that church and served in that position until 1924, when the "Supreme Directional Control" controversy flared up.

In essence, Frederick M. Smith, RLDS Church President, had asked for more direct managerial authority over the programs of the church. Williams and others felt this move was dangerous in that giving the president of the church too much power, the members would lose their voice in the affairs of the church—which was a very important facet of church government.

Originally the Protest Movement attempted to bring about a change but when this was found impossible, *The Church of Jesus Christ* was organized in an attempt to "reconstruct the church according to the original pattern."

Early history of this protest movement appeared in the official publication *The Messenger*:

"About ten days prior to the convening of the General Conference in 1925 a number of old-time and well-known ministers of the church met for a season of prayer and meditation. This continued almost daily, until Saturday April 4, when after a prolonged season of earnest supplication to God for light, at which time the illumination of the Spirit was clearly manifested to the comfort and joy of all present, the number being about twenty-five, a document was drafted and signed as follows:

"Complete Text of the Protest Document

"Whereas, the document on church government, now before the General Conference of the Reorganized Church of Jesus Christ of Latter Day Saints, grants to the First Presidency supreme directional control over all the affairs of the church, spiritual and temporal; and

"Whereas, because of the irregularities attending the introduction and development of the doctrine of supreme directional control, together with the threat of 'elimination' made by the President of the church against some of the leading church officials who are opposed to the document on church government, and because of the illegal selection and instruction of certain delegations to the General Conference; and

"Whereas, this document on church government limits the legislative rights of the General Conference to assenting or consenting to the proposals of an autocratically controlled priesthood; and

"Whereas, this demand for a completely centralized government with supreme directional control, which would in fact rest in the President, would fundamentally change the established order of the church; and

"Whereas, this change from a theocratic democracy to an autocracy—a hierarchy with final and supreme directional control in the hands of one man strikes at the very heart of the principles of church government contained in our standard books (The Bible, the Book of Mormon, and the Doctrine and Covenants) and General Conference enactments, by which the Reorganized Church in the Temple Lot Suit established its rights and claim to be the true church in succession; and

"Whereas, should this document be indorsed it would be tantamount to apostasy—a departure from the accepted principles and practices of the Reorganized Church;

"Therefore, we solemnly declare that we will not support nor countenance this attempt to change the fundamental principles of government given of God and will consider ourselves justified in taking such steps as will protect the constitutional rights of the officers and members of the church against this insidious departure from the faith.

"Further, as a group holding allegiance to the faith and principles established from the beginning of the Reorganized Church, we pledge ourselves to carry on the work of God in harmony with his law." (*The Messenger,* Volume 1, Number 1, Independence, Missouri, October 1925, pp. 1, 5)

Hundreds of church members put their signatures to this document. Many prominent leaders of the RLDS Church transferred their membership to the Church of Christ (Temple Lot) and others joined the Protest Movement. Many were active in both.

Joint meetings were held on occasion between the protestors and the Temple Lot people, but it would be several years before many of the protestors would officially join forces with the church on the Temple Lot.

It is important to note that Williams did not seek to lead and did not actively seek followers. Even when The Church of Jesus Christ became an entity separate from the RLDS Church, the organization was quite informal.

By February 1926, the protestors realized that reconciliation with the RLDS Church was impossible. That month's issue of *The Messenger* contains the announcement of a special general conference to be held on April 6, 1926 at Independence. The call begins: "We are assured it is the desire of our Father in heaven that all those who believe in the angel's message, who are willing to build upon the foundation of the Bible and the Book of Mormon and are opposed to the supreme directional control heresy, should unite in one common purpose and fellowship to interpret in their lives his mind and will to establish his kingdom on the earth."

On the announced date The Church of Jesus Christ was organized. For the first few years general conferences were held faithfully each April and October. The church was led by an Executive Committee which was elected at the conferences. As things evolved, regular conferences became a thing of the past—to be called only in a specific need. Williams seems to have lost interest in the movement. He returned to his home in Los Angeles, California and was elected to the city council. He died there on April 11, 1931.

After Williams' death the movement disbanded with many of its members uniting with the Temple Lot church.

Many of those who will be discussed in a later section in this volume as "independent" were prominent in the protest movement.

Doctrine

Acceptance of the Bible and the Book of Mormon as scriptural foundations was preeminent. The Doctrine and Covenants was accepted with some reservations at first, but later acceptance moved toward the Book of Commandments.

A statement of belief was published in the church paper in november 1926:

"We believe in God the Eternal Father, Creator of the heavens and the earth, unchangeable and without respect of persons, who speaks to every human heart and would have all men come into fellowship with Him.

"We believe in Jesus Christ, the Son, in whom the God of love was manifest in the flesh, whom we own as our Leader, Witness and Commander, and the head of the Church militant and triumphant. He is an example unto us in all things, having revealed unto us what we may become.

"We believe in the Holy Ghost, the Spirit of Truth, the Comforter, which makes known the deep things of God, brings to our minds things which are past, reveals things to come, and is the medium by which we receive the revelation of Jesus Christ.

"We believe that all men may be saved by a compliance with the gospel of Jesus Christ, the inductive principles of which embrace:

> "Faith in God and in his Son, Jesus Christ and in the Holy Ghost; repentance and baptism for the remission of sins, the laying on of hands for the reception of the Holy Ghost.

"We believe in continuous and pervasive revelation, that God inspires men in every age and among all people 'and that He speaks when, where, and through whom He may elect and without respect of persons.

"We believe in the literal second coming of Jesus Christ; in the resurrection of the dead, and in eternal judgment, and that men will be rewarded and punished according to the good or evil they may have done.

"We believe the signs and gifts of the everlasting gospel, the heritage of all of the followers of Christ, are: the word of wisdom, the gift of knowledge, the gift of healing, the working of miracles, prophecy, discernment of spirits, divers kinds of tongues, interpretation of tongues.

"We believe the fruits of the Spirit should be manifest in all. They are: love, joy, peace, long-suffering, gentleness, goodness, faith, meekness, and temperance."

CHURCH OF CHRIST, INDEPENDENT-INFORMAL (Frank F. Wipper)

Following his withdrawal from the RLDS Church during the Supreme Directional Control controversy in the mid-1920s, Frank F. Wipper united with the Church of Christ (Temple Lot). He was one of the seven men called to the Apostleship in that church in the spring of 1926.

His tenure in office was short, tendering his resignation the following September. A few members followed him and they organized the Church of Christ, Independent-Informal in 1927 with about 20 members. The group rapidly disintegrated—perhaps because of the very fact that it was "independent and informal."

Later Wipper organized the Book of Mormon Foundation, which is covered later in this volume.

PAUL FEIL

In September of 1928, Paul Feil claimed to have received a revelation from God directing him to present himself at the General

Conference of the LDS Church in Salt Lake City and give the church and its leaders a warning.

Feil claimed that President Heber J. Grant had allowed the priesthood to become priest-craft ridden, and had become an opponent of the law of the plurality of wives and the United Order.

Close associates claimed that Feil was the messenger of the New and Everlasting Covenant whom the Lord promised would come and set the House of God in order. It was further stated that Feil was to be the next president of the LDS Church.

All church presidents up to but excepting Heber J. Grant were accepted.

Feil and his followers used the Book of Mormon, Doctrine and Covenants and the Inspired Version of the Bible for their scriptural standards.

Doctrine

The following statement of beliefs was received by Feil through revelation in 1930 and in 1934:

We believe and sustain all the thirteen Articles of Faith, as they stand and were written by Joseph Smith, Jr., the Prophet of God, as true and defend them in all their plainness and simplicity.

We believe and claim that Joseph Smith, Jr., the Prophet, was truly inspired from on High to write these 13 Articles of Faith for the guidance of the Church of Jesus Christ of Latter-day Saints and that he defended all the truths contained therein, as well as all the other revealed truths in the Bible (Inspired Translation), Book of Mormon and all the revelations in the Doctrine and Covenants, and also in the Pearl of Great Price as he received them by God, and by Holy revelations, by the sacrifice of his life and blood through his Martyrdom on the 27th day of June, 1844, in Carthage jail, Illinois, U.S. of America.

We believe and claim, not to be ashamed to defend all the glorious truths, holy heavenly, and all redemptive principles as brought forth through him his great, noble divine Mission and Sacrificing Work, as a true Ambassador and mouthpiece of Jesus Christ, the Redeemer of the World, upon the Earth, who closed his noble work and mission, by laying down his life for the truth alike his Lord and Master Himself did!

We believe and claim to honor, sustain and exalt Jesus Christ the Saviour and Redeemer of the World in His glorious Work, Mission and far-reaching atoning sacrifice for the salvation and redemption of the Children of Man and also all the noble Martyrs from the time of Abel (the just) up to His own crucifixion and also all the noble followers of Him, who sacrificed their lives for the truth's sake in martyrdom after Him; and so likewise all the noble martyrs since the beginning of the opening of "the dispensation of the fullness of times." David W. Patten the noble, first; Joseph Smith, Jr., the Prophet; Hyrum Smith, Parley P. Pratt, Joseph Standing and many other true braves, unknown at present unto us and all others, the noble "pioneers," who, through their suffering, lost their lives for the truth. And, we fully believe and know, that the time is nigh upon us, and the Children of Men, when a just and avenging God will judge, vindicate, and justify their sacrifices and noble, exemplary lives upon the inhabitants of the Earth until all their sacrifices are fully avenged and atoned for; and the truthfulness of their God-fearing lives and all the truths and holy principles as revealed in The Plan of Life and Salvation "The Everlasting Gospel" and the New and Everlasting Covenant as plainly brought forth and established through the choice Seer of the Lord: Joseph Smith, Jr., the Prophet of the 19th Century and will be gloriously vindicated unto the greatest victory for the salvation and greatest happiness of all the nations upon the earth, and all this will and shall be done, with an Eye single to the Glory of God; and to the exaltation of the name of the Lord Jesus Christ and His redemptive work, His Church upon the Earth, for the redemption of all the human race and the redemption of the Earth itself; and the glorious establishment of His Righteousness, His Kingdom of Peace and Justice upon the earth, Yea: "the establishment of His Zion upon this choice and chosen land of the Lord!"

We believe and claim, that a departure from the original child-like faith in God unto repentance, as delivered through Joseph Smith, Jr., the Prophet of God, unto the Church has taken place in the same by the plain evidence before all the faithful Saints; and that "The Church of Jesus Christ of Latter-day Saints" is indeed out of order now!

We believe and claim that the sure promises of the Lord unto His Church and redemptive work in these last days, as they were given and revealed in the 85th, 103rd and the 113th Sections of the Doctrine and Covenants, as well as through the Angel Moroni in His remarkable solemn visitations in the night of 21-22 September 1823, concerning the 11th Chapter of Isaiah, the 3rd and 4th Chapters of Malachi, the 3rd Chapter of Acts, 22-23 verses, and the 2nd Chapter of Joel in the Bible, were not fulfilled at any time in the History of the Church previously, but are now at our very door to be fulfilled for they contain the sure promises, decrees and Covenants of the Lord as were made unto "The House of Israel" through his ancient holy prophets and will now all be fulfilled through His divinely chosen promised Servants and Instruments with an eye single to His everlasting glory and exaltation of His holy name and work forever and ever!

We believe and claim therefore, that "The Church of Jesus Christ of Latter-day Saints" must now come to a speedy awakening, return to the Lord their true God and Redeemer, repent speedily, yea, repent, reform and accept fully all the glorious principles of everlasting truths as were given their Prophet Joseph Smith, Jr., and also accept their humble and faithful servant now among them, for their deliverance, redemption and salvation; and then learn to be truly converted, unto the Lord their God, and become a truly united people, according to the revealed righteousness of "The Everlasting Gospel" and all help, as instruments of honor in His hands, to bring forth and establish the Lord's Kingdom and Zion upon this chosen land of the Lord!

We believe and claim that the 11th Chapter of Isaiah must be fulfilled by the true and full conversion unto the Lord of the Saints of the most High God, "The Lord's Own Elect," yea, "the elect according to the Covenant in the Church, or out of the Church! in order to bring to pass the glorious Blessings as contained in that remarkable solemn 11th Chapter of Isaiah," the Kingdom of God, of Peace, Love, Justice and of full righteousness to be established upon the Earth, and: "The knowledge of the Lord," shall cover the Earth, as the waters cover the Sea; and therefore the great necessity of a speedy repentance and a thorough Reformation among all Israel in bondage!

We believe, claim and know, by the perusals of the sacred History of our Forefathers of The House of Israel, that all their bondages, oppression, drivings, sore judgments, curses, captivities and scatterings, among the nations of the earth, was all on account of their disobedient hearts unto the Lord, their God, His holy laws, Commandments and Statutes, and would have saved themselves from all these calamities. If they would have obeyed their true and faithful Servants and Messengers, divine, humble men and prophets as raised up by their Lord for them, as well as by their Saviour Himself, but they did not so; and hence their awful calamities came upon them! And we know by the present experiences among present-day Israel yea, Ephraim, that they are inclined to be stubborn likewise, again, and their hearts are hard towards their glorious redemptive message of Salvation, and deliverance as held out again unto them by the instrumentality of One of their chosen and promised servants; among them now; and will, we believe, again bring upon themselves the sore chastisements of the Lord. If they willfully reject their saving and redemptive message until all they, who remain, are willing to yield by a true and full obedience to the same and soften and offer their hearts fully for a true conversion unto the Lord and His Plan of Life and Salvation!

The following four Articles were received on Tuesday, March 13th, 1934:

We believe as citizens of this great Nation—The United States of America, that it is our full right to defend our Constitutional rights, our Liberty, our Freedom, as guaranteed, secured and declared in the Declaration of Independence to express and defend our belief, our faith in God unto repentance, as revealed and delivered by Joseph Smith, Jr., the Prophet of God, unto this Nation and unto "The Church of Jesus Christ of Latter-day Saints," and now fully believe that the set time to do so has fully arrived!

Therefore, we believe as the Saints of God and humble followers of Jesus Christ the God of this chosen Land; and as the only true defenders of the true Faith in God, unto true practice; and also of "The Church of Jesus Christ of Latter-day Saints" in its divine, original order, and also likewise all, what God has granted, blessed and given unto this Nation—the United States of America—in those two original sacred documents, or Constitutions as stated in Article 10, that now true and full justice must be met and be dealt out, and the true facts and evidences plainly be acknowledged that the House of God, The Church of Jesus Christ of Latter-day Saints, is truly out of order, and now must be called to order and set in order, and even be called upon by a true Messenger of the Lord unto a true and full repentance, reformation and full return unto their Lord and God and His Holy Laws, plainly given and revealed unto them by their Prophet Joseph Smith, Jr.

We believe and know that the solemn hour and set time has now fully arrived, in order, that true Justice and Righteousness as so plainly revealed in "The full of the Gospel of Christ in this, the Dispensation of the fullness of times, and so long entrusted unto "The Church of Jesus Christ of Latter-day Saints," but not upheld, neither sustained nor defended as a true remedy against all the evils, oppressions, bondages, injustices and unrighteousness in this detracted, now suffering world, under great pains and pangs of distress unbearable unto all the suffering poor upon the face of the earth, among all the Nations, thereof, by a misdirecting and misleading Priesthood of said Church, and we hereby claim as the true Saints of God and followers of Jesus Christ, that all these many leading Prophets and Leaders of His Church are without the true light, and are poverty-stricken of all divine Wisdom, Power and Influence for the defense of the only pleasing justice and righteousness before the God of Heaven and before all the Children of Men upon the face of the earth. And that it is now the most solemn duty and obligation of all the God-fearing, upon this chosen and choice land of the Lord's promised Zion to require and appeal unto these present leaders of said Church that a promised Messenger now among them must be heard before all Israel, the body of said Church, in order that said Church shall be delivered from the great ills and ailments of such sorrowful misleadings by its present misdirecting Priesthood and be brought and led back again unto its true pasture and plain doctrines of Christ, and be rescued and delivered out of the hands of a cruel and despotic Priesthood and remodeled and recovered again and then fulfill its great and nobler destiny, as God's representative Work of Deliverance and Redemption unto all the Nations and Children of Men, and establishment of true and full justice and righteousness upon the Earth and help to usher in the long foretold and promised Reign of Peace, Love and Justice of a thousand years!

We as the Saints of the Most High God, believe and know that the God of Heaven is on our side and will stand by us and His heavenly hosts will attend all our noble, humble efforts, and He will hear and answer our affectionate supplications and petitions of true faith in Him unto repentance, and that He will fulfill all His sure promises unto His God-fearing people upon this His chosen Land of Zion, and that He will overrule for the fulfillment of His greater purposes with Israel and Zion, and overthrow and overcome all His and His true people's opponents, enemies and foes against His great redeeming cause for the deliverance of His Israel as well as the Earth itself!

Finally, we, the Saints of the Most High know (with great Sorrows in our hearts) most solemnly, at these the Last Times of Great Tribulations rolling fast over all the Earth at this day of the Lord's Grace on Tuesday, August 12, 1941. Above all us poor helpless mortals, that all the Sure and Solemn Decrees of the Lord as they were uttered under the Holy Zeal of the Lord upon the Holy Prophets—Moses, Apostle Peter—that every soul which will not hear that Prophet (which is Christ, the Lord), shall be destroyed from among the people. Solemnly compare Acts 3:22-23. And that these great destructions that will remove all despisers of our beloved Redeemer and Lord, all the hard-hearted, unbelieving defiant and rebellious people of mankind, will consist of these Great Wars now raging upon the Earth, of Sword, Famine and Pestilence and other many destroying means of Tempest, Fires, Floods, Earthquakes, desolating sickness and all kinds of epidemics in order to cleanse off our destined Mother Earth for the Kingdom of Christ the Lord and His promised Zion of Peace and Love ever more from all wickedness. Most solemnly compare solemn visits of Angel Moroni unto the Prophet Joseph Smith, Jr., September 21-22, 1823, page 88-94 and learn. Pearl of Great Price. And we now most humbly and solemnly declare hereby and that in the holy name of the Lord of Hosts the true and Living God now angry and offended about rebellious mankind, and now preaches His own sermons of the Gospel of Great Judgments upon all the nations of the earth, that the only safety, deliverance and redemption for the remaining children of men upon the earth, is to turn fully unto the Lord, their inviting Redeemer, and, repent O repent, speedily, and be baptized, for the remission of their sins and pollutions in the name of the Father, of the Son and of the Holy Ghost, before Him by immersion in water by a true Servant of the Lord and receive the Holy Ghost by laying on of hands, be baptized by Fire and the Holy Ghost and thereby receive a true re-birth in Christ, the Lord, and thus enter into the Door of His Sheepfold into His Kingdom of Peace, Truth, Love, Justice and Righteousness evermore, and then continue to work out their salvation before Him with fear and with trembling and learn daily the precepts of the Lord, line upon line, precept upon precept alike a child learns from a loving teaching Father obediently, and thus such humble obedient truth-loving and God-fearing souls can become noble instruments in the hands of the Lord to help to establish His revealed Righteousness upon the Earth and a reign of peace of a thousand years, the glorious promised Zion, a Millennial Sabbath Day!

And as the humble receiver of all these most solemn lines of pure inspiration, and as the promised servant of the Lord unto Zion all Israel in a great bondage here in the Rocky Mountains, pray that many of you humble readers shall make themselves speedily worthy for preservation, safety, deliverance, redemption; and be found on the side of the Lord; and act obediently now in the fear of the Lord. Amen. (Paul Feil, The Messenger, The Lord's Servant, August, 1941, Salt Lake City, Utah.)

LDS DEPRESSION YEARS MOVEMENT

Not really a church or a religious group, this movement began in Utah during the depression. It became a concerted protest against the LDS Church's welfare program, which was just starting, and the manner in which it was being administrated. Other items of concern were brought forth, including the changing of the temple "garment" (the sacred article of underclothing worn by members of the LDS Church who had received temple endowments) and the mortgaging of church properties, including the temple, to financial institutions in New York.

Many of these people later identified with the Davis County Co-op Society and other groups of Fundamentalist persuasion.

The following petition, with a space left at the bottom for signatures, etc., was circulated during this time:

"To the First Presidency and Council of the Twelve:

"Undersigned do hereby petition you that the Church Relief be raised from the $11.36½ a year per person as quoted by Reuben J. [sic] Clark while in New York and printed in the Deseret News for May 29, 1936, to $20 per month per person which would require not one million dollars but Twenty One Million One Hundred Twenty Thousand Dollars ($21,120,000) a year for the 88,000 persons.

"However President Grant we do not desire Relief (Relief is what Lazarus had, as Jesus told in Luke 16) but would much rather earn our daily bread by the sweat of our brow as God has told us to do, at a fair rate of pay. We are willing to work for the same rate of pay as you are receiving, for our bodies are of exactly the same materials as yours and our bodies require the services of Doctors, Dentists, also clothing, shelter and nourishment very much the same as yours does.

"For remember God had said that we should be equal in earthly things else we can not be equal in heavenly things, which is to say if there is division among us there is discord, hate and envyings or Hell on Earth as we will have Hell in the hereafter if we can not do as the Lord has said that we should do, but if we are united we can make this Earth a Heaven for ourselves.

"President Grant, please tell us why it is that a person can go into most any shop in Salt Lake City and buy a so-called Union Suit, and in the same shop can also buy another identical Union Suit with the approved Garment Label sewed on it but at an extra cost of 50 cents?

"Is the L.D.S. Garment without the Label only a common underwear and after being marked is there any difference in the labeled or unlabeled apparel?

"If the labeled Garment is holier than the unlabeled then has not that which is holy been turned into a thing of merchandise at 4900 per cent profit as the extra cost of the label can not possibly be more than one cent?"

THE CHURCH OF CHRIST (Otto Fetting)

A long time member of the RLDS Church, Otto Fetting was ordained to the office of High Priest in accordance with action taken at the 1920 conference of that body. However, Fetting joined the great exodus to the Temple Lot church during the Supreme Directional Control problems and gained prominence there due to his leadership abilities. He was one of the seven men called and ordained Apostles in the Temple Lot church in the spring of 1926.

The following February he received what was to be the first of a series of thirty visitations from an heavenly messenger. Later it was learned that this messenger was John the Baptist. Over the next two years, Fetting received 11 more messages. In accordance with the practice of the Temple Lot group, these revelations were duly considered and at first accepted. Even his call to begin building the temple in Independence in 1929 was accepted with excitement and work was begun. The temple was never finished.

Events soon took another course, for with the twelfth message, received July 18, 1929, a doctrine that was unacceptable to many in the church was introduced. This doctrine was that of re-baptism, and it became the cause of heated debate and eventually fragmentation of the church. Fetting and his followers were removed from the church.

The Church of Christ was officially established and organized in 1929 in obedience to the 12th message. God said he had waited 100 years since the time John the Baptist laid his hands on Joseph Smith, Jr. (See *Message* 19:12; 30:6) The complete text of the Twelfth Message is contained in the Appendix. Almost one-third the total membership of the Temple Lot group followed Brother Fetting, and at that time the number of people involved was about 1400.

Two days before his demise on January 30, 1933, Fetting received the thirtieth message.

The church continued its work, beset at times by factionalism. One of the most significant problems was the situation with W. A. Draves, who will be discussed at length later. Brother Draves had left the Mormon Church and joined the Temple Lot group, but followed Otto Fetting in 1929. In 1937 Draves began receiving visits from the Messenger. These were neither accepted nor rejected by the church, but allowed to stand on their own merits. Certain facts eventually came to light which some of the leadership of the church were unable to reconcile. Draves led a group from the church and formed another church after losing a court battle.

A missionary minded church, The Church of Christ has always strived to spread the gospel message when and where it could. A mission in Nigeria has been established, for example, and one of the Twelve Apostles is a Nigerian brother.

Doctrine

Articles of Faith and Practice

These are identical to those in use by the Church of Christ (Temple Lot). In the first message the Messenger said not to change them since God had inspired the men who had written them.

The Sabbath

Sunday was originally the accepted day of worship, but the practice had been questioned for a number of years in light of the scriptural record. About 1956, the Twelve Apostles were in agreement on this question and the Seventh Day Sabbath (Saturday) was initiated as a standard church practice.

The Temple

"As yet there is no temple built but I believe it is not too far distant. People have to be prepared spiritually to build it." (R. T.

The Church of Christ has built this headquarters building on East Gudgell Street in Independence, Missouri.

Bronson, Apostle, in a letter to the author, April 14, 1975.)

Other Beliefs

"We believe in the one God head, the Book of Mormon making this very clear. We believe the Seventh Day was the Sabbath of our Lord. We believe in the same Church organization that existed when Christ set up His Church, First Apostles, etc. We do not have High Priests, Presidents, etc. We believe as Message 12:8 states that Christ is at the head of the church." (Bronson, letter to the author, December 12, 1974.)

A similar church organization and priesthood structure as exists with the Temple Lot group is followed.

Publications

The church accepts the Bible and the Book of Mormon, but does not prints its own editions. Most members prefer the RLDS 1908 Authorized Edition of the Book of Mormon. The thirty messages received by Otto Fetting are printed in a separate book entitled, *The Word of the Lord.*

The *Voice of Warning* is the official church paper, being published monthly since 1930.

Several tracts explaining church doctrine are also available.

CHURCH OF CHRIST (E. J. Trapp)

The April 1930 conference of the Church of Christ (Temple Lot) selected Brother E. J. Trapp to fill one of the vacancies in the Council of Twevle Apostles. Apostle Samuel Wood was sent to England to ordain Trapp to the Apostleship.

Ernest John Trapp was called the father of the Reorganization in Gloucester, England by Samuel Wood in the January 1930 *Zion's Advocate*. Wood had been in England for some time organizing branches of the church.

"However, here again dissension was ready to break out. Wood seems to have become imbued with the "One Person Godhead" heresy, and made that a part of his teaching while in Britain, on this, his second trip over there. This resulted in creating a serious division among the membership of that country. They had already been disturbed and divided by the defection of Fetting and Gates, and a number had been rebaptized and become members of the Fetting group. Now this new heresy of there being no trinity in the Godhead, again caused a split over there. A special conference was held by the Apostolic Quorum in Independence, Missouri, and again they were met with defiance; and Apostles Samuel Wood, C. W. Morgan and E. J. Trapp, who were teaching this new cause of division were dismissed from the Council, and Samuel Wood was disfellowshipped after an Elder's Court trial, and E. J. Trapp left the church." (Flint, B. C., *An Outline Hitory of the Church of Christ (Temple Lot)*, Independence, Missouri: Board of Publications-The Church of Christ (Temple Lot), 1953, p. 142.)

Further details of Trapp's religious experiences and what became of the followers he had obtained in England is unknown.

DAVIS COUNTY CO-OP SOCIETY (Charles W. Kingston)

In the 1930s, a group of people residing mainly in Davis County, Utah, organized themselves economically and religiously under the leadership of Charles W. Kingston. Divine guidance was claimed in the organization of this communal order, in which the true principles of the United Order are adhered to. Plural marriage is also practiced.

The leadership of the group has rested with members of the Kingston family.

Heavily involved in business, the group owns stores, land, farms, commercial printing facilities, clothing factory, a bank and a mine. It is reported that the group is quite wealthy, although individual members live only with the basic necessities.

The group is very secretive, and generally in order to gain membership one must be born into it. Several attempts at contact have been unsuccessful.

The purpose of the group, quoting from the articles of incorporation is: "..to establish the long-looked-for ideal condition known as the Golden Rule (Do unto others as you would have others do unto you.) To abolish war and bloodshed of all kinds. It being our absolute belief that God cannot under any condition be pleased with any types of action of this kind or anyone engaged in the same; that it is better for the individual concerned to be killed rather than to kill. To bring about the condition so that all incorporators are self-sustaining by means of their own labors which labors are performed in perfect harmony with all other incorporators. To establish peace, good-will, and brotherly love between all men as well as all incorporators. To obtain, operate, and own lands, homes, factories, equipment, machinery of production and raw materials; all for the purpose of producing the every day necessities and comforts of life for the incorporators. To cooperate with the State self-help Cooperative Board in devising and executing plans for the oranization, financing, and operation of this corporation, to work in harmony with the Resettlement Administration and other government organizations which have the self-help plan included in their programs.

The corporation shall produce goods and services to be used by members, and to be exchanged with and sold to other cooperatives and the public for other goods, services, or cash." (From the Articles of Incorporation of the Davis County Cooperative Society, February 7, 1941.)

CHURCH OF CHRIST (RESTORED)

In 1936 A. C. DeWolf, a missionary from Otto Fetting's church was laboring in Mississippi and Louisiana. Many were baptized and several branches of the church were organized. Later the same year W. A. Draves began telling members of the church that he had dreamed the Messenger would return again. The main body of the church went along with this, but those in the south could not accept these claims on the grounds of *Message* 30:6, which says:
"I have established my church in 1929 anew. I have given the message and it must be obeyed. All else is of man and I cannot, and will not accept the follies and traditions of men for my work is a holy work and man must first be made holy."

The final split came in 1939, and this group maintains that they are the original branch of the Fettingite church—the other being apostate, although they took with them the church paper and properties. When S. T. Bronson introduced the Saturday Sabbath into the church in the 1950s (the two churches having already separated), this became final proof that the group under his direction was in error, and had left the original path which this group maintains they are following today.

The church is somewhat loosely organized and its apostles are in many different areas of the country laboring in their fields. Church offices are maintained whereever the officers of the church are residing. Annual assemblies (conferences) have been held in Independence and other areas.

Doctrine

Articles of Faith and Practice

These are the same as those used by the Temple Lot Church.

Other Beliefs

Doctrinally, with the exception of the sabbath queston, this group believes and practices the same doctrines as does the previously mentioned Fetting group. Current and on-going revelation is commonplace—with many leaders and members partaking of this blessing. A temple will some day be built in Independence. The church has Apostles at the head—no high priests or first presidency.

Publications

The Bible, Book of Mormon and Word of the Lord (Fetting's 30 Messages) are accepted scriptural works. A monthly paper, *The Gospel Herald* is published by the church.

CHURCH OF CHRIST (E. E. Long/Thomas Nerren)

Elmer E. Long and others, including Thomas Nerren, led a break from the Church of Christ (Temple Lot) in 1936. The Temple Lot group had again brought forth the problems concerning the disposition of the 12 messages Otto Fetting had brought to them. Long and Nerren formally organized the Church of Christ in 1938. The Denver, Colorado branch of the Temple Lot church was used as the headquarters and formed the main nucleus of the new church. The Church paper *The Arimat* made its appearance in April 1938 at Independence, Missouri.

At the General Conference of the church, convened at Independence on April 6, 1938, the following resolution was adopted:

"Whereas, the Articles of Faith and Practice provide that where one or more local churches of six members, one of whom is an elder, are walking in harmony with the law of God, there the Church of Christ exists with full power of church extension, and

"Whereas, such a local church exists at Denver, Colorado.

"Whereas, the general body at headquarters, Independence, Missouri, have denied and repudiated the Messenger and Messages, therefore

"Resolved, that the local Church of Christ of Denver is hereby recognized as the authorized Body of Christ with power to carry on the Lord's work until He, the Lord, shall give further direction." (*The Arimat*, Volume 1, Number 2, May 1938.)

This group accepted Fetting's messages, but was unable to unite with that church. The Messenger began visiting Thomas Nerren, and through messages given to him Bishops, Apostles and other church leaders were selected.

A message given to Thomas Nerren on June 14, 1939, is titled a last warning to the Fetting group:

"At 2:30 a.m., the Messenger came to my bedside at the home of Bishop James Hedrick, Oak Grove, Missouri, with words of comfort, and stated that he would soon come again. In the Morning we drove into Independence and between 7:30 and 8:00 a.m., the Messenger came again, to my room at the E. E. Long home, 424 East Walnut, and gave the following message.

"I went to the Fetting Assembly and stated that the Messenger had been with me that morning and had commanded me to go and deliver a message to them, which I asked permission to do, but was refused by Joseph Camp, who was presiding over the meeting. I said, I have come just like Samuel did to the Nephites, and now the blood is upon your own heads. I am free. The message as given, follows:

"I come to you again to deliver the instructions of the Lord. I am John the Baptist, the prophet of the Most High, to prepare His ways, to prophecy,

"Thus saith the Spirit unto you, O My People, I have sent My servant, Thomas B. Nerren, to you, as I sent My servant, Otto Fetting. (As I laid my hands upon Otto Fetting, I have laid my hands upon Thomas Nerren, and set him apart for the work that has been entrusted to him.) Yea, I did send my word to you, O My Children. I gave command that you should meet in your assembly and cry mightily unto Me, but you did not obey My words; but you did disobey where I did say, Man cannot legislate laws; and by your legislation and false prophecies, have gone away from Me, your God and Father, as did my people in the past. They too, treated lightly the things they received; and their minds were darkened, and a curse was sent upon them that would remain until they repented. So it is with you, My children. You have failed, you became unworthy; for you did not heed my commands, and your minds became darkened; and you have been misled by false dreams, visions, prophecies; and the devil has appeared as an angel of light; and you are deceived, yea, many of My children; but there are some of My true servants and handmaidens that have not followed the whisperings of Satan.

"I did send My servant, Thomas B. Nerren, to you once, and you treated him unkindly; for you shut him out of your meeting. I sent him again the second time, and he was again not wanted—yea, I sent him again the third time. Those servants that were in their council meeting, oh I heard their statements that were against him; and he was told by one, You had your chance; so they did not permit him to deliver My word—therefore Satan has led with a high hand. I have sent him again, for the last time, with this message to you, O My Children. If you heed it, and repent, and obey all of My Commandments that I have sent, you can be numbered with those that I am raising up to do My work.

"I gave them seven years—those in charge; and the work was to start in 1929. That time ended in 1936. I stated plainly in the first message to you; that if they did not build the temple, I would raise up a people that would build it.

"I stated I would come from time to time until the Church was fully established, and the Temple built, and a people prepared to meet Christ when He comes, and a real Zion established. I have come from time to time to Thomas B. Nerren, since Otto Fetting's departure; for he was one of the Lord's choosing, and the only one remaining of the three; and he has been true and faithful to the trust that has been placed upon him. He truly has become the marred servant; for he has delivered the Lord's words faithfully. Though few believed them, yet he has declared them. Those who have heeded are blessed.

"Those of My true servants that I have called and set in My Church by My Messenger, that have not followed the cunning of the devil—I extend to them the invitation to come and be baptized and have their garments washed clean and white, and go forth with those who have been chosen and set in My Church. Let it be done quickly, for this is the time to hasten. My work must be quickly done, the Church fully established, the people prepared. I say let all repent and be obedient, lest they are lost, and great shall be their sorrow and suffering.

"I will come to you again." (*The Arimat*, Volume 2, Number 4, 1939.)

In 1940 a revelation was received directing the church to gather to Halley's Bluff, near Schell City, Missouri. Here a temple was built. My sources have indicated that this structure has since been destroyed by fire.

E. E. Long split with Nerren in the 1960s.

In 1946 *The Arimat* ceased publicaton. A new paper, *Zion's Restorer* began publication in 1964. At this time Gerald A. Hall and Dan Gayman were prominent in the leadership of this church.

A serious split between the two men occurred circa 1973. A long court battle ensued. Hall won the paper and most of the property. Both of these new groups will be disussed later. (See *Church of Christ at Zion's Retreat* and *Church of Israel.)*

The Articles of Faith and Practice common to the Church of Christ (Temple Lot) were used as well as the Bible, Book of Mormon, Fetting's thirty messages. Subsequent revelations to Nerren and others were also used as spiritual guidelines.

THE CHURCH OF JESUS CHRIST OF LATTER DAY SAINTS (Third Convention)

The Third Convention movement had its beginnings with Rey L. Pratt, who served an outstanding job as president of the Mexican Mission of the Mormon Church in the 1920s and 1930s. The members of the church liked him and found him good to work with. However, when his brother Harold replaced him, many members of the church found him to be so different from Rey that they could not work with him.

Under the direction of such able leaders as Isaias Juarez, Abel Paez and Margarito Bautista, a conference was called in order to petition the First Presidency of the church for a change in mission leadership. The petition was rejected and one-third of the more than 2000 members of the church in Mexico withdrew their allegience from Salt Lake City.

The Third Convention met on April 26, 1936, with Abel Paez presiding over the meeting. With seven hundred members at the outset and having taken records, furniture and church buildings with them, this movement was off to a great start.

Tensions mounted in the group as Margarito Bautista began advocating plural marriage and the United Order. He was removed from the group and established his own church and a colony at Ozumba, Mexico.

The Conventionists sustained all leaders of the LDS Church with the exception of the mission president, Harold Pratt. However, this loyalty was insufficient. In May 1937, all the leaders of this movement were excommunicated from the LDS Church on the grounds of rebellion, insubordination and apostacy.

The doctrine and organization of this group was identical to that of the LDS Church. They built chapels, produced some literature and baptized many converts.

In May of 1942, a new man became president of the Mexican Mission, Arwell L. Pierce. He extended a hand of friendship to the Third Conventionists and obtained needed church literature in the Spanish language for them which Pratt and his successors had refused to do. Pierce's acceptance grew and he began to frequent their meetings as a guest and speaker.

George Albert Smith, President of the LDS Church called a conference in Mexico in 1946. The Third Conventionists were invited to attend and rejoin the LDS Church. The invitation was accepted and 1200 Third Conventionists returned to full membership with the Mormon church. (Information was based on a paper by F. Lamond Tullis and Elizabeth Hernandez, *Mormonism Comes of Age: The Third Convention in Mexico*. By permission.)

THE CHURCH OF JESUS CHRIST OF ISRAEL (J. H. Sherwood)

J. H. Sherwood was excommunicated from the Mormon Church in 1936 for claiming to be the only man who held the legal right to the office of Presiding Bishop of the church. According to the Doctrine and Covenants, this office rightfully and automatically belongs to a literal descendant of Aaron. Sherwood claimed he was just this person. He also taught that he had been sent by the Savior to reclaim the rights of the priesthood.

Sherwood taught that on September 13, 1936, the Lord "cut-off" the sacrament and took the priesthood authority from all Mormon leaders. This was done, he said, because they failed to recognize his right to the office of Presiding Bishop. Since the authority was withdrawn on this date, all ordinances performed after the above mentioned date in the Mormon church were invalid.

A letter dated February 14, 1954, was written by Sherwood to the leaders of the Mormon Church requesting permission to use the Salt Lake Temple to perform a baptism for the dead. This request was refused. Sherwood proceeded to a lake in Ventura County, California, on April 4, 1954 and at 6 p.m. performed a baptismal ceremony for all those who were dead up to that time. Sherwood stated that the Lord commanded him to do this in order that the laborious and costly work of genealogy could be done away with.

Sherwood claimed to receive revelation as "Jasper #7." The meaning of which is not certain.

Just how many followers Sherwood had and when this group ceased to exist is unknown.

Doctrine

There were two "glories" established in The Church of Jesus Christ of Israel. The Celestial and the Terrestrial.

The celestial glory was a glory of equality. Members of the church in this category were required to live the United Order. These were to be stewards, or managers, of the property of the Lord. To obtain the Celestial glory one had to obey every one of God's commandments. Those who were obedient were sealed by the Holy Spirit of Promise into the Book of the Law of God.

Members of the lesser, or Terrestrial glory were required only to live the law of tithing. Those who entered into this covenant were sealed into the Book of Remembrance.

The priesthood, or authority to act in the name of the Lord, was given only to those who entered into the Celestial covenant.

Blessings of the Celestial Order

"Spiritual: Entrants are sealed into the Celestial kingdom and endowments are given as stated in Doctrine and Covenants 132:7; husband and wife are sealed in marriage for time and eternity, to their eternal salvation—as stated in Doctrine and Covenants 132:19, 20; children are sealed to parents. The children thus becoming heirs to the covenant with its attendant blessings; retention of rightfully obtained priesthood authority; Book of the Law entry provides automatic forward genealogy record.

"Temporal: An inheritance assignment from the church for every member of the family, at the accountable age; full support for widows by the church; freedom from the economic bondage of the world; abundance and surplus of the earth's fruits as a blessing; opportunity to be a steward of the Lord."

Blessings of the Terrestrial Order

"Spiritual: Opportunity to learn the gospel and laws of God. The window to a better way of life; promise of Terrestrial reward; genealogy not automatic, but does provide a record of entrants.

"Temporal: Assistance from the Lord's storehouse for those in need.

"The following conditions provided a way for members of the Mormon Church to renew and continue their priesthood and stewardship to the Lord:

"Their names must be enrolled in the Book of the Law of God as given in the Doctrine and Covenants 85:7-11. This means that the priesthood, both the Melchizedek and the Aaronic must live the United Order.

"Others, not of the priesthood, not wishing to live the United Order, the Order of Enoch, embracing the Celestial, may be enrolled in the Book of Remembrance, which is the law of tithing, embracing only the Terrestrial Order. However, each may, at any time, enroll into the Book of the Law, thus becoming stewards, instead of servants, and from Terrestrial to Celestial laws and sealing.

"Priesthood ordinations, baptisms, blessings and temple marriage made and entered into, on or before September 13, 1936, will be recognized and honored upon renewal of their priesthood and enrollment into the Book of the Law of God.

"Priesthood work of any description cannot be acceptable that was made or entered into after September 13, 1936.

"Through complete disobedience and disregard to the laws of the Lord, by The Church of Jesus Christ of Latter-day Saints, members and presidency, the Word of God is to them as written, the stone which the builders refused, the same is become the head of the cornerstone. This is the Lord's doing and it is marvelous in our eyes. The Doctrine and Covenants 132:7, is written against them also.

"Enrollment into the Book of the Law of God and renewal of priesthood, is also renewing of the covenants of the Lord Jesus Christ, under the Church of Jesus Christ of Israel, and agreeable to the laws and covenants as given by the Lord to Joseph Smith, Junior, in the Doctrine and Covenants.

"All members must recognize the abolishment of the sacrament which was over-turned and cut-off in the Vermont Ward of The Church of Jesus Christ of Latter-day Saints in Los Angeles on September 13, 1936, by commandment of the Lord Jesus Christ to Jasper #7 and will not be renewed by Him until the Temple of New Jerusalem at Independence, Missouri, is built. Those disregarding this will be as written in 1 Corinthians 11:29 and Doctrine and Covenants 85:9." (From a publication of the church.)

CHURCH OF JESUS CHRIST OF LATTER DAY SAINTS
(Margarito Bautista)

Margarito Bautista led this group from The Church of Jesus Christ of Latter Day Saints (Third Convention) in the mid-1930s when he was removed from that body for advocating plural marriage and the united order. An agricultural colony was established in Mexico.

All doctrines of the church remained basically the same as those of the Mormon church. It was claimed that President Wilford Woodruff had no authority to stop the practice of polygamy and his declaration, known as the Manifesto, was not a revelation from God but a decree inspired by the desires of the church for the recognition of Utah as a state.

Further claims were made that the Gentiles who belonged to the LDS Church had had their chance to obey God and build up His Kingdom properly but because of the Manifesto lost it and the Lamanites were once again given the opportunity.

Bautista was a prolific writer and many books and tracts were produced in English as well as Spanish.

In 1951, Margarito Bautista was chosen to a position in Joseph W. Musser's new Council of Seven, and since that time Bautista's followers have associated with that group.

Bautista died on August 4, 1961.

BENJAMIN T. LEBARON

A member of the famous LeBaron family, Benjamin T. LeBaron is credited with claiming to be a prophet and establishing a small following in the late 1930s. Although he was committed to the Utah State Hospital, and actually spent time in and out of various hospitals for most of his adult life, it seems that he was sincere in his beliefs.

Claiming to be receiving revelations from time to time, Benjamin tried to discredit his brother Joel, after Joel organized the Church of the Firstborn of the Fullness of Times.

An interesting letter written to Rulon C. Allred Follows:

"Dear Brother Allred:

"I am the Prophet Mighty and Strong of Chap. 28 of Isaiah; 85 of D & C, and the branch in Isa. 11:1; as also spoken of by Zachariah.

"The Lord is healing me of the marring of Doctorcraft.

"Joseph Smith is the rod of Jesse, and Jesus is the Stem. Thus saith the Lord. I am King of Kings today.

"You are next to me in the Ancient of Days Order of Priesthood...

"I am God, the third; the Holy Ghost; or the 3rd member of the Trinity since Adam went to Mars nearly 300 years ago, leaving Jesus and Joseph Smith and myself in charge. Jesus was killed for saying He was the Son of God. Joseph Smith was killed for inferring he was one of the Trinity.

"I was killed for the same reason—but an angel of God has raised me from the dead, and I stand truthful in all things.

"John the Revelator was killed three times, and raised by an angel, and then finally died. I will be translated as were Enoch, Moses and Elijah.

"I am the Lord's anointed, and hold the sceptre of power. Moroni was not as great as I am; and neither is McKay.

"B. T.

"P. S. Your duty is to gather all the tithing of the earth to give to me to build temples and churches and maintain them. The Bishops should use all legally consecrated to the United Order as I tell them by revelation.

"The President of the Church should collect the fast offerings only to help the poor saints.

"Ervil is King of Israel; and Alma is Church President; F. O. Spencer, Bishop, and Marion Hammond, Patriarch.

"Take two more wives. Thus saith the Lord.

"Ben T. LeBaron" (Quoted in LeBaron, Verlan M., *The LeBaron Story,* published by the author, 1981, pp. 61-62.)

Benjamin was killed in an accident on August 16, 1978 in Arkansas at the age of 65.

THE CHURCH OF CHRIST WITH THE ELIJAH MESSAGE
(W. A. Draves)

Just four and one-half years after Otto Fetting's passing, the church he had organized once again began receiving visitations from the Messenger. A young elder in the church residing at Nucla, Colorado, W. A. Draves, received his first visit from the angel on October 4, 1937. In the six years which were to follow, Draves would receive thirty more messages, before a disastrous division was to occur in the church.

Not all members of Fetting's church were willing to accept the messages received by Draves. The positon of most however was one of acceptance. After some of the church leaders began to question the validity of the revelations, a growing division began to split the church. The growing factionalism came to a head at the June 1943 annual General Assembly of the church in Independence, Missouri. Draves and his followers filed suit against the others claiming they were the legal organization of the church and demanded possession of the church properties and newspaper.

When the matter was finally settled many months later, the court ruled against Draves and his followers.

The messenger continued to come, and by June 1944, a general church organization had been arranged. With the group's general assembly in that month, nine apostles were sustained and much of the business transacted dealt with the church making an official record of accepted practices. By this time Draves had relocated his residence to Independence.

During the court proceedings, both the Fetting and Draves groups had been concurrently publishing a *Voice of Warning* with the same volume numbers and same dates. Careful scrutiny of the articles and people associated therewith is required to discern which paper belongs to which group. By June 1844 the matter had been settled and with that month's issue of the paper the name *The Voice of Peace* was used.

The church has progressed considerably since 1944 and boasts a sizeable membership, a very nice church headquarters building in Independence, and missions to Africa and India in addition to the work being conducted in many parts of the American continent.

The church is directed by a council of Twelve Apostles, much the same as the other bodies coming out of the Temple Lot group.

Doctrine

Articles of Faith and Practice

These are the same as those used by the Temple Lot church.

The Temple

While the purpose of the temple was brought forth in the messages received by Otto Fetting, its time has still not been set. This church believes they are the ones who have remained faithful and will be called upon to build the temple in the due time of the Lord.

The most recent reference, specifically, to the temple is in Message 80, received August 15, 1964. Verse 10 says: "Fear not and worry not about the Temple of the Lord, for the Lord can choose the place, the time to build, and direct in His work when He desires His Temple to be built..."

Built in the 1960s, church headquarters have been maintained at this building on Lacy Road in Independence, Missouri.

Other Practices

A very brief, yet comprehensive overview of the church's practices was reported in the first issue of *The Voice of Peace,* June 1944. As the church was formally organizing itself, it went on record as follows:

"Resolved that the ministry of this Church be instructed to preach and teach nothing regarding the God-head that is out of harmony with the first three paragraphs of the Articles of Faith and Practice.

"Moved that we go on record as favoring Sunday as our Sabbath day.

"Resolved that we take a stand against the teaching in public or private of the doctrine of abstinence as being in no wise linked with our soul's salvation nor with sanctification and that we consider it a dangerous subject for a missionary to discuss with members of the opposite sex, even in the presence of their husbands.

"Resolved that we go on record as opposed to the idea that sanctification can free one from sins or temptations yet to be met, but rather that sanctification is a continuous process embodying purification, dedication, and devotion to the service of God.

"Moved that the laying on of hands be confined to those occasions as referred to in paragraph 5 of the Articles of Faith and Practice.

"Resolved that in our understanding of the scriptures Christ intended that the sacrament should be administered only to those who are baptized members of the Church of Christ.

"Moved that we believe in the duties of the General Officers of the Church as found outlined in the Articles of Faith and Practice and the messages to date and that we resolve to be in accord therewith."

Publications

In addition to using the Holy Bible, the Book of Mormon, Book of Commandments and The Word of the Lord form the basic scriptures in use by the church.

The church publishes its own edition of the Book of Mormon under the title *The Record of the Nephites.* The wording follows that of the 1830 Palmyra edition of the Book of Mormon. The church also publishes the book of messages, *The Word of the Lord,* which contains the thirty messages received by Otto Fetting and the messages received since that time by W. A. Draves. The Book of Commandments is the edition printed by the Temple Lot church.

Numerous pamphlets are published by the church. Recently a booklet on the Book of Mormon and archaeology in the central and south Americas was issued.

ORDER OF AARON (Maurice L. Glendenning)

Descended from an old Scottish family surnamed "Glendonwyn" Maurice Lerrie Glendenning was born February 15, 1891, at Randolph, Kansas. This ancient family, it is said, held the lesser Priesthood which has ruled on the earth since the days of Moses and members of the tribe of Levi passed this priesthood authority on to succeeding generations.

Two blessings, acknowledging the lineage of Aaron, have been discovered in recent years. On February 15, 1799, John Glendenning pronounced the following blessing on his son, John, Jr., who was Maurice's Great-great grandfather:

"My beloved son John Glendenning.

"In my desire for righteousness am I persuaded by the spirit of Almighty God to continue in the faith of our Fathers, that through us may be filled the promises of our Father in heaven through the lineage of Joseph Ephraim Aaron and our Fathers unto the coming of our Savior in whom we have not lost faith. Though wayward in thy youth I give this blessing unto you my son John Glendenning in whose seed shall continue the Priesthood of our lineage, and if in thy days thou shalt not serve the Lord thy God, yet through and by the grace of God, shall there be power to bless thy sons for thou art of Aaron. And in this power shalt thy seed be blest and shall serve God and shall glorify His name in power and righteousness unto men in the flesh.

"Righteousness shall come unto thy seed and unto the seed of thy sons, wherein the spirit of our fathers shall dwell to bring forth the good works of our Lord. But in fear of thy weakness my son I pass this blessing unto thee and over thee unto thy son that in him may dwell the spirit of prophecy with the priesthood unto which _____ shall come forth _____ spirit of his calling unto righteousness. Before our heavenly Father and in the name of our Lord Jesus I scribe this blessing and seal it upon thee and thy seed in the year 1799 A. D. and in the 2nd month and in the 15th day and in the early part of that day.

"Amen. John Glendenning." (*Levitical Writings,* EskDale, Utah: Aaronic Order, 1978, p. 255)

And again, on February 15, 1863, Maurice Glendenning's father Milton received a similar blessing from his own father:

"A Blessing.

"Unto you my son Milton Worth Glendenning, as was given unto me by my father, and unto him by his father, and unto him by his father and in this manner it was given from Aaron unto me; do I now give in your infantcy unto you; but in your seed shall it cease and shall come forth the restoration of the fullness of the keys of the priesthood of Aaron.

"Thou art of Aaron, the first born of our Lord in the flesh, and God shall give unto you a first born through whom the restoration of the keys of the priesthood of Aaron shall be made unto man in the flesh. Throughout all thy days thou shalt serve the Lord thy God.

"And in the sorrow of my future departure from which I shall not return, I seal this blessing upon thee in the name of our Lord and inscribe it in this stone.

"And thus is it done according to the will of our Father, in the year 1863 A.D. and in the 2nd month, and in the 15th day and in the first part of that day. Amen. Henry Glendenning." (ibid. p. 256)

At a very young age, Maurice began hearing music, then later a voice spoke to him, directing that the words should be written down. Others were unable to hear these things. When he was fourteen he began receiving and writing poems—which a school teacher claimed were of such an advanced degree that the young boy could not have possibly written them, but copied them from books. However, Glendenning had no access to such books in his home or at school. When he was almost sixteen, these poems took on a new form. They became messages in prose form, which Glendenning faithfully copied down but could not comprehend.

After marriage in 1915, he was reluctant to share his experiences with his wife, but eventually relented. Others he had shown them to had caused him a degree of suffering because he was unable to explain the meaning, and at first his wife reacted in the same manner—but later her heart was changed and she became an ardent supporter of her husband in all his doings.

These various persecutions, however, caused Glendenning to stop writing for awhile, and in the first message received after this time, which later became the first part, Section 137, of the Book of Elias, Glendenning is called to repentance. This occurred on January 20, 1923.

A practicing chiropractic doctor, Glendenning settled in Provo, Utah in 1928 after moving about in search of employment. Here he came in contact with the Mormons and on April 14, 1929 he and his wife were baptized into that church.

Looking forward to the day when he might serve in the church, receive the priesthood and participate in the various temple ordinances, Glendenning hoped that his revelations would be received by the church leaders and that they would be able to give some meaning to them. However, this dream was not fulfilled.

Glendenning's revelations were publicly, although not specifically, rejected at the April 1931 conference of the LDS Church. That same afternoon Glendenning received a revelation which stated in part:

"Now that my works have been declared to be of Satan, and that they of the house of the Lord have fulfilled these things, and do attempt to limit the Lord in the things which are pleasing unto Himself, I say unto you prepare the works which have not been sealed and have been witnessed by others...And I delcare unto you that I shall bring them forth unto the house of Levi, that they may know for a surety that I am truth..." (Ibid., p. 79)

Many people became interested in the works of Dr. Glendenning, and study groups were formed from which came the first of the converts to the Order of Aaron. Many were former members of the Mormon Church.

The keys of the priesthood were restored to Glendenning on March 21, 1938. Articles of Incorporation for the Order of Aaron were filed with the State of Utah on August 19, 1943. Glendenning was formally excommunicated from the Mormon church on January 15, 1945.

The Order of Aaron has several hundred followers, and although they state they are not a faction or a break from the Mormon Church, many of the principles practiced by this group are common to Mormonism.

In addition to a gathering of members in Salt Lake City, Utah, where the order maintains legal headquarters, several United Order communities have been established in the southwestern Utah desert, primary of which is EskDale.

These people have been very successful in managing and living the United Order, and are revered in the area for their honesty, integrity and educational standards.

Members of the order wear a uniform dress, very modest, with the word "Levi" embroidered onto the clothing (usually caps for women, shirts for men) which signifies their calling into the House of Aaron and serves to remind the members of their consecration.

Missionaries are not sent out because the order is the "tribe of Levi." It is maintained that God will proselyte those whom He knows to be Levites.

A firm belief in Jesus Christ is maintained and the members of the order strive to be a witness for Christ and to set a Christian example in their every day lives.

When Glendenning passed away on October 5, 1969, he did not leave a successor "in the full sense as his mission was unique. He was a messenger with the mission of an Elias, much as John the Baptist, who also had no successor. He was a Bishop, a Chief High Priest..." (letter to the author from Robert J. Conrad, Chief High Priest of the Aaronic Order, March 6, 1975.)

The following names of the group have been approved for use by the members: Order of Aaron, Aaronic Order, House of Aaron, House of Levi, The True Church of God, The Church of the First Born, Kingdom of God, The Church of Christ, The Church in the Wilderness. (Erickson, Ralph D., *History and Doctrinal Development of the Order of Aaron,* Masters Thesis, Brigham Young University, Provo, Utah, 1969.)

Doctrine

Priesthood and Organization

Jesus Christ is the Great High Priest and all officers and members are subordinate to Him. He is the only one who has the rights and powers of this office and is in control of the entire earth.

The Order is directed by a president who holds the office of Chief High Priest. He is in charge of the spiritual affairs of the church.

The temporal affairs of the church are directed by the First High Priest who is directly under the Chief High Priest, and who succeeds to the higher office on the death or removal of the person in that position.

Under these two officers are the Second High Priests. These men direct the ordinances of the church—marriages, baptisms, etc. As Many Second High Priests as necessary may be appointed.

Directly subordinate to the First High Priest is a group known as the Twelve Councilors. They provide counsel and assistance to the two leading officers of the Order. Local branches are presided over by a priest.

Headquarters of the Aaronic Order is maintained in this building in the western part of Salt Lake City, Utah.

Qualifications for Membership

In the Order there are three stages of membership. The first of these is the tithing member. A person is baptized, confirmed and placed on the records of the church. He is in a probationary state for one year and is required to pay ten percent of his income and his time to the Order.

If after one year the individual wishes to continue with the Order, he may become a Consecrated Member. All of his properties are deeded to the church, which then become the sole property of the church. A person may still leave the order, but the properties previously consecrated can not be returned. A one year probationary period also applies to this membership status.

At the end of the second year, the member becomes a United Order Member. He may now be called to a position of responsibility in the church. If he accepts his callings and lives satisfactorily during another year's probation, he becomes a full United Order Member.

Baptism

Members are usually baptized within one year after application for membership in the Order.

The baptismal ceremony is administered once a year on New Year's Eve in a mountain valley named Eden, located a few miles north of the Order's main community of EskDale, Utah.

In this ceremony all new members are baptized by immersion and confirmed prior to midnight in order for them to be eligible to partake of the sacrament as the new year begins.

Proxy Baptism

Proxy baptisms are performed for those who died before reaching the age of accountability—8 years. Worthy family members are generally selected for this ordinance, and it must be performed no earlier than the time which the deceased would have been eight years of age had he lived. Adults who died after the age of eight, who did not accept the gospel and were not baptized, are lost.

Godhead

Jesus Christ is viewed as having a Heavenly Father, but he is also thought of as the Father. The Holy Ghost is the spirit of God or Christ. All three beings of the godhead form one god.

Sabbath Day

In the early days of its history, the Order acknowledged Sunday as the day of rest and worship, but in September of 1958 Dr. Glendenning received a revelation directing the change to Saturday.

Sacrament

The Sacrament of the Lord's Supper is observed, but with

somewhat different procedures than some other church groups. Wine and bread (unbroken wafers) is used, which become the actual flesh and blood of Christ. Sacramental prayers were revealed to Dr. Glendenning.

The reason for using wafers of bread rather than broken bread is recorded in Chapter 211 of Levitical Writings (1978) page 101:

"For ye are now commanded to do this thing in remembrance of your long waiting and that ye may keep in your remembrance that when your Lord Jesus appears, it shall be in the fullness of His Body; and He shall be whole. Therefore your bread shall not be broken, nor your wine new."

Word of Wisdom

The Order is a very health oriented group, observing the laws of Moses regarding food and drink. In addition, the counsel found in Section 89 of the LDS Doctrine and Covenants, known as the Word of Wisdom, is strictly adhered to.

Publications

Accepted works of scripture include the following: Holy Bible, some parts of the Book of Mormon and some sections of the Doctrine and Covenants, Dead Sea Scriptures found near Qumran in 1947, and Glendenning's works—Book of Elias, Book of New Revelations, and Disciple Book. (These three works of scripture were reprinted by the order in 1978 in one combined volume entitled *Levitical Writings*.)

A periodical entitled *Aaron's Star* has been published for a number of years.

CHURCH OF CHRIST (Pauline Hancock)

Having left the RLDS Church with the Protest Group under T. W. Williams then later joining the Temple Lot church, Pauline Hancock was a dynamic woman with great leadership ability. Circa 1946 she became dissatisfied with her affiliation with the Temple Lot group and organized a Bible and Book of Mormon study group with several friends. This group quickly evolved into an organized church.

Pauline Hancock's spiritual experience, which caused her to proceed in this manner, follows:

"For many years I had a hungering in my heart that had not been satisfied. These things I had been taught to believe did not give peace to my soul. I had gone into business hoping to drown the cry of my heart that I could not still. God in His infinite mercy visited me. No other but He sought to help and relieve my need.

I had never understood the blood of Christ or the way of salvation until one day in His great love opened my blind eyes to the following: I was in our living room, when all of a sudden I saw a marvelous vision. It seemed that I was taken to Jerusalem and I saw a man seated upon what looked like a stool. All around and about him, men were mocking, bowing, and making fun of this individual. They spit in his face, they laughed at him with scorn. I watched and I watched and I had never in all my life beheld such love as that which shone on his face.

"I continued to watch as he was condemned to death and a crown of thorns was placed on his head. I followed as they led him to Calvary and nailed him to the cross, my eyes were fixed upon him and for the first time in my life I beheld the blood of the Lamb of Calvary. I knew all of a sudden my own vile and sinful nature—my lost condition. I knew that there was nothing good in me except God had put it there. I looked and looked at him. I couldn't get enough of what I saw shining from His face. I knew that I was nothing like this wonderful person. When others were cruel and unkind, he was kindness himself. His face reflected love and compassion. I had murmured and complained at my burdens and trials while He, in the greatness of agony, was willing to bear all this, that I might live again a new creature forever, for it was Jesus that I was beholding. Oh, the beauty, the glory, the wonder of such love that I saw in Him. I knew I had to have this Jesus or die. My soul began to thirst and hunger for Him. I fell upon my knees and prayed to God through Jesus and His shed blood, to be forgiven of my sins, that I might have the love I had seen in Him. When my prayer was finished, God baptized me with His own spirit and my soul was on fire with love towards God and mankind—I became a new creature. Oh, Glory to God for such a Redeemer as mine.

"God spoke to me then and said: Now go and teach all people what I have shown you—for I am the way. I answered Him that I couldn't do that and He said, I will be with you. I said, I am a woman and they won't receive me. He said, I wasn't a woman and they didn't receive me—go teach and I'll be with you.

"Blessed be the name of God. Yes, he calls women. He called me. I know for He lives in my soul. I would rather have Jesus than anything. I pray that I shall faithfully teach what God in His mercy has shown me. May God help each one of you is my prayer in Jesus' name." (Carter, *Denominations...*, pp. 49-50.)

Due to the prominence of one associate, H. Irvin Luke, this group is sometimes referred to as "Lukeite."

Further history is taken from a letter to the author from Darrel

W. Clow, a church representative, dated December 17, 1974:

"We began meeting in homes as a small group of families studying the scriptures to see what God would have us to do. Most of us at this time were or had been members of the RLDS Church and had become disenchanted with one or more of their teachings. These meetings began in the late 40s. (Approximately 1947 or 1948). These meetings or get-togethers gradually evolved into regularly scheduled meetings in one of the member's basements. Later we rented an older church building for a few years and then still later we built our own church building at 723 S. Crysler [Independence, Missouri] where we still meet."

Mrs. Hancock died several years ago.

Sometimes locally referred to as the "basement church," this building is located just a few blocks from the RLDS Auditorium.

Doctrine

Authority

"We get our authority from the Word of God. Actually, man of himself does not have any authority. God is all authority. We do not pretend to be holier or more upright than any other person anywhere." (From above mentioned letter.)

The church does not believe that the gospel of Christ was ever taken from the earth, and disclaims any ties whatsoever with the restoration of the gospel through Joseph Smith, Jr.

Other Beliefs

Using the Bible exclusively as scripture, this group teaches that Christ is God, the Trinity is one manifestation, and there are but two places for man's existence after death—heaven or hell.

Baptism by immersion is practiced.

Publications

In addition to a few small tracts, this group publishes a regular advertisement in the *Independence Examiner.*

Until November 1973, this group believed in and taught from the Book of Mormon. However, in 1973 evidence was discovered which seemed to indicate Joseph Smith, Jr. was a fraud, and the group decided it had no choice but to cease using the Book of Mormon. The church now promotes itself as a non-denominational, Bible teaching church.

The announcement was made in the November 24, 1973 issue of the Independence Examiner as follows:

"So as a group of believers in Jesus Christ and His glorious salvation, we can no longer accept the claim that the Book of Mormon is of divine origin. In the future the Bible alone will be our scriptures.

"May God help all Book of Mormon believers to understand the truth and realize who it is that has been falsifying historical facts.

"Book of Mormon believers we have been deceived."

CHURCH OF FREEDOM OF LATTER DAY SAINTS

Organized circa 1950. No further information available.

ZION'S ORDER OF THE SONS OF LEVI (Marl V. Kilgore)

Organized at Phoenix, Arizona on June 21, 1951, Zion's Order of the Sons of Levi has attempted to live a communal way of life, everyone sharing the fruits of their labors. Marl V. Kilgore and his family had had previous experience with Mormonism before joining Maurice L. Glendenning's Aaronic Order in 1950. However, it seems that Marl was unable to find adequate outlet for his leadership talents and a break occurred. Some 19 members left the Aaronic Order and established the new group.

In 1952 the group moved to Mansfield, Missouri. The corporation was later amended in that state to "Zion's Order, Inc."

Lifestyles and religious practices are similar to the Aaronic Order. There are no specific uniforms to wear, except that modesty prevails.

In 1969 Marl resigned as president in order to do missionary work among the Indians in the Southwest United States. His son Douglas took his place as the administrative head of the group.

According to a personal visit with the leaders of this group by a source, quite a large number of people are now ministering among the Navajo indians, with 11 churches having been established.

The current size of the group in specific numbers is unknown.

Doctrine

Declaration of Essential Beliefs

Quoting from a pamphlet written by Marl V. Kilgore:

I believe in being just, fair and charitable towards all men, and claim the right to be treated likewise. Matthew 5:1 through 18; 1st Cor. 13; Romans 14 and first three verses of chapter 15 are the basis for such beliefs and essential to promotion and maintenance of this united order work.

I believe in kindness and pure holy love towards all humanity regardless of nationality, race, color, or politics, and liberty to all according to their obedience to eternal laws and tenable laws of our land.

I believe in equal rights to all humanity according to their abilities and adaptabilities, efficiency and cooperation with the management, and necessary tenacious qualities that must be in whatever business or other any seeks employment, and that all adults should have a right to vote except they that are mentally deranged, incompetent, or criminals, or aliens.

I believe in looking for the good in all persons. Good thoughts make good, joyous feelings. We all have evil as well as good in our makeup, or at least what some thinks of as evil. The proclaimed Savior of perfection was found fault with so much that they crucified him. Thinking of evil in others makes us feel evil or bad, thus let us look for, and think good.

I believe if we claim freedom in a nation for ourselves, to keep that freedom we must zealously allow and maintain and foster just as much freedom for every other human dwelling in that nation, else we lose our freedom.

I believe in accepting truth no matter where it is found and rejecting error likewise. Though rejecting such errors, I do not condemn the maker of such, but seek a way if possible to help that one in an orderly and unoffensive way to see their error and correct such to their joy.

I believe in eternal and divine Creators and worship them. I feel that all peoples that believe in such are worshipping the same creators, whether they call them by the same names as I do or not. And also that all will be rewarded for the good they do regardless of what religion they claim or do not claim; and that we must all suffer for evils or broken laws according to our understanding or lack thereof. Thus degrees of glory. (Ref. 1st Cor. 15:40-42; and Mark 4:20)

I believe that Christ Jesus will return, at which time the willful wicked shall be destroyed for a period of time until they learn their lesson and return or are resurrected to a repentant life in a degree of glory.

I believe the Savior shall also at His return redeem the righteous and they shall dwell with Him a thousand years in progressive joy and the devil and his chief followers shall be bound for a thousand years. During that time all of the inventions of marvel will be put to good usage of purity and holiness: television and radio programs then will be all good.

I believe in the ultimate end of the thousand years reign of the Savior that the leader of evils shall be loosed again for a short time, and great multitudes of followers will make their great stand against the righteous and their defeat shall be such that nearly all will return to the Lord and reject the great deceivers. And only a terrible end shall be for the devil and they with beastly natures and false prophets. (Ref. Rev. 7:9)

I believe all methods of doctoring and healing arts hold a worthy place, and what is good and an aid for one is not so for another. And that all should be used judiciously without prejudice. My choice is Physical Culture methods.

I believe from years of experience in dealing with uncounted thousands seeking help physically, mentally, and spiritually that happiness, success, and joy only can be obtained by a balancing of the three above mentioned, plus a balanced education, free from racial, religious, cultural, color, nationality, tribal, personal, continental, or family bias or prejudice whether one is religious or not so. Yet moral decency must prevail always with an inner responsibility of fairness felt towards all our fellow men. This takes faith coupled with works of love. (Ref. Ephes. 2:5 thru 10.)

I believe last but not least in the redemptive powers of Jesus Christ through the Law of Grace, and that Faith, Repentance, Baptism by immersion for the remission of sins, and the laying on of hands of the gift of the Holy Ghost was essential for me because of my convictions.

Publications

Literally scores of various writings, sermons and other items of doctrinal and historical interest have been published by this group.

In addition to the Bible, the Book of Mormon and the Doctrine and Covenants (Joseph Smith, Jr.) are accepted works of scripture.

ANNALEE SKARIN

A prolific writer, Annalee Skarin's first book *Ye Are Gods* was published in New York in 1948. Upon coming to Utah, apparently having been a member of the LDS Church for a number of years (she refers to the Book of Mormon and other LDS teachings in her book), she gathered quite a following as she traveled from place to place lecturing. Mrs. Skarin was excommunicated from the LDS Church on June 11, 1952 for preaching false doctrine.

She has since become "translated," that is passed from this life into perfection (resurrection) without having died, as did the Three Nephites in the Book of Mormon writings. Her books, now numbering a set of eight volumes (*Ye Are Gods* being the first in the series), are of a metaphysical nature and no longer make references to Mormonism.

Among some of her teachings is that one can become perfected in this earth life and when one overcomes sin, he overcomes death. Being a recipient of divine revelation, she claims that she has been given the same calling as the Three Nephite Apostles of Christ.

CHURCH OF JESUS CHRIST (Clyde Fletcher)

A split between the Minnesota and Missouri congregations of the church organized by Alpheus Cutler in 1953 regarding the question of leadership of the church resulted in the Minnesota congregation selecting and ordaining Clyde Fletcher to the presidency of the Church. The two churches remained divided over this question until Fletcher's death in November 1969. Since that time the membership in Minnesota has dwindled and in 1975 I was told that but 2 members were left, with no priesthood authority.

Since Fletcher's death, the split in the church became mended. Title to all church properties never changed hands during the disagreement.

Please see the previous entry for further details on history and doctrinal subjects.

CHURCH OF JESUS CHRIST OF LATTER DAY SAINTS (STRANGITE)
(Theron Drew)

A leader in the Strangite movement, Theron Drew and his wife accepted baptism from Marl V. Kilgore (Zion's Order of the Sons of Levi) in the early 1950s. They believed him to be the "one mighty and strong" who was prophesied to come to the last days. Sometime after the baptism, however, Drew became convinced that Kilgore was in error and attempted to return to his former position with the Strangite church.

Unfortunately, the leadership of the church had already excommunicated Drew. This action took place during the 1955 conference of the church.

A legal battle ensued and Drew was declared successful and obtained ownership of most of the church properties. Few of the church members, however, followed Drew. Subsequently Drew's following consisted mainly of his family and close associates.

Upon Theron Drew's demise in May, 1978, his son Leonard took charge of the group.

For further historical and doctrinal material regarding the Strangite movement, please see an earlier entry.

THE CHURCH OF THE FIRSTBORN OF THE FULNESS OF TIMES
(Joel F. LeBaron)

Born and raised in the Mormon colonies of northern Mexico, Joel F. LeBaron and his family had been members of the LDS Church, but under their father's influence the family held to several practices of the church, namely plural marriage, which had been officially condemned by church authorities. Names like Rulon C. Allred and Margarito Bautista hold a prominent place in the LeBaron family history. Both men were revered as great spiritual leaders, and several members of the LeBaron family adhered to their priesthood claims.

Claiming a special priesthood authority, traced back to Joseph Smith, Jr., Joel F. LeBaron was directed of the Lord to officially incorporate The Church of the Firstborn of the Fulness of Times on September 21, 1955, in Salt Lake City, Utah. According to the family history, Joseph Smith, Jr. had ordained Benjamin F. Johnson to a special priesthood authority which was to be held dormant until the Lord directed its use in reestablishing the church. This special priesthood authority was passed on to Alma Dayer LeBaron, Joel's father. He in turn passed this priesthood to Joel. An older brother, Ross Wesley LeBaron, claims that he actually received this authority before Joel, although he followed Joel for a short two months before officially incorporating his own church.

The actual organization of the church took place on April 3, 1956, although it took a number of years before the full organization could be completed. Most of Joel's brothers occupied prominent leadership positions in the church.

In 1958, an unsettling chain of events took place in France among LDS missionaries laboring there. Some of the missionaries had become converted to the fundamentalist teachings of one of the mission leaders. Several were sent home. Many of these became converted to Joel's teachings and were baptized into his church.

When the Quorum of Twelve Apostles was organized, half were former LDS missionaries who had labored in France. Since Joel's untimely assassination in 1972, the church has dwindled and Verlan M. LeBaron indicated in a history published in 1981 that all of these former LDS missionaries are no longer affiliated with the church.

Ervil LeBaron, who had held the office of Patriarch of the Church, was accused of masterminding Joel's death, and about 1974 organized his own church, which will be discussed later.

The church, which is headquartered in Colonia LeBaron, Chihuahua, Mexico, established missions in Mexico, California and Salt Lake City in the early 1960s, and for a number of years published a small magazine, *The Ensign.*

From 1969, when Joel turned leadership of the church to him until his accidental death in August, 1981, Verlan M. LeBaron was the President of the Church. He also held the keys of the Second Grand Head of the priesthood, that of Patriarch of the Church. Verlan did not appoint a successor to head the church. One of his counselors, Siegfried Widmar, now heads the church as Presiding Elder.

The LeBaron Story by Verlan M. LeBaron, which was published in 1981, is well written and the best current source material for details concerning the church.

Doctrine

Priesthood and Church Government

"...Important among Joel's teachings were those concerning priesthood—the authority to act in the name of God and under His direction for the betterment of mankind. Joel taught that since the time of Adam, certain men had held the highest priesthood office with authority to organize God's children on the earth. Each man holding this office was appointed to it by one who held it before him.

Joel called the man who holds this office the First Grand Head. This man holds what is spoken of as the right of the Firstborn, or the right to act in the stead of Christ upon the earth, being His representative and responsible to Him. This office has come down in an unbroken chain from the time of Adam. It was held by Enoch, Melchizedek, Moses and others.

"Joel claimed this highest office through appointment from our father who received it from Benjamin F. Johnson, who, in turn, received it from Joseph Smith. He received it from John the Beloved, who remained on the earth in a translated state after having received it from Christ.

"Joel taught that when God's kingdom is fully organized the man holding the highest office will legally organize God's children in three distinct and separate areas—spiritual, economic and civil. It was the right of the first office to appoint a man over each of these areas. They in turn were responsible to him as the grand head. This doctrine, which Joel claimed to have received by revelation, became the basis for his reform movement. It was powerfully convincing and he never deviated from it.

"Directly under the First Grand Head is the Patriarch who holds the second office and is over the church or spiritual branch of God's kingdom. In priesthood these are the only two offices which hold the right to perpetuate themselves. The first can appoint the second as well as any or all lower offices, but the second cannot appoint the first." (LeBaron, Verlan M., *The LeBaron Story,* 1981, pp. 179-180)

A church organization consisting of a First Presidency, Twelve Apostles, Seventy, etc. was affected. Many of these leading offices of the church are no longer functioning.

Kingdom of God

"It was my father's belief and Joel's teaching, that the gentile nation of the United States would collapse and that great destructions and sufferings would take place. These things would come as a natural result of rejecting the gospel or laws that could have established the nation in peace and security forever.

"Joel truly believed that the responsibility rested upon him and his associates to warn the righteous in the United States, first, and then the other nations, of the judgments that were to come.

"Eight months before his death, Joel spoke again upon the subject of God's kingdom. He told the Saints that it was their duty to pray for that kingdom to come.

"'That kingdom has not yet come, but is around the corner. The time has come for us as a people, for the Mormon people, and especially the Protestant nations, to realize these truths, acknowledge them and prepare for the time when this kingdom will come, that there might be a nation prepared with enough knowledge for the basic principles of liberty to again be brought in force." (LeBaron, Verlan M., *The LeBaron Story,* pp. 178-179)

Law of Consecration

Along with plural marriage, the gathering, and other doctrines considered by "popular" Mormons to be fundamentalist in nature, the United Order, or the Law of Consecration is very important.

Faithful members of the church consecrate property to the church. Each member is given a stewardship of property (deeded to him), which is sufficient for the support of his family. All properties above and beyond the stewardship are retained by the church to use as needed. Such uses might include providing stewardships for the poor and needy, for the building of the church and kingdom.

Each year, after the initial consecration, each member is to give of his surplus to the church. During Joel's administration this was still a theoretical goal, although attempts have been made to live this law.

Publications

In addition to more than a score of tracts, the church published a monthly called *The Ensign* from March 1961 to February 1965.

Those scriptures in use by the LDS Church are used, along with the volume compiled by Joseph Fielding Smith entitled *Teachings of the Prophet Joseph Smith.*

THE CHURCH OF THE FIRSTBORN (Ross Wesley LeBaron)

An older brother to Joel F. LeBaron, Ross claimed that he had received the special mantle of authority from his father prior to Joel. After a brief period of accepting his brother's authority, Ross proceeded to file articles of incorporation for The Church of The Firstborn on December 1, 1955 in Salt Lake City, Utah.

Although it has been learned that he recently disincorporated, he did have a small following. He has resided in Salt Lake City for a number of years.

Doctrine

Articles of Faith

1. We believe in Michael, the Eternal Father, and in his Son Jesus Christ, and in Joseph Smith, the Witness and Testator.

2. We believe that men will be punished for their own sins and not

for Adam's transgression. For He partook of mortality that He might bring forth mortal bodies for his spirit offspring.

3. We believe that through the Atonement of Christ, all mankind may be saved, by obedience to the laws and ordinances of the Gospel of the First Born.

4. We believe that the first principles and ordinances of the Gospel are: First, Faith in Michael the Archangel, and in his son Jesus Christ, and in Joseph the Testator; second, repentance; third, Baptism by immersion for the remission of sins; fourth, Laying on of hands for the gift of the Holy Ghost.

5. We believe that a man must be called of God, by prophecy, and by the laying on of hands, by those who are in authority to preach the Gospel and administer in the ordinances thereof.

6. We believe in the same organization that Adam first established upon this earth, viz: The Right of the First-born, Patriarchs, Prophets, Priests, etc.; and that the Church of Jesus Christ is an appendage thereto, that the Gentiles might be heirs of salvation.

7. We believe in the Holy Spirit of Promise, the gift of tongues, prophecy, revelation, visions, healing, interpretation of tongues, etc.

8. We believe the Bible to be the word of God as far as it is translated correctly; we also believe the Book of Mormon to be the word of God; we also believe that the fullness of the everlasting gospel was restored by the Prophet Joseph Smith and that any departure therefrom is apostasy.

9. We believe all that God has revealed, all that he does now reveal, and we believe that he will yet reveal many great and important things pertaining to the Church and Kingdom of the First Born.

10. We believe that the literal descendants of Israel are legal heirs of the Church and Kingdom of the First Born; and that the Patriarchal reign shall be re-established upon this continent as in Adam's day.

11. We claim the privilege of worshipping Almighty God according to the dictates of our own conscience, and allow all men the same privilege, let them worship how, where or what they may.

12. We believe in being subject to kings, presidents, rulers and magistrates, in obeying and sustaining the law as declared in the 98th section of the Doctrine and Covenants.

13. We believe that this is the dispensation of the fullness of times, when all things shall be revealed, and that men are required to obey all the laws and ordinances; we also believe that the Lord will send one mighty and strong, to set in order the House of God. (Quoted in Carter, *Denominations...* pp. 60-61)

Those scriptures commonly used by the LDS church are accepted as scriptural standards. Plural marriage is practiced.

THE NEW AMERICAN'S MOUNT ZION (John Leabo)

Although not specifcally a church organization, John Leabo's corporation might best be described as a religiously oriented scientific and political association.

What began in 1956 as the *Antarctica Development Interests* from Port Angeles, Washington, has grown through the years, with various changes in name and scope. For the past several years Leabo has been developing an energy source which uses nuclear fusion, rather than fission.

John Leabo was raised in the RLDS Church, but in 1944 transferred to the Church of Christ, Temple Lot. In 1955 he joined with W. A. Draves, and although he now indicates that he accepts the messages given to Draves, he does not accept Draves' interpretation of them. Some years ago Leabo was interested in Maurice L. Glendenning's Aaronic Order. Marl Kilgore, Zion's Order of the Sons of Levi, has administered baptism to Leabo, but Leabo has never been a part of that organization. He believes that baptism is not the way to join a church, but rather the door to enter the kingdom. (From a personal letter to the author, March 22, 1975.)

The Antarctica Development Interests was begun in order to attract interest in the Lord's development of Antarctica by the righteous people who reside there. (Not meaning the scientific researchers stationed there.)

Leabo incorporated in 1957 under the name *Universal Cooperative Fellowship.* A paper, the *Christian Zion Equalitarian* was begun and published under that name for about one year. A name change was effected and has since been known as the *Christian Zion Advocate.* The paper has been sporadic and of various forms of reproduction over the past years.

It is maintained by this group that the New Jerusalem will be built at Salt Lake City, Utah and that the City of Zion will be built in Independence, Missouri.

Leabo has been witness to several UFO sightings, and explains them by reasoning that there is either another race of people on this planet—unknown to us—or there is another planet similar to ours in the nearby universe. In addition, reincarnation is held as the true meaning of the biblical phrase "born again." Man continues to reincarnate until he develops the highest condition he is capable of attaining.

The purpose of the corporation, as stated in the articles, is:

To teach and advance the Christian religion, To teach and advance science, to participate in government and politics, to educate the people and promote their general welfare, to develop farm communities for self help and welfare of the participants.

In addition to the several issues of his periodical, Leabo has authored a full length book, *The Harmonizing of Science and the Bible.*

The LDS Doctrine and Covenants, Book of Mormon, Book of Commandments, and the angel messages to Otto Fetting and W. A. Draves are accepted scripture.

UNITED OUTCASTS OF ISRAEL (Noel B. Pratt)

A descendant of Parley P. Pratt, prominent Apostle in the early days of the LDS Church, Noel B. Pratt associated with Joel F. LeBaron's Church of the Firstborn of the Fulness of Times early in its history. He began editing and publishing a periodical in the interests of the church called *The Rolling Stone* beginning in June 1957. However, by the time issue number eleven made its appearance in December 1958, Noel had changed and in the short 5 page issue, lashed out strongly against Joel and his brothers, for which he was subsequently removed from the church.

Pratt became the promoter of various credit associatons over the following few years, where the barter system was the rule. He admonished all who would listen to put their money into a tangible asset, such as real estate.

For two years Pratt published various newsletters and attempted to promote his ideas for a sound economic system which did not rely on the use of money.

This organization gave way in November 1960, with the following notice: "The Credit Association is dissolved. Dissolved also are the Bank of the Covenants, the Sovereign Citizen's Party and the Church vs Mammon. My records and books are burned, as a testimony that I no longer shall seek to set myself up as a light unto the world."

Pratt was located in Alexandria, Virginia at this time, and would remain there for the next few years as the American Indian Restoration Enterprises was launched. (See a later entry.)

PERFECTED CHURCH OF JESUS CHRIST OF IMMACULATE LATTER DAY SAINTS

Claiming to have been appointed as a spokesman to the LDS people by a group of American Indians, William C. Conway wrote a letter to all the leaders of the LDS Church in 1958, which called them to repentance and described this group of divinely appointed Indian followers of Christ. Conway's further claims include being the host of Moroni, Joseph Smith, Jr., the One Mighty, Wise and Strong, Mulek, son of Zedekiah and the Three Nephites during the open house of the LDS Los Angeles Temple.

These Indians, while gathered at Walker Lake, Nevada in 1890, were blessed with a visit from Jesus Christ, who rejected the LDS Church at that time and gave them all the blessings previously promised to that church. One of these Indians was designated the "One Mighty, Wise and Strong." Twelve Disciples and 70 Apostles were chosen by the Savior from among this righteous group of Indians.

On April 7, 1932, Lorin C. Woolley is said to have conferred the keys of the Kingdom of God upon this Indian Prophet.

These actions were taken because the LDS Church was not living the United Order, had rejected Plural Marriage and other laws of God.

At a special festival held by this group at the sacred hill of Ku-Ma-Ra (in Central America) on May 3, 1958, Christ again visited them and brought with him Joseph Smith, Jr., Moroni, Mulek and the Three Nephite Disciples. These men remained among the Indians to assist in the work of building the Kingdom of God.

Doctrine

This group lives the United Order and Plural Marriage. They have abolished menstruation, claiming it to be a crime against the law of God and the cause of sickness and death. All children are immaculately conceived.

It is maintained that Mulek, the son of Zedekiah, who came to Central America 2000 years ago, established a string of communities beginning in Central America and proceeding up the western coast of Mexico into present day California. These communities were set apart for the establishment of the New Jerusalem. Many of these communities are still marked today by the old missions of the Catholic Church.

The term New Jerusalem, it is said, literally means "City of Angels," and the spot Mulek dedicated for this city is today known as Los Angeles, California.

William Conway has passed away, and although his wife resides at the Redondo Beach address in California, the actual whereabouts of this group is unknown.

Other names of the group include *Restored Apostolic Church of Jesus Christ of Immaculate Latter Day Saints* and *Consolidated American Indian Institute.*

CHURCH OF CHRIST (E. E. Long)

In the 1930s, E. E. Long and Thomas Nerren were leaders of a group in Denver, Colorado. A move was made in the 1940s to Halley's Bluff, Missouri (near Schell City), but a disagreement circa 1960 between Long and Nerren led to a split.

Long had a small group with headquarters in Allen's Grove, Wisconsin. Two prominent leaders, Milton Funk and Jess Cruse followed Long.

I have been told that since Long's death, Milton Funk became the leader of a current membership of about 20 individuals.

AMERICAN INDIAN RESTORATION ENTERPRISES (Noel B. Pratt)

After the failure of *United Outcasts of Israel* in 1960, a new organization centered mainly on restoring the Indians, rightful heirs of the house of Israel, to their proper position in the world began to take shape.

The AIRE Newsletter made its first appearance on July 15, 1961 and continued on a sporadic basis until July of 1962. Thereafter, Pratt attempted to resurrect his money-less bank, but with short-lived success. It should be noted that this venture was not particularly a religious movement, but a religiously oriented politcal attempt at organizing the American Indians into a self-governing body.

Pratt revised the Book of Mormon, and re-published it in several mimeographed volumes under the title *The Indian Bible.* It was billed as a history of the American Indians, rather than a book of religious teachings.

AIRE presented the belief that the Indians would once again be restored to their white skins, after which they would build a great city and therein a temple to the Great Spirit.

This movement further contended that the white man was destroying the good laws of the U. S. Constitution and the Indians were to save it from total destruction.

The return of all lands owned by the white man to their rightful owners, the Indians, was advocated.

The organization disbanded within a few years after its inception.

PAUL SOLEM

The last known whereabouts of Paul Solem was in Utah County, Utah in 1974.

Although not connected with the John Koyle Dream Mine people, Solem had shown an interest in it and on several occasions in the fall of 1974, gathered with curious and faithful alike at the site of the dream mine in order to make contact with the people of the planet Venus. Solem alledged that these people were the lost ten tribes of Israel. Considerable publicity was given to Solem's visit and claims in the local media, but no contact was made.

Solem's story was printed in *Restoration Reporter*, November, 1974:

"His first contact with flying saucers was in June, 1944, at Howe, Idaho, where he had a ranch. He at one time was a member of the Utah Church, but is not a member of any group at the present time. [He was excommunicated c. 1960 for teaching plural marriage.] He considers himself of fundamentalist leanings, believing that the Utah Church is in error now, since they don't follow the practice of polygamy and living the United Order. In 1952, he was contacted by angels from the planet Venus, who are of the Lost Ten Tribes. They were humans about 20 years of age. Paul believes that he lived before, during the time of Christ, [in Palestine] and was ordained by Christ to preach the purity of the gospel. He was born this time in Western Springs, Illinois, and grew up in Monrovia, California. He was converted to Mormonism (Utah Church) shortly after the Short Creek raids—the raids having made him curious about Mormonism. He believes that the LDS Church went into bondage during the presidency of Heber J. Grant, that most of the important church properties were mortgaged to the Chase-Manhattan Bank, etc. Solem indicated that he had been severely persecuted for his beliefs, having been jailed, and spent considerable time in the Idaho State Mental Hospital in Blackfoot, because of his preachings about flying saucers." (Martin, David C., *Restoration Reporter* Volume 3, Number 3, Provo, Utah: November, 1974.)

BRUCE DAVID LONGO

Known by several other names, such as Immanuel David, Bruce David Longo and his family created a sensation in downtown Salt Lake City, Utah, on August 3, 1978. Longo had driven to a nearby canyon and asphyxiated himself with carbon monoxide fumes from an automobile earlier in the week. After learning of this, his wife pushed their seven children from the 11th floor suite balcony of a downtown Salt Lake City hotel, then jumped off herself. All but one daughter died in the incident.

Bruce David Longo was born in 1939 in New York and was raised in the Episcopal Church. In 1960 he converted to the LDS Church and served as a missionary in Uruguay. He was excommunicated shortly thereafter for claiming to be the Holy Ghost. In the May 13, 1972 LDS Church News, he formally apologized for this and disappeared for about one year, only to reappear as Eloheim (God).

Gathering a small following, he claimed to receive revelation. In addition, he contended that each prophet of the LDS Church since Joseph Smith, Jr., had been progressively weaker. He taught that God allowed Joseph Smith to be killed in order to atone for his sins.

The following revelation is representative of Longo. It was received circa 1971:

"Thus saith the Lord God of Israel unto the high minded leaders of the Church of Jesus Christ of Latter Day Saints: You have professed to know my name and have blasphemed in my name in the midst of my own house. Because of this blasphemy I have taken my tabernacle from among you and I have ceased to speak unto you and I have withheld the gifts of my spirit and you are left as blind guides. Do you think that I shall speak and not fulfill? Have you not heard that I am God? Eternal is my name, Man of Counsel is my name and Holiness is my name also. Will I be mocked by the works of my hands? From the day that you were born in Joseph Smith you have been an offense to me. Your necks were stiff and your hearts were hard that I could not establish my Zion among you but took you from the place of my Zion until a generation should arise that would receive my gospel again as it was restored to my servant Joseph; whose blood I will require at your hands if you do not speedily repent. That which you teach is not my gospel nor do you bear witness of me in Spirit and Truth. I have rejected you and your works. Your sacrifices and offerings have become like unto my people in days of old when their offerings were rejected of me because of their wicked hearts of unbelief. Even more; your offerings have become like the offering of Cain which Satan inspired. Shall I receive your converts that knew me not, neither worship me, nor will they obey my voice when I speak. But I have promised and I will fulfill and my covenant people, who are the House of Israel, shall hear my voice and I will manifest myself unto them in might power and they will know that I am the same yesterday, today and forever and that I am no respecter of persons: only he that worketh righteousness is received of me. They will also know that I am he that was revealed unto their fathers and gave their fathers; Abraham, Isaac and Jacob, the promises and that I will fulfill. Now hear my voice you Gentiles: You have polluted your inheritance; you have rejected my gospel and acted presumptuously before me. For this cause I have taken my priesthood from among you and by so doing, cut you off from my presence. For without this priesthood you cannot see the face of God the Father and live. And except you repent and put away your abominations far from you and cleave unto my words which have been brought for you who repent not, and you shall abide there a thousand years. Then you shall be judged and sent to that kingdom which is telestial. This is a promise I make unto you who will not repent. But if you will repent with all your heart, might, mind and strength I will work a mighty work for your deliverance and salvation and will restore unto you that priesthood which you have lost and allow you to receive an inheritance and be united with my people of the covenant, even the lost sheep of the House of Israel. Concerning Joseph Fielding Smith: he is not my prophet. I did not call him. I do not speak to him and I do not bear witness of him. All your witnesses that you bear of him are your own and are false. Behold I am God and I am a God of Miracles and I will do signs and wonders and mighty works, as I did by the hand of my servant Moses, to bring about the salvation of mine elect. And those who will not listen to my voice or the voice of my servants shall surely die even as Pharoah in the midst of the Red Sea. For my judgments shall cover the earth as a flame of fire consuming the wicked before me. My anger is kindled against you wicked shepherds and you are about to partake of the fulness of my wrath if you do not repent even according to my words. Search the scriptures, see if these things are not so. Ask me in the name of mine only Begotten and I will testify. But repent speedily least the summer be over, the harvest ended and your souls not saved. What I say unto one I say unto all the Church of Jesus Christ of Latter Day Saints. Amen." (From *Restoration Reporter,* Volume 1, Number 4, Janesville, Wisconsin: December 1971)

LDS SCRIPTURE RESEARCHERS/BELIEVE GOD SOCIETY
(Sherman Russell Lloyd)

Founded in the 1960s by Sherman Russell Lloyd, the Believe God Society or the Angel Elias Study Class claimed that Joseph Smith, Jr. had returned to earth and that Elias had been on the earth for some forty years preparing for the second phase of the Dispensation of the Fullness of Times.

All the standard works of the LDS Church were accepted as scripture. Several volumes of scripture references and doctrinally oriented interpretations were published. These included *This is that Day for the Promised Return of Joseph Smith in the Flesh,* and *Has the LDS Church Completely Apostatized from the Gospel of Jesus Christ as it was Restored Through Joseph Smith? Here is Proof that it Has!!*

Some complaints included the LDS Church was not living the United Order or the Law of Consecration; the building of temples in foreign lands, and the purpose of temples having been distorted; a change in teaching concerning the nature of God and the godhead.

The group also used revelations given in 1916/1917 to Harry Edgar Baker of Chicago, Illinois, and in their publications quote from the Book of Elias (compilation of revelations given to Maurice L. Glendenning of the Order of Aaron).

A statement of purpose is contained in one of their publications:

"To learn all about his foretold work of the Father, that this reincarnated Joseph Smith is now preparing to do. To become posted on all the early day predictions of the return of Joseph Smith, in the flesh.

"To learn of the Word of the Lord, through H. E. Baker of Chicago consisting of some of the greatest revelations of all time being the Word of Jesus Christ, given in 1916-1917. These reiterate among other things that the raising up of the man like Moses, is future to the giving of Revelations.

"To study the complete religious works of Emanuel Swedenborg, who was a great Seer, of the 18th century, writing over thirty huge volumes of his experiences in the Three Degrees of Glory.

"To become informed of the teachings of the Prophet Joseph Smith as they pertain to the Three Grand Powers, of Elias, Elijah, and Messiah.

"To read and study the fabulous book, *This Is That Day*, which proves that God foretold that Joseph Smith would return to the earth."

This group was not formally organized as a church, but attempted to reform or call the LDS Church to repentance.

It is presently unknown how long this group existed, or the degree of their success.

THE CHURCH OF THE BODY AND OF THE SPIRIT OF JESUS CHRIST (Max E. Powers)

Sometime in the 1960s, Max E. Powers formed this church, with headquarters in Kansas City, Missouri. In the mid-1970s he admitted that he had no followers. The current status of the church is unknown.

According to information I have obtained, Powers appeared before the Council of Apostles of the Church of Christ (Temple Lot) some years ago and gave them an account of how he had been present at the Grand Council of Heaven before the world was created, in the presence of God, Jesus Christ, the Devil and all the angels. Powers claimed that Jesus Christ's pronouncement that he would come to earth and redeem mankind was personally witnessed by himself. He further claimed that Christ did not accomplish his mission and Powers had been appointed to complete the task.

Doctrine

The following information is taken from an undated, mimeographed leaflet by Mr. Powers.

Faith

Faith is the first requirement of the gospel of Jesus Christ, for it is not by knowledge of the spiritual that we enter into the spiritual world. We enter in by faith through the assurance and evidence of things not actually seen. No man can show for the pleasure of viewing by others that which is invisible. Neither can the heft and feel of that which has no earthly element be tried. The power of spiritual knowledge cannot be obtained without entering into the spiritual.

For a foundation of faith man has the logic of natural order in the universe of which he is a part, and the witness of the scriptures testifying of God. "In the beginning God created the heaven and the earth." (Genesis 1:1). The earth, sun and moon and stars are clearly evident and visible to the natural eye. The divine power by which these visible objects are created and established in their revolutions and orbits is invisible. The life and existence of all things known to man are dependent upon the immutable, irrevocable and invisible power of God.

There are three facts concerning the life of man which may be likened to the stars, the moon and the sun. There is the carnal law of evil and good. There is the spiritual law of truth and power of existence. At night you observe the stars and the moon, during the day the light of the sun is so bright that the lights of the stars and moon are invisible.

God has established irrevocable laws of regeneration by which all things bring forth newness of life after their own likeness. The principle of one being the same as the principle of another yet there is a difference of kinds.

The law governing the existence of man comprehends three spiritual kinds. The kingdom of evil, the kingdom of good and the kingdom of truth. Each kingdom has a law by which it is governed. The trust men have in God is inspired by the spirit and confirmed by the existence and order of visible objects.

Priesthood

Reading of the experience of others, or the revelations given to them, can never give us a comprehensive view of our condition and relation to God. Knowledge of this kind can be obtained by self-experience alone. The beginning of this kind of knowledge is in the mediatory authority of the priest. The laws of God were given by unalterable decree before the world existed. By being subject to certain principles and ordinances men acquire the power of the priesthood.

Webster's Dictionary informs us that "A priest is a person authorized to perform the sacred rites of a religion, especially as a mediatory agent between man and god."

Priesthood is the whole body of priests and they form a sacerdotal system for the promulgation of the gospel, the administering of ordinances and the good order of society.

John the Baptist was one man yet he was the priest, church and the kingdom of God. I am informed of the gospel and power of John by revelation given to Joseph Smith, Junior, on September 22-3, 1832.

"Which gospel is the gospel of repentance and of baptism, and the remission of sins, and the law of carnal commandments, which the Lord in his wrath caused to continue with the house of Aaron among the children of Israel until John, whom God raised up, being filled with the Holy Ghost from his mother's womb. For he was baptized while he was yet in his childhood, and ordained by the Angel of God at the time he was eight days old unto this power, to overthrow the Jews, and to make straight the way of the Lord before the face of his people, to prepare them for the coming of the Lord, in whose hand is given all power."

John the Baptist was ordained of angel, but Jesus, when he was baptized, went straightway out of the water; and lo; the heavens were opened unto him, and he saw the Spirit of God descending like a dove, and lighting upon Him and lo a voice out of the heavens saying, This is My Beloved Son, in whom I am well pleased. (Matthew 3:16-17)

The announcement: "This is My Beloved Son" was the announcement of a greater priesthood than that of Aaron. A power of salvation greater than that of John the Baptist. The law of carnal commandments which the Lord in his wrath caused to continue with the children of Israel, was at an end.

[Mr. Powers goes on to relate the story of Joseph Smith, Jr. and Oliver Cowdery, wherein they were praying about baptism, John the Baptist appeared to them, ordained them to the Aaronic Priesthood and commanded them to baptize each other.]

Baptism

The word baptism is defined in Webster's Dictionary: "A Christian sacrament signifying spiritual rebirth and admitting the recipient to the Christian community through the ritual use of water."

Men are born into the world through the principles of regeneration which are common to all mankind. If there were but one Christian community all men would be endowed through nature with membership. For the birth into the world would also be the birth into the community of Christ.

The apostle Paul informs us that there is one glory of the sun, and another glory of the moon, and another glory of the stars: for one star differs from another in glory. So also is the resurrection of the dead. (1 Corinthians 15:41-42)

Christ is the resurrection and all men must come forth from the grave by his power. Hence all men are endowed by nature with Christian membership. In the resurrection all men shall not have the same glory. Some shall be as the stars, a community here and another community there all based on the same principles but having different leaders and different forms of the same testimony.

In resurrection some shall be as the glory of the moon. Receiving their knowledge and understanding from God. Living their lives in accordance to the carnal laws of Aaron. These are they who were obedient to John the Baptist and were baptized by him but they rejected Jesus Christ.

Then above all and through all and in all the resurrection of Christ. The glory of the sun. The principle of regeneration must be complied with in baptism as well as in natural birth. Hence there are three Christian communities each having a glory separate and distinct from the other. Admittance to one is by natural birth. Admittance into either one of the others is by baptism.

The baptism of John the Baptist was a rebirth by flesh. The baptism of Jesus Christ was a rebirth of spirit. In the other case men were immersed by the spirit. For in the one case John immersed the men who came to him.

The scriptures abound with testimony of the distinctly different baptism of regeneration. Who can understand the scriptures? He who enters into the spiritual communities of Christ by baptism.

CHURCH OF CHRIST (Howard Leighton-Floyd/H. H. Burt)

At the 1965 General Assembly of the Church of Christ With the Elijah Message (W. A. Draves) in Independence, Missouri, one-half of the members of the Twelve Apostles withdrew from the church, as did three of the members of the Quorum of Bishops. Prominent leaders in this action were Apostle Howard Leighton-Floyd of Noel, Missouri and Bishop H. H. Burt of Colorado Springs, Colorado.

The point of contention arose over the name of the church. Initially the church had been incorporated as the *Church of Christ*

Established Anew, Inc. but between the 1964 and 1965 General Assemblies, Draves reincorporated the church, with a new name: *Church of Christ With the Elijah Message.* The dissenters felt this was improper in view of the fact that members had been baptized into the *Church of Christ Established Anew.*

For several years prior to this action, members of the church in the Holden, Missouri vicinity had established an agricultural cooperative which became the central area of Leighton-Floyd's group.

Brother Leighton-Floyd states that he did not attempt to lead another church, and that the group has never made claims to being the only true church. For a short time the church published a paper called the *Banner of Truth.*

H. H. Burt assumed unofficial leadership of the group when Leighton-Floyd joined the Church of Christ (Temple Lot).

In 1975 this group made moves to combine with the Church of Christ at Zion's Retreat (to be discussed hereafter), but whether this was effected is unknown.

This group has about 35 members.

Doctrine

The same Articles of Faith and Practice currently in use in the Temple Lot, Fetting and Draves groups are accepted as valid guidelines for faith.

It is held that someday yet future the Lord will command a temple to be built at Independence, Missouri. The church also believes that Christ will someday give them Twelve Apostles. There are presently no Apostles functioning.

Tithing, baptism by immersion, and the laying on of hands for the gift of the Holy Ghost are all important practices of the church.

The Sacrament of the Lords' Supper is practiced, as in many other restoration churches. This group believes that wine should be used. The sacramental prayers found in the Book of Mormon, Moroni 4 and 5 are used.

Any member of the church can receive revelation. Many of these have been printed, but not widely distributed.

Scriptures include the Bible, Book of Mormon, parts of the Doctrine and Covenants, Otto Fetting's and some of W. A. Draves' messages. Parts of the book of Commandments are also in use. (From conversations and correspondence with church leader, Don Henson of Holden, Missouri.)

UNITED ORDER OF THE FAMILY OF CHRIST (David E. Desmond)

This group was organized in 1966 by homosexual members of the

LDS Church. At one time located in Denver, Colorado, recent attempts at contact have failed. I assume that the group is no longer functioning but has probably assimilated into some of the more recent Gay LDS movements.

The information available is taken from a letter from the leader of the group:

"We received your letter today and thought that we would take the time to write you and tell you what we are and what we hope to do. First let me tell you that we are not a new group that has not stood under the test of time. We have been together for over six years and in that time our Order has grown stronger and stronger and stronger. We are Gay and we are LDS. We love our Father in Heaven and serve him but we do not serve our Church as it now stands. We were given the commandment to love our brothers and when we find it easy to obey that command, we are told by the Church that we misunderstand the meaning of love.

"The United Order is just what the name says. We are united and we are an Order. We hold everything in common. We have one checking account and one savings account. Everything is in common for the common good. The ages of our Order are from 18 to 30. Only one member of the Family is over 25. The family is made up of officers (called keys) and members of the Family. The Keys hold council with the Father and direct the Family in the way that brings them union and peace with the will of the Father in Heaven. The leader of the Family is the First Key. He is the same as the First President of the Church. He is the mind, the will, and the heart of the Order. He has given the Order an understanding of the will of the Father that we have never known before the union of the Family. He is so close to the Father that there is no question in the minds of the Order that he and the Father think and live as one. It is known when he is in mind with the Father because members of the United Order see a golden light around his head and we know that the Family is about to grow in knowledge and wisdom.

"This family is not for the great majority of the Gay LDS for it belongs only to those who can put themselves in second place and the will of Father and Family in first place. Those who must own and do on their own will find service and Union with the United Order is hard and not rewarding. Those who see life as a time of service to the Almighty Father and not themselves and feel that common living and loving with others is the way for them, these people should belong to the family.

"Write soon, your brothers, United Order/Family of Christ, David-Edward Desmond, First Key of the Order."

THE TRUE CHURCH OF JESUS CHRIST OF LATTER DAY SAINTS
(David L. Roberts)

Claiming to be the successor of the church restored in 1830 through the Prophet Joseph Smith, Jr., David L. Roberts of Independence, Missouri, contends he is the direct prophetic successor to James J. Strang.

Teaching what he terms *Hebrew Mormonism*, Brother Roberts received a visition from the ancient American prohphet Nephi, now an angel, on November 17, 1967. Just more than one year prior to this heavenly visitation, Roberts was baptized into W. A. Draves' organization and ordained to the office of Elder and Evangelist in the priesthood. After his angelic visitation he resigned and became associated for a time with the Strangite church in Wisconsin. The Strangite *Gospel Herald* for January 1979 comments on his excommunication from the church.

After his visit with the Angel Nephi, Roberts was directed by the Lord to go to Independence, Missouri and rededicate the Temple Lot, which he did.

On July 14, 1974, Roberts was directed by the Prophet Elijah to officially organize the True Church of Jesus Christ Restored. Roberts' own testimony:

"July 14, 1974-The Prophet Elijah appeared to David and Denise Roberts about twelve midnight.

"The Prophet Elijah said, I have come to give you the keys and authorities for the salvation of the dead and to ordain you to the office of Moses.

"The Prophet Elijah anointed me, David, with the heavenly anointing oil and laid his hands on my head and ordained me to the office of Moses and king over the kingdom of God on the earth until Jesus Christ comes again and he handed me the king's scepter and the shepherd's rod to hold in my hands, I held the king's scepter in my right hand and the shepherd's rod in my left hand and I felt all the power and authority of Almighty God. Then I returned the king's scepter and the shepherd's rod back into the hands of the prophet Elijah and he also told me to start my work in Newark, Ohio and move there soon as possible as we can.

"Denise, my wife, witnessed that the Prophet Elijah appeared to me, because she saw him and she also shook his hands and he remained unto day light." (Roberts, David L., *The Angel Nephi Appears to David L. Roberts*, Nashport, Ohio: The True Church of Jesus Christ Restored, nd)

In 1977, Roberts moved the headquarters of his church to Independence, Missouri, where he plans to build a temple. All other restoration churches are considered to be in a state of apostasy. A newspaper article which appeared in the October 15, 1977 issue of the *Independence Examiner*, quotes Roberts as stating that his church has a worldwide membership of 11,000, most of which are in India.

A new revelation, received on May 15, 1981, directed Roberts as follows:

"Thus saith the Lord God of Israel unto thee, the time has come to call my church even, The True Church of Jesus Christ of Latter Day Saints, and the gates of hell shall not prevail against it and I will manifest my glory and power through it.

"Let the Holy Melchizedek Priesthood and the Aaronic Priesthood acknowledge my will to The Whole Church World Wide that The True Church of Jesus Christ of Latter Day Saints has been restored again on the face of the earth and shall never be destroyed again.

"I have reserved a remnant of my servant the Prophet James J. Strang through my servant the Prophet David L. Roberts and he is the one chosen to build the Temple of the Lord even, The House of The Lord in the land of Zion in the Center Place, saith The Lord God of Israel and Zion.

"Let my servant Johan J. Schut be called to the office of Apostle and High Priest, and serve me faithfully and establish the European Mission and preach the True Gospel to all of the continent of Europe for the glory of Almighty God.

"Let my servant the Prophetess Denise L. Roberts preach and sing my Gospel to the inhabitants in the land of Zion and she shall receive the desires of her heart. Thus saith the Lord Jesus Christ unto thee. Amen." (Roberts, David L., *The Oracles of God Book*, Independence, Missouri: The True Church of Jesus Christ Restored)

Doctrine

Articles of Faith

1. We believe in God the Eternal Father, and His Son Jesus Christ, and in the Holy Ghost, which is the glory and power of God. It is neither a person nor a personage in the godhead.

2. We believe that men and women will be punished for their own sins, and not for Adam's transgressions.

3. We believe that through the atonement of Jesus Christ all of the human race is saved by obedience to the laws and ordinances of the true gospel of Jesus Christ.

4. We believe and practice these ordinances of the true gospel of Jesus Christ are: 1st, Faith in the Lord Jesus Christ; 2nd, Repentance;

3rd, water baptism for the remission of sins by immersion; 4th, laying on of hands for the true gift of the holy ghost, with the physical evidence of speaking in other tongues and the baptism of fire with the evidence of cloven tongues of fire coming upon our physical body in order to receive divine health; 5th, the Lord's Supper by the miracle of consubstantiation communion and washing of the saints feet during the new moon sabbaths and the seven annual feasts of the Lord our God.

5. We believe that men and women must be called of God by inspiration and ordained by the laying on of hands by those who are duly commissioned to preach the true gospel of Jesus Christ and administer in the ordinances thereof.

6. We believe in the same organization that existed in the primitive church of Jesus Christ, viz., Apostles, Prophets, Evangelists, Pastors, Teachers, etc.

7. We believe and practice the powers and gifts of the everlasting gospel, viz., the word of wisdom, the word of knowledge, the gift of great faith, the gifts of healing, the gift of mighty miracles, the gift of prophesy, the gift of beholding of angels and ministering spirits, the gift of all kinds of tongues, the gift of the interpretation of languages and of divers kinds of tongues, dreams, visions, the gift of revelation, and the fruit of the spirit is love, joy, peace, long-suffering, gentleness, goodness, faith, meekness and temperance.

8. We believe in the word of God recorded in the Holy Bible and the word of God recorded in the Book of Mormon (the Nephite Record), and in the revelations of Joseph Smith, Jr. and James J. Strang.

9. We believe all that God has revealed, all that he does now reveal, and all that God will yet reveal many more great and important things pertaining to the theocratic kingdom of God, and the second coming of Jesus Christ.

10. We believe in the literal gathering of Israel, and in the restoration of the ten tribes, that Zion (New Jerusalem) will be established upon the western continent; that Jesus Christ will reign personally upon the earth a thousand years; and that the earth will be renewed, and receive its paradisaical glory.

11. We believe in the literal resurrection of the body, and that the dead in Jesus Christ will rise first, and that the rest of the dead live not again until the thousand years are expired.

12. We claim the privilege of worshipping Almighty God according to the dictates of our conscience unmolested, and allow all men and women the same privilege, let them worship how or where they may.

13. We believe in being subject to kings, queens, presidents, rulers, and magistrates, in obeying, honoring, and sustaining the law of the land according to the word of God.

14. We believe in being honest, true, chaste, temperate, benevolent, virtuous, and upright, and in doing good to all; indeed, we may say that we follow the admonition of Paul, we believe all things, we hope all things, we have endured very many things, and hope to be able to endure all things. Everything virtuous, lovely, praiseworthy, and of good report, we seek after, looking forward to the recompense of reward.

15. We believe that the seventh day is the true sabbath of the Lord our God and the seventh day sabbath begins at sunset Friday to sunset Saturday and all believers in Christ Jesus must keep this day as the true Sabbath day and no other day ever.

16. We believe that the new moon sabbaths, the seven annual feasts, the seventh year sabbath, and the jubilee year sabbath of the Lord our God must be observed and kept by all believers in Christ Jesus forever.

17. We believe that the law of clean and unclean meats and all other laws of health must be observed and kept by all believers in Christ Jesus forever.

18. We believe in salvation for the living and the dead and in building temples and in performing temple ordinances for both the living and the dead, such as, the baptism for the dead, washings, anointings, sealings and marriage for time and for all eternity, etc.

19. We believe in the virgin birth of Jesus Christ. We believe that he was conceived by the power of the holy spirit and that neither the seed of Mary nor the seed of Joseph was used in the virgin birth. Also that the virgin Mary only encompasseth the child Jesus. Read St. Matt. 1:18-25; St. Luke 1:26-38; Isaiah 66:7 and Jeremiah 31:22.

20. We believe and practice all things common, even the united firm of Zion in all our stakes of Zion, according to the Holy Scriptures.

21. We believe in the translation of the saints, such as Enoch, Elijah, John the Beloved and the Three Nephite Disciples; also that the faithful saints on earth will obtain complete Christ-like righteousness and be caught up in the air to meet our Lord Jesus Christ at His Second Coming. (*Articles of Faith of The True Church of Jesus Christ Restored,* Independence: The First Presidency, nd)

Priesthood and Church Government

The church has both the Aaronic and Melchizedek Priesthoods, which include the offices common to the LDS Church of Joseph

Smith's day.

The church is directed by a First Presidency. The general church leadership includes a Presiding Patriarch, Apostles who hold the office of High Priest, etc. Both men and women may hold priesthood offices. Roberts' wife Denise is the Presiding Patriarch.

The Prophet must be ordained of God by an angel—others cannot pass this authority to anyone.

The Sabbath

Citing Old Testament, New Testament and modern references, the church has established Saturday as the true Sabbath. Church members gather on this day for worship. Additional information on the seventh-day Sabbath can be found in an earlier segment of this volume which reports James J. Strang's organization, of which this church claims to be the successor.

God's Holy Feasts

There are many references in the scriptures concerning special feasts which were observed by the house of Israel. The True Church of Jesus Christ Restored, in keeping with its observance of Hebrew Mormonism, also observes these special feasts and sabbath days. These include: the feast of the Lord's Passover, the feast of Unleavened Bread, the feast of Pentecost, the feast of Trumpets, the day of Atonement, the feast of Tabernacles, the great day feast. Other special occasions include the new moons, the seventh year sabbath and the year of jubilee sabbath.

Health

The Mosaic health laws—that of clean and unclean foods, is observed as is the Word of Wisdom, as given by the Lord through Joseph Smith, Jr.

United Order

The practice of having all things in common, or "The United Firm of Zion" as it is designated by the church, is taught much in the same way as was originally outlined in the early history of the church under Joseph Smith, Jr.

The law of tithing figures prominently in this teaching, but it is taught differently than in other restoration churches. Citing the book of Leviticus 27:30-34 in the Inspired Version of the Bible, the first tithe given to the Lord is one tenth of a man's possessions. Thereafter he is responsible for the Second and Third Tithes, referring to Deuteronomy chapter 14, Inspired Version. Every year after the first tithe is paid, two tithes, or 20 percent of increase is paid. Every third year, the Third Tithe is paid, or 30 percent of increase. The Third Tithe is "for the fatherless, widow, stranger and the Levite may eat and be satisfied..."

Other Doctrine

The church teaches salvation for the dead, through baptism for the dead and the eternity of the marriage covenant. This eternity of the marriage covenant is supported by Chapter 143 from Volume 3 of the Book of the Lord's Commandments. It is very similar to Section 132 of the Utah Doctrine and Covenants, but all references to the plurality of the marriage covenant have been deleted.

Publications

The church uses as its scriptures the Book of Mormon, or as is preferred, the Nephite Record, the Holy Bible (generally the Inspired Version), the Book of Abraham (as translated by Joseph Smith, Jr.), the Book of the Law of the Lord (translated by James J. Strang), the Voree Plates (translated by Strang), and The Book of the Lord's Commandments, which include the revelations given to Joseph Smith, Jr., and the Oracles of God Book, which contains the revelations given to David L. Roberts. All of these items, with the exception of the Bible and the Book of Mormon are printed by the church.

Other church publications include a large selection of leaflets introducing the doctrine and practices of the church. For a time a church periodical was published, entitled *Voice of Eternal Life.*

SPLIT FROM MARL KILGORE'S ZION'S ORDER OF THE SONS OF LEVI

In summer 1969, Eldon Taylor, a leader in Marl Kilgore's Zion's Order, and his family left the church and filed formal charges in the county court against Kilgore. The Taylor's alleged that their children had been assaulted by Kilgore and his son Nathan with a battery operated cattle prod, while living at the order's Missouri ranch.

The Taylors and some others, including some members of the Kilgore family, left the group and made their way to Washington State. (See *Douglas County Herald,* Ava, Missouri, September 4, 1969)

WORLD REDEMPTION (Barney Fuller)

In 1969, Barney Fuller and others formed a group called World Redemption in California. This organization was not a church, but was formed to publish what Fuller and his associates felt were important issues regarding what was seen as a dangerously fast-growing liberalism within the RLDS Church.

One aim of the group was to bring church members into line with the scriptures, so they might once again enjoy the workings of the Holy Spirit and come to know Christ as the Savior.

Although Fuller, and some others involved with World Redemption had been "silenced" by the RLDS Church (officially unable to preach in the church), they found another way to reach church members. From 1970 until mid-1976, *Zion's Warning* made its appearance about five times each year.

World Redemption came to an end on April 18, 1975 when Fuller organized the *New Jerusalem Church of Jesus Christ.* (To be presented later.)

In addition to the paper, several pamphlets and a full length book on the Book of Mormon were published.

CHURCH OF JESUS CHRIST RESTORED (Stanley M. King)

On April 26, 1970, a group of members of the RLDS Church in Owen Sound, Ontario, Canada, began holding meetings separate from the church. Six weeks later, on June 6, 1970, Stanley M. King was called to preside over the newly organized Church and steps were taken to complete the organization and missionary efforts of the Church of Jesus Christ Restored (Latter Day Saints). Direct revelation from God gives King his instructions pertaining to building the kingdom and the church.

This group believes that the RLDS Church was the second church chosen by God in this dispensation, but having been rejected, they are now the third chosen church.

In the mid-1970s a mission in Independence, Missouri was opened, and later a very successful mission in India was begun. Total church membership is not known at this time.

Doctrine

Faith and Doctrine

"We believe in God, the Creator of all things, our Father, who is unchangeable, from everlasting to everlasting, without beginning of days or end of years, the source of all righteous inspiration, whose capacity for love and wrath are beyond man's ability to know or find out. We believe He has given His Son the task of judging each man according to the works and faith they have practiced while on this earth. Therefore, there is no condemnation for the man who lives and dies ignorant of God's laws. Men choosing to ignore God's laws, however, live under the threat of condemnation from day to day and their just judgment is sure, except they repent and live according to all the principles of the gospel of Christ.

"We believe that just as God spoke to man in days past, so he speaks today. We expect it. We experience it. We are grateful because it delivers man's mind from unstability, confusion and anxiety.

"We believe that Jesus of Nazareth was and is the Only Begotten Son of God; that with God He presided in the beginning over the creation of all things and that it was by Jesus Christ that God created all things that are.

"We believe God directs, comforts, teaches, chastizes and/or reproves men by the ministry of His Holy Spirit, either directly or through divinely called ministers.

"We believe that as man 'feels after God' by diligent study and constant prayer, he is practicing faith and that by willfully enduring and gradually overcoming all things, under the protection and guidance of divinely called ministers, his faith will become knowledge.

"We believe that Jesus built His own church for the purpose of making men perfect in this life. Anything less than this, is not of Jesus Christ. The church that preaches the fullness of His gospel, accordingly promises the perfection of the soul in this life on condition of total obedience to godly principles.

"We believe repentance from doing sin and living an unproductive life (dead works), is essential for any man, woman or youth who by reason of intelligence (knowing right from wrong) are accountable before God and therefore as often as may be necessary, must conscientiously practice sincere repentance.

"Baptism by immersion in water, as performed by the Son of God in the river Jordan by an authoritative minister of God, for the remisson of sins, is absolutely necessary to man's salvation. Without it there is no membership in the church and kingdom of Christ.

"We believe the Eucharist or Sacrament of the Lord's Supper, properly observed by authoritative ministers of God, provides for those who are members of Jesus' church and them alone, the opportunity to consider the blessed sacrifice of the Lamb, Jesus, to give thanks for that atonement His death made possible, and to confess to God publicly or privately the sins that separate man from his Maker and the Holy Ghost.

"The physical body and the spirit (or intelligence) in every man born into this world constitutes the soul of man and because God so loved the world (the souls of men), He allowed His Only Begotten Son to come in the meridian of time, to offer the only acceptable sacrifice for the sins of the world—His death on a cross and by so doing He gave His Father (and our Father) an acceptable offering and a complete and effectual reconciliation and mediation for mankind. Men may lay claim to this atonement only in the church that bears His name and teaches all He taught.

"We believe the fullness of the doctrine of Christ Jesus, is the only way by which man may be saved, and that giving support to any church which does not preach the fullness of the doctrine of Jesus is supporting that which may be well-intentioned perhaps but nevertheless, a counterfeit and therefore, her promises are vain.

"Man is required (if he desires the salvation of his soul) to live by every word that proceedeth forth out of the mouth of God. We believe those words as they are found recorded in the Inspired Correction of the Scriptures (Bible)—even though all biblical references in this tract are to the King James Version—plus the Book of Mormon, the Doctrine and Covenants, and the latest revelations (called Supplements), received by our present prophet, Elder Stanley King and sanctioned by the saints.

"We believe that just as the original Church of Christ as organized by Jesus himself, apostacized, so also the Reorganized Church of Jesus Christ of Latter Day Saints—lawful successor to the church restored by Joseph Smith, Jr. in 1830—has also apostacized administratively. There are many good honorable people within that denomination as there are in many other denominations of the world today but this fact does not negate the evidences of her unfortunate apostacy.

"We believe Joseph Smith, Jr. was and is the great Prophet of this last dispensation and that as a man he may possibly have erred from time to time but as God's servant, ordained from before the foundation of the world, to speak forth His Word, He did not err.

"We believe Sanctification must be attained by the honest in heart. It is the process of perfection. Attaining perfection while living in a system of houses, stores, streets and divisive devilish influences of this present age is impossible. We believe the only way to effectively live in the world but not be part of it, is in the stake; the stake as revealed by God through Joseph Smith, Jr., not those promoted by the RLDS or Utah churches. The Stakes divinely organized always start with the building of the House of the Lord (temple) first. This church has prepared for five years to do this and at this writing (1975) are very near to commencing such a work in obedience to His word and to His glory.

"The obligation upon the saint (member of the church) is to become independent above every other creature or system beneath the Celestial world. Practicing daily the attributes of God is a way of life in the Stake. The Law of Preference is taught and lived.

"We believe in being good stewards over all God gives us. Sacrifice is expected and desired by members in this church so that

God's final glorious chapter of His strange act might be completed. There is no perfection without sacrifice and where there is no perfection there is no church. Man must not fail to please God. Jesus willingly sacrificed all for His Father. So must we.

"We believe heaven is a place of varied glories. There is the Celestial, Terrestrial and Telestial glory that man may attain. We believe that when this earth has fulfilled itself in the present system of things that it will be changed and provide for the righteous the greatest glory of all—Celestial glory.

"We believe there are no authoritative High Priests on the earth today (1975) but that very soon this ministry will be restored to the salvation of man, the redemption of Zion and the everlasting glory of God.

"There is historical support for Presidencies in the Church of Christ. We do believe they are acceptable to God and necessary for the church to function orderly.

"There are other tenets of faith that make up the fullness of the doctrine of Jesus such as Ministerial Authority (who really are the servants of God?), the gifts and fruits of God's Holy Spirit, Baptism for the dead (by revelation through a prophet), Endowments, and other temple ordinances, Celestial Priesthood Education (School of the Prophets), equality, the gathering of scattered Israel, plus many many more." (From a tract introducing the church.)

Priesthood and Church Organization

"We believe that a fully organized church must contain the following: High Priests, Elders, Priests, Teachers, Deacons: a First Presidency, consisting of three Elders (High Priests): the Council of Twelve Apostles, with one called to be the President: Twelve High Priests to form the Standing High Council of the Church, mainly a high judicial council: A Presiding Bishopric, consisting of three: A Presiding Patriarch, with two councilors: and also, the quorums of Seventy, to work under the direction of The Twelve as the leading missionary arm of the church."

"...the second presidency of the church is the council of the Twelve, and...their prime function is to take the church into all the world, and preach the gospel unto every creature...Those whom they send, are the several quorums of the Seventy who are really an extension of this second presidency." (Letter to the author from S. M. King, March 25, 1975)

Temples

"The fullness of the gospel cannot be achieved without temples. They are the only Houses of worship which were employed in the first church. They did not build churches after the fashion of the world...The Temple had many functions which are not well understood by the people of the restoration, and those people who do believe in them, and those who do build them, do not build them like the ones built in the old days. Neither are they used for entirely the same purpose or for the same reasons.

"All Stakes which are to be built up unto the Lord are to have in the centre square of the city, the House or the Houses of the Lord (Temples)....There were to have been twenty-four in all [referring to the city of Zion], all built the same size, which again bespeaks the equality of the church...The first three, for the First Presidency and his Councillors: Three for the Presiding Bishopric and his Councillors: Three for the Presiding Patriarch: Three for the Elders in Zion: Three for the Presidency of the Order of Aaron: and also, three more for the Priests of Aaron: Three for the Teachers: and Three for the Presidents of Deacons...

"Temples are Holy Houses...These are the only places which God can come to, and reveal His presence...Temples are the only place where the high ordinances can be performed...such as, the anointings, washings, receiving of the endowment [not the same as taught by the Utah Church], baptism for the dead, and the receiving of the Holy Spirit of Promise, which in effect, is the Sealing Ordinance performed by the Patriarch, which is the sealing up unto eternal life, which is being saved, or as the scriptures more often call it, being sanctified..." (From letter referred to above.)

Publications

Although the church does not print its own editions, it uses the Inspired Version of the Bible, Book of Mormon (1908 RLDS Edition), and the 1844 edition of the Doctrine and Covenants. President S. M. King has stated that he believes the Book of Abraham to be scripture and plans were made to incorporate that book as part of the accepted scripture of the church. An additional book, printed by the church, is called *Supplement to the Doctrine and Covenants* which contains the revelations given to the church since its organization in 1970.

For a number of years, from January 1974 until 1978, the church published a quarterly magazine, *The New Times and Seasons.*

RESTORED CHURCH OF JESUS CHRIST OF LATTER DAY SAINTS
(F. Elwood Russell)

Beginning in the late 1960s, F. Elwood Russell of San Diego, California, began receiving revelations which directed him in a course that the leaders of the LDS Church in Salt Lake City considered contrary to the will of God, for which Russell was excommunicated.

On October 24, 1971, ten members gathered and sustained Brother Russell as the Presiding Elder of the church. Russell is prompt to point out that the church, as yet, is but potential and not functional.

Having been called by God to restore the power of the priesthood to the LDS Church in Utah, Russell maintains that the church has not had the priesthood power since the administration of Joseph Fielding Smith.

All four standard works, common to the LDS Church, are the accepted books of scripture.

In addition to the thirteen articles of faith of the LDS Church, eight additional articles have been added. These are as follows:

"We believe that, in fulfillment of numerous prophecies, the original church organized by Joseph Smith has strayed from many of the commandments of God and as foretold by the Prophet Isaiah, has transgressed the laws, changed the ordinances, and broken the everlasting covenant.

"We believe Elwood Russell to be the Messenger of the Covenant, foretold by the Prophet Malachi, who was sent by the Lord to restore all things from which the original church has fallen, and to prepare the world for the coming of the Lord on the great and dreadful day, to be followed by His Millennial reign.

"We believe the original church to be guilty of priestcraft and of raising up churches to get gain, as evidenced by the existence of a paid ministry among the General Authorities and by their investment of church funds in numerous forms of business enterprise.

"We believe that Jesus Christ is now living on the earth in the flesh and know that there are numerous witnesses to that effect.

"We believe that the keys of the Holy Priesthood have been withdrawn from the original church of Jesus Christ and are now transferred by the Lord into the hands of the members of the Restored Church to set in order the House of God, as foretold in Section 85 of the Doctrine and Covenants.

"We believe San Diego County of California to be the place foretold in many prophecies as the New Jerusalem, where the Tribes of Israel are to gather, so as to escape the time of the destruction of the wicked by fire that is at hand, and as a place of refuge from the wars that will continue until the end.

"We believe that the gathering of Israel can only be accomplished by the exercise of the covenant of Abraham, to separate the wicked from the righteous, without any prejudice as to race or the color of a man's skin.

"We believe ourselves to be the Elders of Israel who shall be directed by the Lord to save the Constitution of this land, and be instrumental in setting up the theocratic government, foretold by the prophet Daniel, that shall consume all other kingdoms and be the means by which the Lord shall rule and reign for a thousand years." (From an undated article, *The Articles of Faith of the Restored Church of Jesus Christ of Latter Day Saints*)

HOMOSEXUAL CHURCH OF JESUS CHRIST

Organized in 1972 in the Denver, Colorado area. No further details are available at this writing.

LATTER DAY SAINTS CHURCH (N. S. Park)

Sometime in 1972, Mr. No-sup Park, of South Korea, came into contact with some Mormon missionaries who were laboring in that land, purchased a copy of the Book of Mormon and became converted to many of its teachings. He never accepted baptism, however, from these Mormon missionaries, although many attempts were made to obtain his commitment to the Mormon Church.

For a short time, Park regularly attended Mormon meetings in his hometown, which is about 100 miles south of Seoul.

He believes the Book of Mormon, Doctrine and Covenants, Pearl of Great Price and the Holy Bible. Worship services, which are held in his home, consist of preachings from these books and hymn singing.

Claiming to be a prophet of God, he believes that Jesus Christ has commanded him to write an additional book of scripture, in addition to recording the various revelations he has received from time to time. He has received visits from Christ, and also from Satan—who attempted to thwart his work.

A 1976 revelation told Park that Christ will make his Second Coming to Park's home, from which the Savior will reign over the earth during the Millennium.

Park's activities at this writing are not known. (Information from personal visits with Mr. Park, and from manuscript documents in the author's possession.)

THE CHURCH OF THE LAMB OF GOD (Ervil M. LeBaron)

Sometime after his removal from Joel F. LeBaron's Church of the Firstborn of the Fullness of Times, between 1972 and 1974, Ervil M. LeBaron organized the Church of the Lamb of God. Many prominent leaders of Joel's church followed him.

This group has been accused of the murder of Joel F. LeBaron, Rulon C. Allred, and many others who claimed to possess the true priesthood authority. Threats against many public servants have also been discovered.

Considered the mastermind behind the murders and threats, particularly the assassination of Dr. Rulon C. Allred in 1977, a Utah court convicted Ervil and placed him in the custody of the Utah State Prison. LeBaron was found dead in his cell at 5:30 a.m., Sunday, August 16, 1981. The medical examiner's office concluded that the cause of death was a heart seizure.

Without his charismatic leadership, the future of his church is in question.

Teaching that all should obey the civil law of God, the church found in the scriptures its call to rid the world of false prophets and non-believers. These people were very sincere in their belief, and Ervil claimed to be directed by revelation from God in all that was done.

Quoting LDS Doctrine and Covenants 133:63-64, "And upon them that hearken not to the voice of the Lord shall be fulfilled that which was written by the prophet Moses, that they should be cut off from among the people...," this group taught that "the great work of carrying out the judgments and destructions that the Lord would send forth by His divine command just prior to His coming in the clouds of Heaven in power and great glory was to be performed by those among His people who feared His name and obeyed His law." *(The Saints of Latter Days—Their Rise in Power at the Last Time, nd)*

THE NEW JERUSALEM GROUP (Kathryn Carter)

Started in 1972 in the Los Angeles, California area, recent reports place this group in Blanding, Utah. Available information is from a printed document issued by the group:

"Important notice for members of the Church of Jesus Christ of Latter Day Saints. God will let you know this is the truth by the power of the Holy Ghost. Ask God if the things I say here are the truth and God will let you know by the power of the Holy Ghost.

"A New Church Starting

"Help us to start The New Jerusalem Group, to be started in the Los Angeles, California area and eventually in the Utah mountains.

"We have been let know by revelation of God that my son, descendent of Utah, Mormon Pioneers, is Chapter 12, Verse 5 of Revelations of the Bible (King James Version and other Versions). I quote

Chapter 12 Verse 5 of Revelations of the Bible:

"Chapter 12, Verse 5: And she brought forth a man child, who was to rule all nations with a rod of iron: and her child was caught up to God and His throne.

"The Rod of Iron spoken of in this verse in the True Gospel of God on Earth or The Book of Mormon as translated correctly, so the child will obviously rule the world with the Book of Mormon as translated correctly by my son. Anyone who knows Mormon prophecies well would probably see that this fits in perfectly with Mormon Prophecies. (See Book of Mormon, 1 Nephi for the rod of iron spoken of in Chapter 12, Verse 5 of Revelations: Rod of Iron, in vision of Lehi, 1 Nephi, Chapter 8, Verse 19; in vision of Nephi, 1 Nephi, Chapter 11, Verse 25; meaning of: 1 Nephi, Chapter 15, verse 23.)

"The time element would be all off in this chapter for the woman described in the chapter to be Mary, Mother of Christ or Verse 5 to be Christ. This is not the Meridian of Time which is spoken of in this chapter, it is now that this chapter is happening and from Chapter 12 on in Revelations is obviously from now on (the year 1972 on).

"To prove this I will discuss this chapter briefly here: See Revelations, Chapter 12, Verse 5 again: And she brought forth a man child who was to rule all nations with a rod of iron, etc. We translate the rod of iron mentioned here to be The Book of Mormon as translated correctly by my son or the true gospel of God on earth and the Mormon Church was not established until the year 1830, consequently this could not possibly have been the time of Christ. Also, see Revelations, Chapter 12, Verse 12....for the Devil is come down unto you, having great wrath, because he knoweth that he hath but a short time. Surely in the time of Christ it would not be said that the Devil had but a short time but right now, the year 1972 would be the time obviously when the Devil has but a short time. According to Mormon Doctrine it is only about 28 years until the beginning of the 7th thousand years when the Millennium or the Second Coming of Christ is expected. And again, see Chapter 12, Verse 14 of Revelations: And to the woman were given two wings of a great eagle, that she may fly into the wilderness, into her place, etc. We have translated the two wings of a great eagle spoken of in this verse as a modern day airplane, so this would indicate that this could not possibly be the time of Christ as there were surely no modern day airplanes in the time of Christ. We can discuss this chapter further, but in order to conserve space will not do so in this short notice.

"My son was baptized at 8 years old in the Church of Jesus Christ of Latter-Day Saints as was his sister in Revelations, one year younger than he is (they are both adults now). I also was baptized into the Church of Jesus Christ of Latter-day Saints in the year 1957.

"We, his sister and mother in Revelations with him, of course, are only female helpers to help him accomplish his great mission in life to rule the whole world eventually with The Book of Mormon, the true gospel of God on earth, or the rod of iron as it is called in Chapter 12, verse 5 of Revelations.

"How can you help?

"Help those in the Bible with money quickly for their protection from the wicked here on earth. You can help also by having copies of this notice made and getting this important information to as many Latter-day Saints as possible, as quickly as possible. We could use donations to get started immediately. Please include your name with any donation you make to the group so that we can keep records of the early donators to the group. Make out any checks or money orders to K. Carter. Also, write to us for our location so that you can come to see us and find out more about how you can help to get the group started.

"We would appreciate any help we can get to get this group started as quickly as possible, because we will be starting another small group on a small farm in Kansas (northwest corner, Near Mt. Sunflower). As soon as we get enough money together to purchase valuable church and genealogy records which will be needed for the new genealogy library which we will eventually build near the temple at Jackson County Missouri and the church records for the future historians of the church and other record keepers of the church, and church libraries we hope to build eventually and for future generations of the church and for the benefit of others in this country and other countries of the world who may surely not have the records in order to preserve them. When enough people have come into the New Jerusalem Group it will eventually become the New True Church of God on Earth, the church the Lord's prayer refers to when it says Thy kingdom come. The church will be the true Kingdom of God on Earth.

"We thought the New Jerusalem Group could use trailers for their camp when they got to the Utah mts., then we would be able to move when necessary without much difficulty. Trailers could well be the new version of the old covered wagons to cross the plains once more, but this time, of course, our destination will be Jackson County, Missouri (to build the New Jerusalem temple and city).

"Don't forget we need donated and consecrated money to get

enough funds together to purchase much needed farm land (a small amount at first) and a small farm on which we can keep these records safely in case of nuclear attack or earthquakes, etc. (See Prophecy Key to the Future by Duane Crowther on sale at Deseret Book Store, mail away to 44 East South Temple, Salt Lake City, Utah for Mormon prophecies.) All should read this book for Mormon prophecies for the next thirty years but consult us for the proper interpretation of these prophecies.

"We will not go out to Jackson County, Missouri until it is completely burned out according to Mormon prophecies for some reason (earthquake and disease which sometimes follows, or some other disaster.) This group (New Jerusalem Group) will not be allowed to take up arms against their neighbors or to do anything against the laws of the land ever.

"We hope to go to Jackson County, Missouri within five years or so, possibly less, but expect severe internal wars (according to Mormon prophecy) (Democrats against the Republicans and the Independent American Party to come out of the internal wars), and World War III (Russia and its allies against the United States of America and its allies) during this time, or at least part of these wars during this time.

"If you want to have a copy or copies made of this notice, the city libraries usually have copier machines which cost 10 cents a copy, or see the yellow pages of your local phone book for lithographers or local printing shops (100 lithographers copies is usually fairly inexpensive if you can use that many.)"

The writer goes on to speak of the "spiritual crucifixion" of her son, etc. and how he will be a great world leader, a man who receives revelation from God.

She concludes..."I, the mother in Chapter 12, Verse 1 to 5 of Revelations of The Bible ask you now to join me on faith because this crucifixion is pathetic and because of bad treatment my son had where he was living with wicked people he has joined the United State Navy and is on a ship. I have got to get him out of the Armed Forces. It is like Jesus Christ in the Navy. It must not be. The sister in the Bible has been forced by the family into a very young marriage and the young man who married her did so for the money in the family and is very cruel to her but she cannot say that he is cruel to her. Please help me, the mother of Chapter 12 of Revelations of the Bible to get enough money together quickly so I can get them to come with me. It is very dangerous for them not to be with me, their mother God chose for them. Do no believe anything the family who raised them tells you. All of them lie and are extremely wicked to him, but he cannot talk to defend himself because of the crucifixion. He just does and says things that hurt himself. Please help quickly. I need an inexpensive used trailer and an inexpensive used car (which looks good enough so that it doesn't shame him) for the three of us so I can make a home for him and his sister quickly so they will come with me. Also, I do not drive myself and will need someone who will drive me around to the different wards in and around Los Angeles in order to deliver these notices to the different wards quickly as possible."

CHURCH OF CHRIST AT ZION'S RETREAT (T. Nerren/Gerald A. Hall)

The beginnings and basic beliefs of this group are those promulgated by E. E. Long and Thomas Nerren in 1938. A revelation directed the church to move to Halley's Bluff, near Schell City, Missouri, where this group maintains their headquarters.

In 1964 the group began publishing a paper called *Zion's Restorer,* which I believe is no longer being issued. I was told that a temple had been built on the bluff, but was destroyed by fire several years ago. In addition to using the Bible and the Book of Mormon, Otto Fetting's thirty messages and more recently revelations from members of the church are used as works of scripture.

A split began to develop in the early 1970s when a radical faction led by Dan Gayman was unable to reconcile with those who chose to follow Gerald A. Hall, even though the two men had both been prominent in the leadership of the church for a number of years. The court contest, settled in 1973, was adjudged in favor of Hall, who was able to retain most of the church properties, including the paper. The name of the church, which had previously been the Church of Jesus Christ, became the Church of Christ at Zion's Retreat.

Although I have been unsuccessful in contacting this group, I believe it is still operating.

Information about Gayman's group follows.

THE CHURCH OF ISRAEL (T. Nerren/Dan Gayman)

The other part of the original Nerren group is now led by Dan Gayman. Although the court battle was lost, this group still retains part of the original church properties at Halley's Bluff.

Making it's debut in 1971, *Zion's Watchman,* became the voice of the more radical population of the colony.

Preaching the supremacy of the white Christian race, the church has been able to regroup its forces and boasts a school where a solid Christian education is available for the children of Christian families. A training program for ministers is also available.

Zion's Watchman makes several appearances each year and contains many articles and recently preached sermons pertaining to the beliefs of the church.

As with the ancient Israelites, several feasts are observed each year, including the Feast of Passover, Feast of Pentecost, Feast of Ingathering, which includes the Feast of Trumpets, Day of Atonement and the Feast of Tabernacles.

Gaining self-sufficiency is a prime concern of the church, as well as healthy attitudes, including avoiding tobacco, caffein (as in Coca-cola), white sugar, etc. Food storage is essential for all.

Gayman's own account of the split of the church is interesting and the following segment is quoted from *Zion's Watchman,* August-September 1974, Volume 2, Number 10, p. 4: "Those of you who have followed Zion's Watchman publication will remember that for a good number of years we published a journal called Zion's Restorer. At that time our group here in Missouri sponsored three National Kingdom Conferences each year, with Christian Israel Patriots coming here from all parts of the nation. Each year these National Conferences were attracting attention and drawing people here to hear the Gospel of the Kingdom proclaimed. Then beginning in 1971, traitors and betrayers of Jesus Christ and the White Race, from our own ranks, arose because of fear, fear of left wing groups, fear of right wing groups, fear of our own governmental agencies, and from fear generated in their own hearts and attempted to close down all National Kingdom Conferences and cease all activities for God and Country. When we opposed this position of fear, and persisted in holding National Conferences during 1971 and 1972, our opposition, led by two men from our own ranks, filed a suit against me personally and against our congregation, and sought to close down all Conferences as well as confiscate the camp ground and buildings, together with all the land upon which the National Conferences were held. After nearly two years of litigation in the courts, our opposition fearing they might lose the case if it came to trial, turned against the White Christian people of this nation, and against the truth of Jesus Christ by framing our group with unbelievable lies, that resulted in our loss of the right to hold National Kingdom Conferences, our loss of all but 20 of the 511 acres of property, and all but two of the buildings that housed our camps and conferences. In all this great struggle we have seen the Sovereign hand of God demonstrated many times. Today we stand liberated from traitors who might have caused irreparable harm in the serious days that lie ahead..."

In addition to the church magazine, several pamphlets explaining various positions of the church have been published and are available. At one time the church accepted part of the Restoration scriptures (Book of Mormon, Otto Fetting, etc.) but currently no reference is made to these in the publications of the church. The Book of Common Prayer of the Episcopal Church (Church of England) is used by the church.

The name of the church was originally *The Church of Our Christian Heritage* but in 1981 the name was changed to *The Church of Israel.*

LUKEITE BREAK-OFF—DAVISON, MICHIGAN

A split occurred in Pauline Hancock's *Church of Christ*, sometimes called the Lukeites, circa 1973 in Davison, Michigan. It may have been over the main body of the church's rejection of the Book of Mormon. (See previous entry on the Hancock organization.)

No further details are available.

THE WATCHMEN ON THE TOWERS OF LATTER DAY ISRAEL
(Miltenberg/Braun)

Preaching Mormon Fundamentalism, but not affiliated with any of the organized fundamentalist groups, the Watchmen have been called of God to "perk up the sleeping membership of the LDS Church."

Elder Arno Miltenberg stated in a personal letter to the author dated December 3, 1974 "...we are not a new splinter group, cult or church, but a few courageous elders who, because of their valiance in believing in the continued validity of the original, doctrinal structure of Mormonism, have been cast out (or disfellowshipped and finally excommunicated) from the society of the constituted LDS Church. As such, we have undertaken to make a study of all the differences now existing between original and modern Mormonism and have stressed the fact that modern Mormonism is absolutely apostate of original Mormonism."

The Watchmen's most gifted writer is Elder Henry Braun. Several publications have been issued, including a two volume set *Mormon Fundamentalism and the LDS Church*, and a three volume series entitled *Thoughts of a Mormon Convert—Pro and Con."*

The Watchmen are located in Salt Lake City, Utah.

MONTE SCOVILL

A possible polygamist group organized circa 1973. No further details are available.

CHURCH OF JESUS CHRIST OF SOLEMN ASSEMBLY
(Alexander Joseph)

Once a prominent leader with Rulon Allred's fundamentalist group, Alexander Joseph withdrew and formed his own church in 1974.

Claiming to be a Latter Day Saint, which has nothing to do with Mormonism, Joseph is a firm believer in plural marriage as a revealed principle of the gospel of Christ.

In the mid-1970s, he and his followers received considerable publicity when the Bureau of Land Management contested their rights as homesteaders in the Kanab, Utah area.

Late in 1979, Joseph published a book entitled *Dry Bones—A Resurrection of Ancient Understandings.* This book is an interesting explanation of the drawings which accompany the Book of Abraham in the LDS Church's volume of scripture, the Pearl of Great Price. Joseph says that his work vindicates the Prophet Joseph Smith, Jr.

With several wives, children and followers, Joseph maintains residence near Glen Canyon City, Utah.

CHURCH OF CHRIST (PATRIARCHAL) (John W. Bryant)

At a young age, John W. Bryant, the Presiding Patriarch of the Church of Christ (Patriarchal), began receiving visions, visitations and other manifestations from heavenly sources. He was given certain knowledge by the Lord which pertained to the temple ordinances. Later in life, he learned this fact when he received his own endowments in the Salt Lake Temple of the LDS Church. Having been baptized into the Mormon Church on August 18, 1964, John traveled to Salt Lake City the following year where he went through the temple, received a patriarchal blessing from Eldred G. Smith, Patriarch to the LDS Church, and was set apart as a missionary to Japan.

In the early 1970s, he became associated with the group of fundamentalist Mormons under the leadership of Rulon C. Allred, and was ordained into the priesthood.

After being active with that group for several years, a break started to form on August 27, 1974, when Bryant received a visitation from John, the Beloved, one of the Savior's original twelve apostles. Bryant was commissioned by the apostle to establish the *Order of the Ancients* among his family and friends and others who would be led by the Holy Ghost. Subsequently additional revelations and visitations were received. In addition to

Bryant, who is referred to as *Samuel* on most occasions, many other members of the church have been used at various times by the Lord for the purpose of revelation and prophecy.

Bryant, through study, learned that after the death of Joseph F. Smith, sixth president of the Mormon Church, only those worthy of the authority and keys held by Joseph Smith, Jr., would be given the opportunity to exercise these keys on his behalf, and then only would they be able to do so through the ministry of translated beings.

On one occasion Bryant was taken to the City of Enoch, where he received his *second anointing* among other special blessings. Later he was sealed to Joseph Smith, Jr. as the "firstborn of his heirs." He received all the keys originally held by Joseph Smith, Jr. on December 31, 1975, when Joseph W. Musser in the presence of the Prophet Joseph, came to Bryant and conferred these keys upon him. In addition to the "fullness of the keys of the Melchizedek Priesthood" which were conferred by Musser, Lorin C. Woolley conferred the "fullness of the keys of the patriarchy to the Church of Christ." Joseph F. Smith conferred the "fullness of the keys of the Presidency of the Church of Christ," and John Taylor conferred the "fullness of the keys of the Kingdom of God."

The church practices polygamy and has strived to live the United order. Several branches have been established in Utah and Nevada, with other groups in various parts of the country. A community was established near Mesquite, Nevada but in 1981 the church headquarters was moved to Oregon. Since the move the publication of the church magazine appears to have ceased.

This group has been commissioned to build temples and the Holy City of Zion, and looks to that as a special goal.

A publication of the church declares the Church of Christ (Patriarchal) "...is not a new church. This is not a new dispensation of truth; nor a restoration of truth to the world, for this has already been done through Joseph Smith when he was living with us.

"The Lord has set his hand, through his Prophet Joseph Smith, merely to renew those laws...rites...and ordinances which have been forsaken, and must be here when he returns.

"The Church of Christ (Patriarchal) is a provisional church; one which can provide a way for God's chosen, to obey and live the laws they are expected to live.

"When the Church of Jesus Christ of Latter-day Saints accepts the 'setting in order' that Joseph will do, then the Church of Christ (Patriarchal) will no longer be needed, or required by the Lord."

The Church recognizes that "many factions have broken off from the Church of Christ which was organized under the direction of the Lord by Joseph Smith, but none have retained the fulness of the gospel which he taught nor the Patriarchal Priesthood under the authority of which the church was organized. Each of them has 'transgressed the laws, changed the ordinance, broken the everlasting covenant.' (Isaiah 24:5). In none of them does the Patriarch, bearing the Patriarchal Priesthood which has been handed down from the Fathers, retain his place at the head of the church, but in every case he has been placed in a subordinate position indicating their departure from the Patriarchal Order. Only in the Church of Christ (Patriarchal) is the pure order of heaven as it was had in the Primitive Church of Christ and among the early Patriarchs preserved. Only in this Church can be found the fulness of those laws, ordinances and instructions which emanate from the Holy Priesthood after the Order of God, through obedience to which mankind may be redeemed from the Fall and the effects of individual sin to return to the presence of our Father in heaven and dwell with him forever and ever." (*What is the Church of Christ (Patriarchal)?*, published by the church, nd, np.)

Doctrine

Church Government

In response to an inquiry on the organization of the church, the following answer was published in the church magazine, *Voice of Zion:*

"The Church of Christ is divided into two parts, the Church of Enoch, consisting of those living the Law of the Melchizedek Priesthood, and the Church of the Latter-day Saints, consisting of those living the law of the Aaronic Priesthood. The Melchizedek Law is administered by the President of the Melchizedek Priesthood assisted by two Assistant Presidents and seven counselors who are known as the Council of Friends. The President of the Melchizedek Priesthood and the Council of Friends function as the Presidency of the Sanhedrim, a body of approximately seventy high priest apostles charged with the responsibility of approving all nominations which are to be placed before the Conferences of the Church of Christ to be sustained as members of the Church hierarchy...

"The man presiding over the administration of the Aaronic Law is the Patriarch to the Church. He is the spiritual head of the Church, responsible for seeing that the Church is governed according to the revelations and administering the keys to the spiritual blessings of the Aaronic Law. (D & C 124:91-94) The Doctrine and Covenants confirms that the Patriarch is the presiding officer in the Church. (D & C 124:124) That this is the correct understanding of this verse was affirmed by President Joseph F. Smith during the special conference held 10 November 1901 at which he was sustained as President of the Church:

"'We have not always carried out strictly the order of the Priesthood; we have varied from it to some extent; but we hope in due time that, by the promptings of the Holy Spirit, we will be led up into the exact channel and course that the Lord has marked out for us to pursue, and adhere strictly to the order that he has established. I will read from a revelation that was given to the Prophet Joseph Smith, at Nauvoo, Hancock County, Illinois, January 19, 1841, which stands as the law of the church in relation to the presentation of the authorities of the Holy Priesthood as they were established in the Church, and from which I feel we have no right to depart. The Lord says: "First, I give unto you Hyrum Smith to be a patriarch unto you, to hold the sealing blessings of my church, even the Holy Spirit of Promise, whereby ye are sealed up unto the day of redemption, that ye may not fall notwithstanding the hour of temptation that may come upon you." (D & C 124:124) It may be considered strange that the Lord should give first of all the Patriarch; yet I do not know any law, any revelation or any commandment from God to the contrary, that has ever been given through any of the Prophets or Presidents of the Church. At the same time we well know that this order has not been strictly followed from the day we came into these valleys until now—and we will not make any change at present.'" (Conference Report, p. 71)

"The administrative head of the Church is the President. He is responsible for directing the affairs of the Church day by day. The Patriarch oversees the Church but the President administers it. There is also an Assistant President who acts as an alter ego to the President. The existence of the Assitant President means that the First Presidency can be full, even in the absence of the President. Oliver Cowdery was the first Assistant President of the Church. Concerning the office he held, President Cowdery wrote:

"'The office of Assistant President is to assist in presiding over the whole church, and to officiate in the absence of the President, according to his rank and appointment, viz, President Cowdery, first; President Rigdon, second; and President Williams, third, as they were severally called. The office of this priesthood is also to act as spokesman, taking Aaron for an example. The virtue of the above priesthood is to hold the keys of the kingdom of heaven or of the church militant.'" (Historian's Book A, p. 17—LDS Church

Historian's Office; see also Doctrines of Salvation 1:212)

"The First Presidency is assisted by two high councils—the Standing High Council consisting of twelve high priests who assist the First Presidency in administering the affairs of the stakes of Zion, and the Traveling High Council consisting of the twelve apostles who administer the affairs of the Branches of the Church as well as supervising its missionary activities under the direction of the First Presidency. The organization of the first Standing High Council is described in Section 102 of the Doctrine and Covenants. That this section does not refer to the organization of a stake high council is shown in verses 9-11 which specify that the President of the Council is the President of the Church. Verse 12 also states that this refers to the high council of the Church of Christ, not a stake high council. The assistants to the Twelve are the Seventy Apostles. These are presided over by seven Presidents known as the First Council of the Seventies.

"The First Presidency is also assisted by a Presiding Bishopric, a high priest and two counselors who are elders or high priests, who preside over the temporal affairs of the church. There are also a General Clerk and Recorder and a Historian appointed from among the elders.

"The Church Financial Council and General Board of the United Order, consisting of the First Presidency, the High Council and the Presiding Bishopric presided over by the Patriarch to the Church, makes policy decisions of the various United Orders. The Church Board of Education is a body of Patriarchs which establishes a curricula and assists in the establishment of Church Parochial Schools in the stakes and branches. The Church Music Committee selects and prepares hymns and spiritual songs to be included in the hymnal.

"The political Kingdom of God, which is responsible for advising the disciples in political affairs, is presided over by a President and a council consisting of forty-eight high priest apostles and at least two gentiles.

"Above all these is the Church of the Firstborn governed by the Presiding Patriarch, four Assistant Patriarchs, a Council of Twelve Patriarchs and an indefinite number of Counselors to the Council of Patriarchs. These Presiding Patriarchs have ultimate and final jurisdiction over all affairs in the Church of God. They are also the trustees of the Church of Christ (Patriarchal), empowered by the Articles of Incorporation to legally represent the Church." (*Voice of Zion,* Volume 6, Number 12, 1981, pp. 397-399)

Publications

Accepted scripture includes the Book of Mormon, the Pearl of Great Price, the Holy Bible and the Doctrine and Covenants. The church prints parts of the Doctrine and Covenants, which includes many of the revelations given to John Bryant and others. Two other books of scripture are published by the church—*The Writings of Abraham* and *The Book of the Order.* The Writings is a translation of some ancient writings in which Abraham recorded his history, and were given to John W. Bryant for translation and publication. The Book of the Order is a record written by Elijah the Prophet, and contains the laws of the patriarchal order, the order of Enoch.

In addition to numerous pamphlets describing various doctrines and practices of the church, a periodical *The Voice of Zion* has been published since the inception of the church. However, as of this writing, there have been no issues released for about one year.

THE NEW JERUSALEM CHURCH OF JESUS CHRIST

(Barney Fuller)

Acting on revelation from God, Barney Fuller and two others officially organized the New Jerusalem Church of Jesus Christ at Independence, Missouri on April 18, 1975. A building, which had been used as the headquarters of Fuller's "World Redemption" organization, became the new church headquarters and worship hall.

Fuller had not intended a complete organizaton with Apostles, Seventies, etc., but maintained that if and when the Lord so directed, he would follow.

Originally accepted as scriptural works were the Inspired Version of the Bible, Book of Mormon and the Book of Commandments, with some reservations. However in 1976 all "restoration" scriptures were dropped.

Originally Fuller had a sizeable following, but the modified scripture practice caused most members to leave.

In the summer of 1977, Fuller stated that only a very small group remained, accepting the Bible only as the Word of God.

This group has now disbanded and Fuller was reported as being in Texas.

BREAK FROM MARL KILGORE'S ZION'S ORDER

A split led circa 1975 by Barton Kilgore. The followers moved to Washington state, where an earlier break from the group had moved.

No further information is available.

AFFIRMATION

A group of gay Mormon organized circa 1975 for the purpose of ministering to each other in the face of rejection from the regularly organized LDS Church.

Called "Affirmation" this group is organized into chapters in various parts of the world in order to provide activities and other services for its members. The national organization publishes a newsletter, *Affinity.* Headquarters is in Los Angeles, California.

CHURCH OF CHRIST WITH THE ELIJAH MESSAGE
(Daniel Aaron Rogers)

Listed as a new elder in the June 1975 issue of the *Voice of Peace* of W. A. Draves' church of the same name, Daniel Aaron Rogers was removed from the church the following year. An announcement to that effect was published in the October 1976 issue of the *Voice of Peace.*

Rogers still preaches under the name of the church and uses much of the church literature including the Record of the Nephites and Word of the Lord book, although he replaces the Independence address with his own.

Rogers has published a newsletter sporadically for several years. He has performed hundreds of faith-healings and preaches gospel of a pentecostal nature.

Although no longer a member of Draves' group, he still teaches the doctrines of the church, the Word of the Lord, and has been witness to countless spiritual manifestations.

THE PROPHET (Ernest Strack)

December 4, 1976 marked the appearance of the first issue of a small magazine entitled *The Prophet* being issued from Provo, Utah. The main topic under discussion in that issue and the only subsequent issue (published March 1, 1977) was the Indian Prophet. In history past, several other Restoration personalities have discussed this topic, including Francis M. Darter, Lorin C. Woolley and William Conway.

In a letter to the author, dated June 2, 1977, Mr. Strack (an avowed polygamist) outlined the purposes of publishing *The Prophet:*

"We...are simply and purely students of the Gospel of Christ. We believe Joseph Smith was a prophet of God and that he restored the Savior's church on the earth. Although we aren't active at the present time we have a sincere belief and testimony that the Lord still recognizes the LDS Church as his own, notwithstanding the fact that his labors are not limited to the Mormon people."

Strack operates a bookshop in Provo, Utah.

AARONIC ORDER BREAK-OFF

About 1977 a group broke with the main body of the Aaronic Order in Utah. The leader of the Aaronic Order, Brother Robert Conrad indicated to the author in a letter dated February 2, 1980: "...there was indeed a time of some excitement in the communities a few years ago which was precipitated by the experience known as baptism in the Holy Spirit. A strong difference of opinion developed and as a result some of our young people went into the city and there affiliated themselves with charismatic or Holy Spirit groups there. They did not start a new group but as a fact have dispersed quite broadly among charismatic churches from Logan in the north to St. George in the south...I am happy to say that practically all the contention and misunderstanding have long since dissipated."

CHRIST'S CHURCH, INC. (Gerald W. Peterson, Sr.)

The "Branch" Church was organized on April 6, 1978 at Provo, Utah by Gerald W. Peterson, Sr. in accordance with divine revelation. Peterson, a former leader with Rulon C. Allred's organizaton, stated that the purpose of the Church is not to replace the Mormon Church (which is considered apostate from the true principles and practices of the gospel of Christ) but to provide a righteous branch wherein those who choose to follow the Lord may experience the gifts of the spirit, the correct organization of the church and kingdom of God and the fullness of the other ordinances and gifts of the gospel.

The establishment of this church is said to be a fulfillment of Section 85 of the Doctrine and Covenants. It is a setting in order of the House of God under the direction of Joseph Smith, Jr., who is the one mighty and strong.

The President of the Church has been ordained to organize and to hold the keys of the priesthood authority which was taken from the Mormon Church beginning with its seventh president, Heber J. Grant and culminating with the "final act of apostasy, the negro entrance into the Temples of God, polluting the same."

The Prophet and President of the Church, Gerald W. Peterson, Sr. left this life on January 9, 1981, but passed the keys of the priesthood to his son, Gerald W. Peterson, Jr., who now leads the church.

Many of the doctrines and claims of this church are familiar to those who have studied the various fundamentalist Mormon groups.

Quoting from a publication of the church, the following claims are worthy of consideration:

"By way of commandment and revelation the prophet John Taylor set apart a few worthy Priesthood brethren to which the keys of the Priesthood were transferred. The church leaders (some of whom were among those set apart) for many years, quietly acknowledged and worked with these special apostles in administering the higher ordinances to worthy saints. This custodial Priesthood body of apostles and their following was not to compete with the 'Mother Church,' but were strictly commissioned to keep the fullness of the gospel alive. They have passed the keys of the Priesthood from one prophet to the next until today they are held by a true living prophet.

"This living prophet has been personally anointed and commissioned by Jesus the Christ and Joseph Smith, Jr. and set apart to organize the righteous branch as foretold in prophecy, to gather out of Zion all the true followers of Christ.

"The gathering of the Lord's people to places of refuge both here in America and in Jerusalem has commenced in preparation for the cleansing of the earth which is to come.

"The fulness of the gospel; including the higher principles as contained in the Book of Mormon, the Doctrine and Covenants, and as restored and taught by the Prophet Joseph Smith are fully available to all saints who desire eternal progression earnestly enough to want to live by every word which has proceeded forth from the mouth of God.

"The gifts of Holy Spirit are present; miracles, signs, and wonders, to them that believe. God reveals Himself to His prophet...

"The branch of Christ's Church is organized with the Prophet and Apostles and is actively fulfilling its mission as foretold; and is making available to the saints, all the principles and ordinances of the fulness of the gospel of Christ; and is directed by the Holy Spirit in all functions." (*A Message to Zion,* Provo, Utah: Christ's Church, Inc., nd, pp. 5-6)

The Church recently moved its headquarters to St. George, Utah.

Doctrine

Articles of Faith of Christ's Church

1. We believe in God the Eternal Father—as Michael-Adam-God, the Creator; and in His Son, Jesus Christ, the Savior of the World; and in the Holy Ghost, Joseph Smith, Jr., the Witness and Testator and third member of the Godhead that rules the Earth!

2. We believe the first principles and ordinances of the Gospel

of Jesus Christ, are:

(1) Faith in the Lord Jesus Christ, His saving blood, that He atoned for our sins if we accept Him and keep His commandments.

(2) That in order to receive effective Baptism and the other ordinances and blessings of the Gospel, all men and women must and shall offer the sacrifice of a broken heart (repentance) and a contrite (teachable) spirit.

(3) Every candidate for receiving the Holy Ghost must be baptised, by immersion in water, by one having authority of Jesus Christ, who himself holds the Priesthood of the Living God and who personally has the Holy Ghost!

(4) The laying on of hands of those who have the Holy Priesthood and the Holy Ghost, for the conferring of the Holy Ghost.

3. We believe that no one shall be confirmed, or accepted as a member of Christ's Church, until they have shown by a righteous walk of life, and have been voted upon by the members of the body of the Church. They are then to be confirmed a member of the Church by the laying on of hands.

4. We believe that men will be punished for their own sins and not for Adam's transgression.

5. We believe that through the Atonement of Christ all mankind may be saved by obedience to the laws and ordinances of the Gospel.

6. We believe that a man must be called of God, by prophecy, and by the laying on of hands by those who are in authority to preach the Gospel and administer in the ordinances thereof.

7. We believe in the Gifts of the Spirit, namely, the gift of tongues, prophecy, revelation, visions, healings, interpretations of tongues, etc.

8. We believe the Holy Bible to be the word of God as far as it is translated correctly; we also believe the Book of Mormon, the Doctrine and Covenants and the Pearl of Great Price to be the word of the Lord.

9. We believe all that God has revealed, all that He does now reveal, and we believe He will yet reveal many great and important things pertaining to the Kingdom of God!

10. We believe in the literal gathering of Israel and in the restoration of the Ten Tribes; that Zion will be built upon this the American continent; that Christ will reign personally upon the earth; and that the earth will be renewed and receive its paradisiacal glory.

11. We claim the privilege of worshipping the Almighty God according to the dictates of our own conscience and allow all men

the same privilege, let them worship how, when, or what they may.

12. We believe in being subject to Almighty God and those kings, presidents, rulers and magistrates who honor and sustain the divine laws of God.

13. We believe in being honest, true, chaste, benevolent, virtuous, and in doing good to all men; indeed we may say that we follow the admonition of Paul—we believe all things, we have endured many things, and hope to be able to endure all things. If there is anything virtuous, lovely, or of good report or praiseworthy, we seek after these things. (*The Branch Magazine*, Volume 1, Number 3, Provo, Utah: Christ's Church, 1979, pp. 2-3)

Church Organization

The House of God is organized with God, the Eternal Father at the head. Next is Jesus Christ who is directly superior to the head of the dispensation, Joseph Smith, Jr. The Keys of the priesthood pertaining to mortality are jointly held by the living prophet and his immediate predecessor, who communicates with and assist him through the veil. The living prophet has a quorum of seven high priest apostles to assist and counsel him. This body, forming the supreme council on the earth hold authority which is superior to that of the church or kingdom. This supreme council presides over two distinct organizations: the Kingdom of God, which consists of the mortal king assisted jointly by the Grand Council of Fifty and the General Assembly. The other, and equal organization is the Church which is presided over by the church presidency, assisted by the Twelve Apostles and the Presiding Bishopric. The Kingdom is the public governmental arm of the priesthood and the church is the public religious arm of the priesthood. In most cases, but not necessarily, the living prophet jointly serves as the president of the church and king of the kingdom. (See *The Branch*, Volume 3, Number 3, St. George, Utah: Christ's Church, May 1981, p. 49)

Publications

In addition to several small leaflets describing various principles of the gospel, the church has been publishing a magazine, *The Branch* since January 1979. At first issued on a regular basis, the publication has lately been very sporadic.

Scriptures common to those used by the LDS Church are accepted.

HOLY CHURCH OF JESUS CHRIST (Alexander Caffiaux)

At a conference of the Church of Jesus Christ of Latter Day Saints (Strangite) in 1978, the following report was issued:

"The claims of Alexander Caffiaux were reviewed and a resolution was passed calling attention to the fact that an error had been committed by the High Priests in 1963 when they sanctioned the ordination of Alexander Caffiaux to the High Priesthood. They did not qualify as a High Council of traveling High Priests abroad, due to a lack of a full quorum, therefore the ordination cannot be considered valid.

"Later in the meetings, the Conference discussed the claims by Alexander Caffiaux to be a prophet of God and head of the Church. It was shown that Alexander Caffiaux had brought forth nothing by which this church could approve of his claims as a prophet, and since he had, in a conference held in France, changed the name of his church to the Holy Church of Jesus Christ, and making that the official name of his church, this conference passed a motion to reject the claims of Alexander Caffiaux as a prophet, seer, revelator and translator to this church, and it was resolved that all those accepting membership in the Holy Church of Jesus Christ are not members of the Church of Jesus Christ of Latter Day Saints (Strangite)." (*The Gospel Herald*, Volume 11, Number 1, Voree (Burlington), Wisconsin: Church of Jesus Christ of Latter Day Saints (Strangite), January 1979, p. 5)

I have been told that this group has built a temple in France, but further details are unknown.

MARRIAGE COUNSELING GROUP

Yet another group breaking with the Strangite Church, on which official action was taken at the Strangite Conference of 1978.

The following is quoted: "A court was convened by Bro. Vernon Swift to try the members of the Marriage Counseling Group (MCG) on charges that had been filed earlier this year.

"The charges were that the members of the MCG were following a system which they claimed was inspired of God, which was leading them to conduct themselves in a manner considered to be contrary to the teachings of the church, and which was bringing shame and disrepute upon the Church." (*The Gospel Herald,* Volume 11, Number 1, as indicated in previous entry.)

All but one member of the MCG was removed from membership in the church.

THE RESTORED CHURCH OF JESUS CHRIST (Eugene O. Walton)

A Baptist convert to the RLDS Church, Eugene O. Walton became a Seventy in that church and actively did missionary work for a number of years. In the late 1960s he became disillusioned with the liberalizing of that body and took a strong stand against the President of the RLDS Church. For so doing he was silenced and then expelled from that body. He was informed by God that the purpose in this was so that Walton might learn how not to organize God's church.

He began an association with another RLDS Elder, Barney Fuller and World Redemption. Fuller was also attempting to awaken the RLDS members to the dangerous changes taking place in the Church. Fuller published *Zion's Warning.* Walton's association with Fuller faded circa 1976 when Fuller completely rejected the message of the Restoration.

When Walton inquired of God what he was to do, he was led by the spirit into the Church of Jesus Christ (Cutlerite). He had a brief association with that church for about two years, during which time he picked up the dormant "Keys of the Kingdom" that had been given that church by Joseph Smith, Jr. through an "Order of Seven." This body was used by God to preserve the Holy Priesthood Authority. After being ordained an Elder, Walton received a command from God by revelation in June of 1977 wherein the Lord told him he was successor to Joseph Smith, Jr. and that he was the "one mighty and strong" spoken of in the scriptures. (See RLDS D & C 100:3; Utah 103:16)

Under Walton's direction, the Church of Jesus Christ published a 600 page volume in 1978 entitled *The Book of Commandments and Covenants* which contains all the sections of the Doctrine and Covenants published in 1835 at Kirtland, Ohio by Joseph Smith, Jr. Also included are items of historical note and several doctrinal expositions.

Shortly after the publication of this book, a disagreement arose and Walton and two other elders, by direction of the Spirit, left the church and organized *Restorationists United,* which was later more fully organized by command of God to be *The Restored Church of Jesus Christ.*

The second revelation, received in January of 1979, called a general conference at Independence, Missouri, to be held the following April. It was at this conference that Walton was set apart and ordained to the office of High Priest, Apostle, and Prophet of the Church. Jack Winegar was ordained as First Counselor and James Rouse as Second Counselor. After the First Presidency was established, further revelation came informing them to seek for a Bishop over Zion, who will establish the Celestial Law of "All Things Common" through the Order of Enoch as commanded in the revelations given to the Prophet Joseph Smith, Jr.

Walton states he was baptized first by the Spirit, without hands, by command of God given in the third revelation, informing them to be rebaptized into a New and Everlasting Covenant. The Church is slowly but surely gathering members who desire to share all things equally. (D & C 51). At this writing (1982) about 25 have committed themselves through baptism.

The Restored Church of Jesus Christ does not consider itself to be a faction of the Restoration. The church is, by God's command, His Restored Church which holds the Keys of the Kingdom.

Doctrine

Statement of Belief

1. We believe in the Godhead there are two personages, God the Father and Christ the Son. They both dwell in Celestial glory. Man was created, male and female, in the image (likeness) of both the Father and the Son, by whom were all things created. (Genesis 1:2, 29; John 1:1, 10, 16 I.V.; 3 Nephi 4:44-48; D & C 17:4-5)

2. We believe there is a Devil-Satan and that he is also from the beginning and that he is a fallen angel spirit and that he has legions of fallen spirits with him, and their stated purpose is to destroy man both body and soul and our disobedience to God gives the Devil power over us. (Genesis 3:1, 4-5; Rev. 12:8 I.V.; 2 Nephi 1:101-103, 120-125; D & C 1:6, 28:10-11; 2 Cor. 4:4)

3. We believe in the Holy Ghost, the Spirit of Truth, which is the life and power of God, to lead men into all truth, and back into the likeness and image of God, even a life of holiness, which is eternal life with God and the Christ. (Genesis 6:59-65, 67-71 I.V.; John 16:13-15; 3 Nephi 5:32-38; D & C 32:3, 34:5b)

4. We believe that men will be punished for their own sins and not for Adam's transgression, and that as a consequence of the atonement of Christ "all little children are alive in Christ, and also all they that are without the law." (Moroni 8:25-26). We believe that through Christ's Law and His Ordinances of the Gospel administered by Priesthood called of God by Revelation.

5. All of His Commandments must be kept! We believe that the Doctrine of Jesus Christ consists of the following laws and ordinances: 1. Faith toward God and in the Lord Jesus Christ; 2. Repentance from all sin; 3. Baptism by immersion, both men and women, and children after 8 years of age, for the remission of sins; 4. Laying on of hands for the gift of the Holy Ghost, according to the scriptures (Acts 2:38, 8:14-19, 19:2-6 and Hebrews 6:1-3); 5. Resurrection of the dead; 6. Eternal judgement.

6. We believe that the "Kingdom Order" can exist without the

church, but the church cannot be without the "Keys of the Kingdom" and through priesthood ordained of God. (Matthew 16:19-20 I.V.; D & C 65 and 87:1-3)

7. We believe Jesus Christ is the same today as He was yesterday, and we believe in the principle of continuous revelation; that the canon of scripture is not full, that God raises up Prophets and inspires them in every age and among all people, and that He speaks when, where and through whom He may choose. (Isaiah 28:10, 13; Hebrews 13:8; Amos 3:7)

8. We believe in the "Holy Order of Enoch" and in sharing all things equal in order to establish Zion. (D & C 51, 77:1). We Believe Zion will be established before Christ returns (D & C 49:4-5) and that only those who keep all of His commandments will be authorized of God. (D & C 81:3b)

9. We believe in the same kind of organization that existed in the primitive church, viz. apostles, evangelists, pastors, teachers, and all other officers provided for in the scriptures. (Ephesians 4:11-15). We believe in the powers and gifts of the everlasting gospel, viz: wisdom, knowledge, faith, healing, and miracles, prophecy, tongues and interpretation of tongues, etc.

10. We believe that a man must be called of God by prophecy and by the laying on of hands, by those in authority to do so, to entitle him to preach the gospel and administer in the ordinances thereof. And that men only are to be ordained to preach the gospel and function in the priesthood ordinances. (Exodus 40:15, John 15:16, Galatians 1:11-12, Hebrews 5:1-6)

11. We believe that in all matters of controversy upon the duty of man toward God, and in reference to preparation and fitness for the world to come, the word of God should be decisive and the end of dispute; and that when God directs, man should obey. We believe in the doctrine of the resurrection of the body, that man will be judged and rewarded or punished according to his works; according to the good or degree of evil he shall have done. (Matthew 7:18-29, 1 Cor. 15:34-42, Rev. 20:12-13)

12. We believe in the Inspired Version of the Bible, and in the Stick of Joseph commonly known as the Nephite Record and in the 1835 first edition of the Doctrine and Covenants containing the Lectures on Faith accepted by the Church in General Assembly at Kirtland, Ohio.

13. We believe a temple will be built in Independence, Missouri, wherein Christ will reveal himself and endow his servants whom He chooses with power to preach the gospel in all the world to every kindred, tongue and people, that the promises of God may

be fulfilled and the tribes of Israel gathered. This temple will be recognized as God's temple by a celestial cloud over it. (D & C 83:2)

14. We believe that marriage is ordained of God; and that the law of God provides for but one companion in wedlock for either man or woman. In cases where the contract of marriage is broken by death the remaining one is free to marry again, and in case of breach of the marriage covenant the innocent one is free to remarry. We believe that the doctrine of a plurality and a community of wives are heresies, and are opposed to the Law of God. (Mark 10:2-12, Jacob 2:36, D & C 49:3a-c)

15. We believe that men should worship God in spirit and in truth; and we claim the privilege for ourselves and all men of worshipping Almighty God according to the dictates of their conscience providing that such worship does not require a violation of the constitutional law of the land. (John 4:23-24) (From an undated tract published by the church.)

Setting the Church in Order

The underlying theme and mission of the church is to bring about a reunited restoraton movement. The church teaches that this disunity has been allowed by God in order for believers to see that things must be done God's way and that a recognition of errors must take place in order to reunite and build Zion together on these points:

1. Taking as our standard of faith the Inspired Version of the Holy Scriptures, the Nephite Record, and the divine revelations given to Joseph Smith, Jr.

2. Affirming that the Nephite Record is a divine record written by men inspired of God, delivered by an angel of God and interpreted by Joseph Smith, Jr., by command of God with the use of ancient instruments of interpretation called the Urim and Thummim.

3. That God has designated Independence, Missouri, as the center place of Zion. That the honest in heart, the saints of God, will begin their gathering here.

4. That Israel shall be gathered and God shall restore the ten lost tribes.

5. That the Law of Consecration is necessary to the establishment of Zion, with God's Bishop, directing a people pure in heart, by sacrifice and covenant.

6. That God is unchangeable and speaks His divine will yesterday, today and forever to an obedient people, and that Christ will reign personally upon the earth, and that the earth will be restored to its paradisiacal glory.

7. That in order to accomplish the work of the Lord committed

to his people, it is necessary for them to unite in "one" organization, in harmony with the Holy and Sacred Law of God. (*Let's Together Set the Church in Order,* published by the church, nd)

Publications

In its short existence, the Restored Church of Jesus Christ has published a dozen tracts and several issues of its newsletter. Publishing programs are currently under consideration which will provide regularly issued newsletters and further publications expounding the doctrines of the church.

ARYAN CHRISTIAN CHURCH

Organized circa 1980 near Hayden, Idaho. Worship and beliefs combine the philosophies of Mormonism and Hitlerism. The swastika and Hitler salute are commonly used.

No further information is available.

TRUE CHURCH OF JESUS CHRIST OF LATTER DAY SAINTS
(Forrest Toney)

Organized in Independence, Missouri in 1980, Forrest Toney heads the True Church of Jesus Christ of Latter Day Saints. He publishes his prophecies and other messages in the local newspapers.

A recent ad, published in the *Independence Examiner* on Saturday, April 3, 1982 proclaims:

"People, if you would just exercise a little faith that I am sent from God, only then can your trust in me unleash this great compassion that is within me. And you shall know that God exists and loves you today; and all your sins will be forgiven, and you shall feel cleansed, and receive the desires of your heart, and know for sure that I am who I am.

"Please don't accept that your condition is impossible to improve; for I don't want Glory or money or patronage; I only want to alleviate you of your cares, and burdens, and loneliness, and suffering; because you are my brothers and sisters, my wife and children, and parents. Simply because I would do more than anyone for you, I would take your place and suffer and die for you. For it is not meant that you should suffer needlessly, but that you would believe. Just believe that you believe. That God's love and power exists here on Earth as in Heaven. Meet me any day at 1:00 p.m., S. E. of the Temple Lot. Love forever, and ever, your servant, Forrest Toney."

Toney claims he is the Elijah, The Lamb of God and Savior to the Gentiles (not to be confused with Jesus Christ) and that only he can defeat death forever and redeem Heaven on earth.

ZION'S FIRST INTERNATIONAL CHURCH

The following article appeared in the *Deseret News,* Salt Lake City, Utah, on Tuesday, December 2, 1980:

"LDS dissidents form new sect.

"Seven people dissatisfied with the Mormon Church's opposition to the Equal Rights Ammendment met in Liberty Park Monday to form Zion's First International Church, calling it 'a positive alternative to Mormonism.'

"The seven founders—three Mormons and four excommunicated Mormons—make up the core of the new sect's governing body—the Quorum of Twelve Apostates. They said they use the word 'apostate' in the sense of 'one who does not follow,' as opposed to an apostle, 'one who follows.'

"In a noon ceremony held under a walnut tree 'because it is self-pollinating,' the seven ordained each other, signed their articles of incorporation and bit into apples.

"The apple ritual, they said, was 'to symbolize a commitment to equality and denounce the use by religions of the Adam and Eve story to discriminate against both man and woman.'

"Church spokeswoman Lee Anne Walker said the new church has grown out of a protest against the Mormon Church just as the Protestant churches grew from a protest movement against the Catholic Church.

"She said the new church believes the Mormon prophet and priesthood are unnecessary, because each person can and should establish his own direct, personal relationship with his source of truth.

"Ms. Walker said Zion's First International Church will have a priesthood, but its priests and priestesses will be called simply to serve and to bless each other—they will have no special access to divinity and no authority over anyone else.

"During the founding ceremony, church members raised a flag bearing the words, 'Liberty, Equality, Family.' Co-founder Byron Marchant, who was excommunicated from the Mormon Church for his oppostion to the church's former policy on blacks, said the flag was in the tradition of the Book of Mormon's 'title of liberty'—'a new standard of liberty.'

"Asked is the new church is Christian or believes in a god, Ms. Walker said individual members can believe whatever they want. She said it's all right for a member to also belong to another church or to be an atheist.

"The church's purpose is to provide a spiritual community for those who believe in liberty and equality for all and in doing good to everyone, she said.

"Ms. Walker said some people may come to the church for temporary comfort and understanding, and others may become life-long members.

"The decision to form a new sect grew out of the concerns of several people who had become involved with pro-ERA protests at LDS October conference, she said. But she said the new church will not engage as an organization in any political activities."

THE FREE WILL MORMON CHURCH (Franklin Lee Coleman)

The following paid advertisement appeared in the Monday, December 8, 1980 issue of the *Waycross (Georgia) Journal-Herald*:

"1. I, Franklin Lee Coleman, first son of Benjamin Franklin Coleman and Lydia Almeda Hurst Coleman, do testify that on the morning of December 4, 1980 while lying on an unmarked gravestone in Hazzard Hill Cemetery in Waycross, Georgia, the United States of America, next to the grave of Mrs. Lula Lewis and next to three cedars, about 2:30 a.m., the Lord spoke to me in tongues.

"2. The Lord said, Think on it, and pray on it, that through thee that I shall soon found a new church so that all my creations shall not be undone in this time of universal turmoil, grief and strife.

"3. I prayed from time to time from that time until about 9:30 a.m. on Friday, December 5, 1980. At that time the Lord said to me, Brother Coleman, are thou ready to found my new church? I answered, Yes, Lord, if thou wilt lead me.

"4. The Lord answered, Go to your typewriter and I will write out what I want to say to all my creations through the means of a one-page advertisement in the Waycross Journal-Herald on Monday, December 8, 1980.

"5. I went into the middle bedroom of my beloved mother's home at 1000 Atlantic Avenue, Waycross, Georgia and turned on my electric typewriter. As the Lord is my God, his fingers led it to write out by my fingers the following:

"On Tuesday morning, December 9, 1980 at 2:30 a.m., thou shalt found a new church in my name. It shall be called at first The Free Will Mormon Church. If this is later not my will, I shall speak to you again.

"My new church shall have the following tenets. If I desire to change these tenets at some later time while your time on this earth is ripe, I shall speak to you again.

"1. My new church is a true church.

"2. All churches that I have founded in my infinite wisdom are true. All churches that I choose to found in the future shall be true.

"3. All creatures shall be welcomed into my new church, regardless of their present religion, beliefs, race, color, sex, age, language, or any other parameters of any kind whatsoever.

"4. There shall be no formal ritual. Each creature shall hear from me how I want him to live his life at every moment in time and space. I may choose to speak to each of my creations in a different manner so that each may hear me truly.

"5. The basic belief in my new church shall be love between all my creations.

"6. There shall be no formal ritual. Every creature shall be free to choose the methods and means that will lead him to the highest form of enlightenment that he, she or it may attain while on this earth. No creature shall at any time impose his beliefs on any other of my creations.

"7. There shall be no formal buildings created solely for meetings. Every point in space shall be holy and therefore suitable for meeting in the name of my new church.

"8. The final aim of each of the members of my new church shall be pure enlightenment as attained by my son, Jesus, born of Mary Magdalene.

"9. The final life style that shall be sought by each of my creations shall be that of Adam and Eve and the creatures of the Garden of Eden. This shall mean eating only the fruits and nuts of the trees and the drinking of pure water.

"10. None of my creations shall be girded in loincloths of any kind.

"11. My creations shall continue to worship me through the church to which they now belong, and at the same time be a member of the Free Will Mormon Church. The purpose of my creating a new church is to unite my creations, not divide them. Have not ye already created amongst thyselves divisioness?

"12. While my creations are on the road to pure enlightenment and final life style, they may be free to eat and drink all foods, liquids and any other substances. Each time they do so, they shall ask themselves: 'Is this act leading me to true enlightenment and final lifestyle?' If so, they shall be free to do so. If not, they shall throw down this substance.

"13. All of my creations shall be free to love one another in any manner that is mutually acceptable.

"14. Until the time all of my creations have achieved true enlightenment and final life style, which shall not be for many days, each of my creations shall continue to obey all the laws of the country, state and province in which they now presently abide. There shall be no revolutions. If one of my creations wishes to pursue the search for pure enlightenment in a manner which is in conflict with the laws of the country, state or province in which they are now abiding, they shall give in to those laws peacefully and without animosity to others. If there is unbearable conflict between themselves and those presently in authority, they shall attempt peacefully to change their physical location.

"15. There shall be no tithing or donations to my new church. Each of my creations shall share as best they can what I have given to each in the way of talents.

"16. There shall be no hierarchy in my new church. No member shall be in authority at any time, and no member shall be higher or lower than another. All members shall be called 'brother' and 'sister' only, followed by their family name or first name, whichever they prefer.

"17. In the order of the priority of love, this shall be followed: First, thou shalt love thy god with all thy heart, soul and might. Secondly, thou shalt love thy mother with all thy heart, soul and might, and thy father also, and thy brothers and sisters also, and thy children also, and thy husband and wife. Each of my creations shall, on their way to pure enlightenment and final life style, feel free to rearrange this order at any point and time in space.

"18. The overriding principle that I want all of my creations to follow every moment of their waking life shall be pure and simply only this: will the following act that I am about to do hurt any other of the Lord's creations? If the answer is no, they shall be free to commit such act. If the answer is yes, they shall not be free to commit such act.

"19. There shall be no world headquarters or formal newspaper. Each of my creations shall be free to communicate with all other creatures in any way that is mutually acceptable and that falls within the laws of the country, state or province in which they are physically located at the time such act is committed.

"20. Baptism may be by any means whatsoever, but the purest baptism shall be by immersion in natural bodies of water such as oceans, rivers, lakes, streams while naked of any garments or by sprinking with pure mineral water.

"21. I shall continue from time to time to speak to Brother Coleman so that my true will be done: to have all of my creations living a life of true love and true happiness and true brotherhood.

I may choose to speak to others and I will not reveal conflicting means or methods to any of my creations.

"I the Lord do not consider myself above or below any of my creations. If any of my creations feel happier by worshipping me as a higher authority, it is alright, but not necessary.

"23. All of the existing beliefs of my Church of Jesus Christ of Latter Day Saints, the Mormon Church, are true as revealed to the Prophet Joseph Smith. There is no conflict between my new church and this existing church. I choose to reveal myself in many ways that may seem mysterious at the present time but will be clear in the future.

"24. As my dear and beloved son, Jesus Christ of Nazareth, said to you: 'Love the little children and let them come to me.' I say unto you this day, love one another with all thy heart, soul and might so that all of the terrible wrongs that my creations are inflicting upon another shall cease, and that pure love shall reign on the earth as shown by my dear and beloved son, Jesus, who laid down his only life in terrible pain and suffering so that one day all of my creations shall be with me in the eternal paradise of heaven.

"And I beseech thee, when thou lovest my little creations, remember that I created them in love, from love, and therefore they are pure when they are born. I cry unto you, do not besmirch their purity by any careless work or deed in thy own selfish interest. Do not perpetuate the hatred thou may now feeleth in thee, for if thou do so, you will be saddened and these little ones will be hurt for the rest of their days on the earth.

"And when thou loveth my little creations, lcve them in the non-verbal way they know so well, for it is not your words only they hear, but your feelings they feel. And always physically place your head as low or lower than theirs, otherwise you appear to be a giant to them, and may frighten them.

"And lastly, and perhaps most importantly, I want to say to you at this point in time and space, simply: when you are in pain and sadness, cry out to me, for I am a just god and full of love, and I will always help you, no matter what.

"I say to you, lovest thou not the children that ye have borne? How then could I call myself God and lovest thee not!

"Verily, I say unto you, the only hell is the hell that you have created amongst yourselves, it is not of my will or doing.

"There are forces of evil that seek constantly to destroy the love ye have for one another. Give ye not in.

"I, Franklin Lee Coleman, do testify in the name of our Lord and Saviour, Jesus Christ, that all of the above was revealed to me..."

CHURCH OF THE RESTORATION (Robert Chambers)

Organized in 1981 at Independence, Missouri, the Church of the Restoration is a group of Restoration and non-Restoration people without specific doctrine or ordinances who are attempting to work in God's purposes in any way available.

No further information is available at this writing.

PART 3—Miscellaneous Groups

This part contains a listing of several groups for which additional information is needed to list them in the main body of this section.

COMMUNITY OF ZION, CENTRAL UTAH DIVISION

Organized by W. A. Miner. Published a pamphlet on the changing of the revelations.

CHURCH OF THE FIRST BORN

Organized by Israel Dennis.

JOHN FORSGREN

Had a small following. Claimed to be a prophet.

LEROY WILSON

Claimed to be the one mighty and strong.

ALONZO LANGFORD

Claimed to be the one mighty and strong.

CHURCH OF THE FIRSTBORN, GENERAL ASSEMBLY

Located in Long Beach, California.

BREAK-OFF FROM STRANGITE CHURCH

Located on Beaver Island, Lake Michigan. Led by a Mr. Spring.

LDS BREAK-OFF

Located in a Mexican border town near El Paso, Texas.

TEMPLE OF SANANDA

Sister Thedra of the Emerald Cross, a recipient of various revelations and other inspired preachings, has had visits from the Angel Moroni. Located at Mt. Shasta, California, her ties with the Latter Day Saint Movement are unknown.

NATIVE INDIAN CHURCH

This church, located in Independence, Missouri, uses Indian customs and teaches the Book of Mormon. I understand that they have no other connection with the Restored Gospel.

PEYOTE WAY CHURCH OF GOD

Organized by Immanuel P. Trujillo and others, The Peyote Way

Church of God is headquartered near Willcox, Arizona.

Quoting from the bylaws of the church as published in the *Eastern Arizona Courier* for Wednesday, March 18, 1981, we learn:

"The functions of the Peyote Way Church of God are:

"1. To maintain, sustain and caretake 160 acres of Sacred Earth as per Vendee's Deed and Gift Assignment, Docket 286, page 521, Graham County Recorder's Office, Safford, Arizona.

"2. To establish economically independent Cottage Industries dedicated to the religious belief in Almighty God, Jehovah.

"3. To practice and promulgate the commandment of God, given in revelation to his servant Joseph Smith, as written in Section 89 of the Doctrine and Covenants of the Church of Jesus Christ of Latter-day Saints; and receive the Blessing as promised therein.

"4. To grow, obtain, steward, protect and defend the Holy Psychedelic Sacrament of Peyote and its religious use; and to regulate the distribution of this Holy Psychedelic Sacrament to other members of this and other churches that use a psychedelic as their Holy Sacrament.

"The goal of the Peyote Way Church of God is to introduce communicants to the Light of Christ. To reach the awareness of the presence of Christ within, we find it necessary to partake of Peyote as Holy Sacrament only. We believe that the holiness of this act and thereby the result, depends upon the purity of the communicant, in his or her environment, motivation, and body."

Very strict rules are enforced regarding the ritual of the sacrament. A vow of poverty and communal way of life are a basic requirement for membership in the church. A highly organized priesthood system, including Apostles, Deacons, Deaconesses, etc. is practiced.

The church teaches the Book of Mormon, Doctrine and Covenants and the History of the LDS Church (Mormon).

SECTION 2

INDEPENDENTS

From the earliest years of the Latter Day Saint Movement many individuals have sought to promote their faith, opinions and scriptural interpretations through the printed word.

Those who have been classified as *independent* are unique in that few were ever appointed as an official spokesman for any particular group of believers.

Many of the individuals discussed in this section belonged to and remained faithful to one of the organized churches; others left the faithful to pursue and publish their beliefs as they best saw fit. Some were more significant than others, but each took his calling seriously and was unashamed to preach the truth as he understood it.

Thousands of pages of source material have been scoured to make this section as complete as possible. I am sure, however, that there are many others who could rightly be included herein. The very nature of an *independent* signficantly reduces the amount of historical background materials available for this type of study.

HUBERT JOHN ARCHAMBAULT

Active in the Supreme Directional Control controversy which flared in the RLDS Church in the 1920s, Hubert J. Archambault became a strong believer in David Whitmer's viewpoints regarding the restoration. Archambault was a convert to the RLDS Church from Catholicism. During SDC he transferred his membership to the Church of Christ (Temple Lot) in 1926. Later he became associated with Frank F. Wipper. He eventually became disillusioned with the various factions of Book of Mormon believing churches and launched a career as a non-denominational preacher.

In almost 50 years of preaching, Archambault published more than a dozen assorted tracts and booklets dealing mainly with the Book of Mormon. He believed the true Church of Christ was composed of those who believe in Christ and follow the patterns of the church exactly as set forth in the Bible and the Book of Mormon.

He had a very strong testimony, as indicated by this comment:

"You that believe in the D & C and in John the Baptist Messages and Pearl of Great Price, did you ever think that you might have deceived yourself that they were the real gold and diamonds when they are only glass and wood covered with varnish.

"Do not cover the precious word of God with all the rubbish Satan pushes on us.

"The value of the Book of Mormon after 60 years of deep study—its word is sweet above all that is sweet and white above all that is white and pure above all that is pure. In other words it is the words of Christ who said: 'I am the way the truth and the life." (Archambault, H. J., *The Great Value of the Book of Mormon,* Rock Island, Illinois, nd, page 17)

Unfortunately, none of Archambault's tracts carry a date of publication.

On February 17, 1977, Archambault met his death in his Rock Island, Illinois home at the hands of three burglars.

CLARK E. CALLEAR

In 1979, Clark E. Callear of West Jordan, Utah, published the first edition of a work entitled *The Falling Away of the Latter-Day Saints.* The book systematically discusses many points of doctrine and practice which the author contends the Mormon Church has either changed or abandoned, causing the church to become apostate from the true gospel of Christ. Among the doctrines, Callear comments that plural marriage and the Adam-God doctrine are true doctrines of the gospel.

From a small advertising leaflet pertaining to the book, Callear comments:

"It is clear that the inhabitants of the earth are ripe in iniquity and will soon be visited with plagues, pestilences, famines, and many other terrors. The wrath of God is kindled against His children and none of us will escape the coming calamities unless we repent of our sins and turn our hearts back to righteousness...

"As a Church, we are falling away from the principles that were restored to us through the Prophet Joseph Smith. We are following the exact trend that has proved to be the pitfall of past dispensations.

"This book...is brought forth with a spirit of love and concern and will help many members of the Church to recognize the magnitude of our apostasy. It will be an aid for those who desire to be free from the false security that Satan has brought into the church..."

D. T. CHAPMAN

At present, the only information I have been able to locate is a copy of a small four page leaflet entitled *Nebuchadnezzar's Image.* It carries no date or place of publication. The only notation is the author's name and a statement that all the Book of Mormon quotations are from the RLDS edition. Comments within the text of of the message, however, indicate that the leaflet was published either during or sometime shortly after the Korean war.

Chapman compares world powers and current history with the story of Nebuchadnezzar from the Bible. He maintained that all religious sects had become polluted. He felt that the last days were upon the earth. Liberal quotes from the Bible and the Book of Mormon are used to support his claims.

FRANCIS M. DARTER

Francis Michael Darter joined the LDS Church in Samoa in 1905 and later became one of the first six members of the Long Beach, California branch of the church in 1912.

A civil engineer by profession, Darter became equally proficient in the scriptures and doctrine of the LDS Church and began writing books and other publications presenting his views on various doctrinal matters.

He was excommunicated from the church on November 2, 1917, for teaching false doctrine. According to Darter, the church felt that his ideas on the return and future mission of the Apostle John and the coming of the one mighty and strong were in error.

In 1924 he was reinstated with all his previous priesthood and temple blessings, but found himself removed again in the spring of 1937.

Darter maintained that while he taught that plural marriage was a command of god, he did not advocate its practice—but the church did not see it in the same light.

Some of the other doctrines he espoused were Adam-God, race segregation as a divine principle, the modification of temple garments as error, etc. He was a proponent of the theory that the Egyptian pyramids were engineered in such a way that they recorded every historically significant event past, present and future. He developed a method of calculating such events as the Second Coming of Christ from the pyramids.

He was a firm believer in the Indian Messiah, wherein it is alleged that Christ spent several days with faithful Indian followers in 1890 at Walker Lake, Nevada, and that at a future unspecified time an Indian prophet would step forth to set the house of God in order.

When he died on September 16, 1968, at nearly 87 years of age, he had published over 32 books and pamphlets, most of them with his own finances.

CHARLOTTE ELAM/CATHERINE PICO

Apparently faithful members of the RLDS Church, but concerned over some of the recent trends in that body, Charlotte Elam and Catherine Pico have published several brochures discussing various problems in the church and have reprinted a number of out of print church titles.

These ladies feel that the RLDS Church has abandoned the Restoration gospel.

GILBERT A. FULTON, JR.

In his 1974 volume *That Manifesto*, Gilbert A. Fulton, Jr. has painstakingly compiled and excerpted from hundreds of documents and historical accounts regarding the issuance of the document by Wilford Woodruff, President of the LDS Church, commonly known as the *Manifesto* on September 24, 1890.

Fulton has gathered considerable evidence to support his contention that the issuance of the Manifesto was only an event in a series of events marking the end of plural marriage in the church, which had begun several years earlier. In addition, the message of that document was not intended for the membership of the church, but as a message to the outside world regarding church intentions.

Much of the information contained in the book would normally be accessible only to the very diligent and patient researcher.

In the foreword to the book, Fulton states: "As the author of this book, I take the position that the Manifesto was a revelation, an emanation from God, a political document, a policy statement for His Church, dictated by God through Wilford Woodruff, and that that policy is inspired by God and is in full force and effect in and by and through His Church and that that Manifesto itself, and the presentation of the action of President Woodruff, in publishing it to the world, to the membership of the Church for their sustaining vote had nothing to do with the formation or establishment of the Church's stand on the plural marriage issue, nothing whatever, for that position and general policy had been dictated and was in effect long before President Woodruff's action was taken in issuing that Manifesto on the 24th of September, 1890."

GEORGE T. HARRISON

Once a faithful member of the Mormon Church, George T. Harrison was excommunicated circa 1935 when he declared he could no longer believe in the church's teachings. Since that time he has actively written and published books and pamphlets.

Most recently a resident of Orem, Utah, Harrison has published such pamphlets as *Do Mormons Believe in Jesus Christ and His Second Coming?, Mormonism? Are You Kidding?,* etc.

The first mentioned tract is most interesting due to a comment Harrison made in a personal letter to David C. Martin on December 15, 1975. Harrison states that "President Harold B. Lee [of the LDS Church] died mysteriously after receiving" the tract. Another interesting factor regarding Harrison's pamphlets is that they are under the authorship of the *Three Nephites.*

Harrison's books attempt to show and document change in the teachings of Mormonism through the years and also a comprehensive analysis of what Harrison calls Joseph Smith's "false prophecies." *Mormons Are Peculiar People* was published in 1954; *Mormonism, Now and Then* was published in 1961. In 1981 Harrison published *That Mormon Book*-an analysis of the Book of Mormon.

One of Harrison's most thought-provoking publications is his updated version of the thirteen "Articles of Faith" of the Mormon Church. His version follows:

"1. We do not believe in God the Eternal Father, and in His Son, Jesus Christ. If we did we would keep their commandments to the Church. But we do believe in our apartments, banks, hotels, insurance companies, motels, plantations, publications, radio and

TV stations, railroads, ranches, sugar companies and wealth.

"2. We believe that mankind will not be punished for their own sins, unless they get caught. We believe that only our members will inherit the best in after-life, if they have a white skin in this life. While we are not always right, we are never wrong. How could we be wrong with the Spirit of God, the Holy Ghost, revelation, the Priesthood, the Only True Church and the Plan of Salvation? Only do not judge us by our "fruits" for they are rotten.

"3. We believe through the atonement of Christ, all mankind may be saved, if they are Mormons, and have a white skin. We are taught that the glory of God is intelligence, and a man cannot be saved in ignorance, if this can be accomplished without thinking, for we are taught Satan wins a great victory if he can just get Mormons to do their own thinking.

"4. We believe that the First Principles of the gospel are: First, tithing; second: money; third, holy money; and fourth, filthy lucre. Any system or principles, or conditions, or fairy-tales that will make us money, must self evidently have the approval and blessing of God. We seek not the greatest good to mankind, but the greatest profits for us, and justification of the Mormon leaders reversal or abandonment of all the early restored gospel principles. In seeking these things we will gladly go to hell.

"5. We believe that in order for a man to be called of God, he must be a relative of a General Authority, or an efficient money maker. Now do not try to confuse us with reason or facts.

"6. We believe in the same organization that existed in the primitive church, namely: A First Presidency with counsellors, Assistant apostles, district apostolic representatives, commissioners of education, Stake presidents, Relief Societies, Fast Offerings, Welfare for over 100,000, and a lot of real dumb teen-ager missionaries, many of them endeavoring to escape military service.

"7. We believe in any and all gifts, particularly tithing, and we believe the greatest "commandment" of all is the Word of Wisdom. We also believe the gospel as far as it is mixed up by professional priestcrafters, and interpreted by ignorant amateurs or conniving opportunists.

"8. We believe the Bible to be the word of God as far as it is mistranslated, with its hundreds of absurdities and contradictions. Examples: Was Jesus born in a house or a manger? (Matt. 2:11; Luke 2:16) Was he crucified on a cross or hung on a tree? (Matt. 27: 40, 42; Acts 5:20) We also believe the Book of Mormon to be the word of God, with its wierd, ridiculous fairy-tales, such as five adults erected a temple like Solomon's (2 Nephi 5:15-16) or that cow-boy serpents tended and herded the livestock. (Ether 9:28-33)

"9. We have been taught and believed that God revealed these principles, that were to be everlasting and endure forever. Plural Marriage (D & C 132); the Gathering (D & C 29:7-11); build a Zion (D & C 6:6), with a United Order (D & C 104:1); Missionaries without purse or scrip (D & C 84:78, 86); Feet washing every priesthood member at every priesthood meeting (D & C 88:127, 133, 139-141) Nauvoo house to be occupied forever (D & C 124:59-60), etc., etc., all of which are now taboo.

"10. We believed that the 'harvesters' were being sent out for the very last time, 143 years ago, in 1831. Purpose: to gather Israel to Zion, to escape the burings and calamities attending Christ's Second Coming and cleansing of the world for the Millennium. (D & C 24:19; 133:4-9; 29:9, 27-28; 29:11) But Mormon leaders stopped the clock long ago to allow the Church to pursue its erroneous worldly ways indefinitely, in pursuit of more fools and greater wealth.

"11. We claim the privilege of worshipping God according to the dictates of our own conscience and pocket book, and allow all men the same privilege, provided they believe what we tell them. We know our beliefs and version of the gospel are true, because we say so. This allows us to ignore the scriptures, God's commandments for a Zion, a Gathering, a Democratic Church, and any sensible real equitable solution for our economic problems.

"12. We believe in being subject to priestcrafters, Church presidents, mission presidents, Stake presidents, Relief Society presidents and all narrow-minded, yes-men bishops. Our sense of fairness and reason has developed to where we send out 18,000 missionaries with our literature, but we are counselled not to read anything written by non-Mormons, for we are to realize, that when our leaders speak that our thinking has been done for us.

"13. We believe all cock-and-bull stories told us by our leaders. We desire to perpetuate inequality and poverty so our Welfare Plan can be justified and receive Babylon's praise. We believe that a system that produces over 100,000 poor Mormons requiring welfare, is good, for it allows us to boast of helping them. If there is anything virtuous, or otherwise, that will pay our leaders a lovely profit, it will receive our praise and a good report, for verily we seek after these things. We believe in being honest, or crooked, when it is to our advantage."

C. J. HUNT

The earliest material in my files written by Charles J. Hunt carries a date of March 4, 1936. It is a one page discussion entitled

Have Utah Mormon Historians Garbled Facts in Church History? In this article, Hunt, a resident of Independence, Missouri and a member of the RLDS Church, makes considerable comment on what is now commonly known as the *Documentary History of the Church,* edited by B. H. Roberts and originally published by the Mormon Church. Hunt points out that although the history was being billed as "one of the most authentic histories ever written," several thousand changes had been made when comparing the history with what had been previously published in the Millennial Star, a Mormon publication in England. He goes on to say, "Thus we see that 'under the strict inspection' of Brigham Young, such men as B. H. Roberts and other Utah Mormon Church historians and writers are unreliable, having falsely and purposely misrepresented Joseph Smith the Martyr on most every page of their designated 'correct' history...a history conceived in Utah, born in a 'salt land,' and published for gratification, deceiving an innocent and unprotected people."

Later in the article, after commenting on the "Utah" edition of the Doctrine and Covenants, Hunt states: "It is very clear that all publications by the Utah Mormon Church, after 1847 should be carefully examined by the search light of facts before being used.

"It is also self evident from Utah Mormon Church history that if Brigham Young and his official church associates in Utah, had had possession of the manuscript of the Inspired Translation of the Bible, and the Book of Mormon, they would have changed and distorted the reading of them to accord with their depraved hearts, characters and personal ambitions. Thank God that both manuscripts are preserved, and in possession of the Reorganized Church at Independence, Missouri.

Other items include a review of Joseph Weston's book, *Those Amazing Mormons, A Brief on Sacred Teachings of the Divine Godhead.* The latter article is dated August 15, 1950 and Hunt lists his age at the time as 89. He is now deceased.

PAUL JOHNSON

A member of the Church of Christ (Temple Lot) for many years, Paul Johnson wrote a number of articles in the church magazine *Zion's Advocate*. He also served as an assistant editor of the magazine. Beginning with the February 1970 issue his name no longer appears with the editorial staff.

Johnson had begun publishing a small magazine entitled *Ask, Seek, Knock* late in 1969. It was a publication that continued for a few years and dealt with Book of Mormon topics.

Johnson has since rejected the restoration message and as of this writing, heads the Kingdom of God Fellowship in Iowa.

PRICE W. JOHNSON

In 1971, at the age of 85, Price W. Johnson, a resident of St. George, Utah, published his testimony of plural marriage in a 28 page booklet entitled *An Open Letter to All Latter Day Saints on Plural Marriage.* Many historical incidents and questions are discussed concerning plural marriage, most of them familiar to any casual student of that phase of Mormon Church history.

In the closing paragraph of the pamphlet, Johnson bears testimony to what he has stated: "As abundantly proved in this letter, the eternity of the marriage covenant as taught by Joseph Smith, and revealed from the heavens to the people of this dispensation, has been rejected by the people of the LDS Church. As foretold by Joseph Fielding Smith, 'The time will come when we will wonder why we could not see the things that are so plainly written,' but it will be too late. There is, and can be no excuse or alibi. If, at the resurrections of our bodies, we are disappointed and bowed down with sorrow, it will be our own fault, as the way to exaltation and eternal glory that is connected with the everlasting covenant of marriage is plainly outlined in the sacred books that we have, or should have, in our homes."

THOMAS JOHN JORDAN

T. J. Jordan was an apostle in the Church of Christ (Temple Lot) from 1936 until his death on June 7, 1969, at the age of 92. Residing in Regina, Saskatchewan, he was the missionary of the church in charge of Western Canada and several north-western states of the United States.

Jordan published an undated pamphlet called *I Beheld a Book* which discusses many interesting facts from and about the Book of Mormon.

A very touching eulogy was published along with his obituary notice in the August 1969 issue of *Zion's Advocate.* In part: "He spent most of his life in the front line of battle, making war against evil, and constantly pointing the way of safety, (the Gospel of Christ) to all who would give ear. The weapons he carried were the Bible and the Book of Mormon, and with the great standard for righteous living contained therein; he constantly forced back the power of evil and was able to cause many to depart from the darkness of sin and to walk in the beautiful light of the Gospel of Christ. Even in the last years of his physical life, tired and almost deaf and blind, he continued in the warfare against wrong."

OGDEN KRAUT

A very prolific and courageous author and publisher, Ogden Kraut publishes under the trade name Pioneer Press from Salt Lake City, Utah.

Many of the books he has written and published could be considered controversial by some, but are in fact some of the only works on many topics of Mormon doctrine and history available.

Some of the titles include: *Michael/Adam; The Seventies; Jesus Was Married; The Three Nephites; The Gift of Dreams; Seers and Seerstones; The Gathering of Israel; Blood Atonement.* The list goes on.

Each book is readable and educational, offering valuable insights to the topic being discussed.

O. E. LAPOINT

I have been unable to obtain very much information concerning the activities of O. E. LaPoint of Flat River, Missouri.

LaPoint died on April 3, 1957. Prior to that he published several dozen mimeographed letters and about three dozen printed leaflets. These included *Much Needed Bible Study, The Simplicity of the Gospel Corrupted, The Everlasting Covenant, Strange Doctrines,* and *The Kingdom.*

The leafets, generously sprinkled with Biblical references, deal mainly with general Christian beliefs. One in particular, however, called *Man's Covenant With Death and Agreement With Hell,* expounds upon several doctrines taught by the Mormon Church. "Now to all who have made an agreement with hell, by your baptism for the dead theory. Set forth by a people who are utterly without excuse for such a doctrine. Of all the blind, leaders of the blind, you lead the parade. Your own Book contradicts your damnable doctrine."

GLADYS BARR LOYD

A resident of Warwick, Rhode Island, Gladys Barr Loyd has published a number of books in duplicated, manuscript form. It is apparent from her references, etc., that she is a member of the RLDS Church. Titles include *Israel's Latter Day Glory, The Seven Kingdoms, Plural Marriage-Is It of God?, The Time of the End, Seven Candlesticks, the Seven Churches of Revelation, Financial law, Celestial vs. Terrestrial.*

JOSEPH LUFF

For many years a very active minister in the RLDS Church, Joseph Luff was instrumental in many of the successes of the church. About 1930 he published a pamphlet entitled *The Book of Mormon-Is It the Stick of Ephraim Referred to in the Thirty-seventh Chapter of Ezekiel, Verses Fifteen to Nineteen.*

In the foreword, Luff explains his objective: "The aim of the author of this pamphlet, in writing it, is to help and not hinder the work of the church. He has been an active minister of the Reorganized Church of Jesus Christ of Latter Day Saints for sixty years...but for the reasons herein assigned, believes it to be his duty to put forth this effort towards correcting what he esteems to be an error in its authorized teaching..." He goes on to explain that all the various branches of the church have improperly used the scriptural reference in Ezekiel in referring to and proving the Book of Mormon. He presents a very rational discussion on why that assumption is incorrect. He asserts that the "Stick of Ephraim" refers to the record of the lost tribes of Israel, while the Book of Mormon is "simply a record of Lehi or Nephi and Zoram and their descendants in America. It is therefore clear from the Bible and especially the passage from Ezekiel itself, that the Book of Mormon cannot be a fulfillment of its prediciton."

B. L. MCKIM

B. L. McKim of Independence, Missouri, wrote and published a series of pamphlets entitled, *The Foundation of the Church.* Each discussed various aspects of Latter Day gospel teachings. He had been a member of the RLDS Church, but joined with the Protest Movement regarding the Supreme Directional Control controvesy in the 1920s. Indeed, his booklets, although published without date, have the appearance of being published during that time of hardship for the church.

In a leaflet published circa 1944, McKim explains: "We do not have to go to Utah now to see the fruits of apostacy as the results of a strongly centralized government.

"Are we not able to see as the result of the centralizing of power, as has been effected by President F. M. Smith, that the same condition is being brought about in the Reorganization as it was in the Old Church.

"That the spiritual power, the spiritual understanding, the spiritual manifestation, or revelation, which came to the honest seeker for truth, in their acceptance of the gospel of Jesus Christ, is gradually being lost by the church...the church by setting up a strongly centralized government, in the hands of few, and introducing many changes in policies and programs, it has created doubt, divisions, and distrust, and killed the Spirit, and thus the Spiritual life or power, that came by the preaching of the Word by faith, is not being passed on to future generations.

"We have before us now not the apostacy of 1844, but the living example of the apostacy of 1940..."

McKim goes on to say: "Since the people, or institution, can rise no higher than their leader, and since he [speaking of the president of the RLDS Church] has no message of peace and love, or the burning urge, for the salvation of man, in seeing that the gospel is carried into all the world, as the first or primary duty of the church, then that urge, or desire, to carry the gospel to those who sit in darkness, also dies with the people of the church..."

D. J. MORGAN

The information available at this writing concerning D. J. Morgan of Independence, Missouri, is limited to but four leaflets under his authorship. Scriptural and other quotations are from materials published by the RLDS Church.

Two of the leaflets are devoted entirely to the Book of Mormon and treat the subject favorably, testifying of its divinity. Another *The Gospel of Christ Restored* deals largely with the Book of Mormon, but expounds on several of the basic gospel principles such as baptism, laying on of hands for the gift of the Holy Ghost, ordination of the ministry, the prayers on the sacrament, etc. and makes comment on some of the difference between the record found in the Book of Mormon and that found in the RLDS Doctrine and Covenants pertaining to these basic principles.

Another larger booklet describes the early history of the church pertaining to the building of temples, etc. Morgan concludes his summary presentation, which indicates his belief that the building of temples was an incorrect principle, with these words: "The work of building material temples has involved a heavy burden of taxation upon the members of the Latter Day Saint churches, and has deprived the worthy poor and needy of just treatment, and if they had relied on the sure word of God in the Bible and Book of Mormon, the peculiar work of men would have been avoided, and right spiritual work of God prevailed." (Morgan, D. J., *Temples-Important Facts About the Building of Temples by Latter Day Saints,* Independence, Missouri, nd, page 24)

None of Morgan's works carry a date, but some sources indicate that Morgan was active in the 1930s and 1940s.

ERNEST W. NINNIS

According to the information I have obtained, Ernest W. Ninnis published all of his works before 1957. His writings include *The Marred Servant of the Book of Mormon* and *Are the Ten Commandments Abolished?* At this writing further information is unknown.

ARCH S. REYNOLDS

During the late 1940s and early 1950s, Arch S. Reynolds, a resident of Springville, Utah and member of the Mormon Church, published a series of lengthy booklets on a variety of gospel subject. Expositions include *The Reorganites (Josephites) by a Utah Mormon*, which was a comparison of the doctrine and practices of the two churches, *The Book of Abraham Brought Forth by Divine Means, How Did Joseph Smith Translate?* and *Minor Sects in the Light of Mormonism,* an examination of beliefs of several Christian churches.

HENRY W. RICHARDS

An avid student of their history and doctrine, Henry W. Richards of Salt Lake City, Utah, is undoubtedly the leading authority in the Mormon Church on the LeBaron Church of the Firstborn of the Fulness of Times and the other Mormon fundamentalist movements.

In 1965 Richards published a series of letters in book format entitled *A Reply to The Church of the Firstborn of the Fulness of Times.* This book goes into great detail concerning the practices and teachings of that church, as well as pointing out what Richards sees as their errors, when viewed in the light of Mormonism.

DAVID A. RICHARDSON

In the early 1970s, David A. Richardson, a member of the Mormon Church, 'published a 24 page booklet entitled *Return to Joseph Smith, II.* It professes to be a comparison of 28 alphabetically arranged points of doctrine and practice of the Mormon Church and the RLDS Church. Taking a definitely pro-Mormon viewpoint, the booklet presents a challenge to members of the RLDS Church to "return to the true church."

In his conclusion, Richardson testifies: "The only defense that the Reorganites can give to the proofs herein that they departed from the true church as taught by Joseph Smith II [Junior] is that he did not always speak doctrinal truths; or that he was so overburdened and harrassed that his mind was distorted during his last few years of life. He said 'God will always protect me until my mission is fulfilled.' HC 6:365. 'Hold out to the end and we shall... become like Gods.' HC 6:500. 'If any man preach any other Gospel than that which I have preached he shall be cursed.' If male children forever was a reward for Jonadab then it is a curse that the Reorganite presidents have few or no male posterity."

JAMES R. SNELL

At one time associated with Frank F. Wipper and the Book of Mormon Foundation, James R. Snell of Kansas City, Kansas, began publishing a small magazine called *An Open Book* in 1970.

Dealing primarily with the Book of Mormon and teaching what might be called "Whitmerite" Mormonism (See David Whitmer's Address to All Believers in Christ, 1887), the magazine appeared several times each year until 1980. According to correspondence with Mr. Snell, Issue 36, March 1980 "will probably be the last one."

LAWRENCE RITCHIE STUBBS

Scant second-hand information has been obtained concerning Lawrence R. Stubbs, a resident of Mexico. It has been learned that he is an independent, although at one time he was a member of the Church of the Firstborn of the Fulness of Times. He was removed from that body on the charge of teaching false doctrine.

A copy of a printed booklet by Stubbs, *Celestial Glory—Eternal Life Can Be Ours,* gives the reader some insight into Stubbs' doctrinal theories, but provides little else. There is no publication date.

C. A. SWENSON

As seems to be the case, none of C. A. Swenson's publications carry a date. Swenson resided in Independence, Missouri.

From some of his remarks, it appears that the booklets may have been published in the 1920s.

Swenson's works, a series called *Seek Ye the Old Path and Walk Therein,* were written "in behalf of the true believers in the Nephite Record." He points out what he felt were differences existing between The Book of Mormon (which he considered to be the final authority on doctrine, practice and church organization) and the Latter Day Saint churches, presumably the RLDS Church. He also touched on some practices of the Mormon church (baptism for the dead, temples).

Other points discussed include Zion, the Gathering, the true mode of Baptism, the Sacrament, the true name of Christ's Church, evidence that there should be only one priesthood and not two, no High Priests, etc. Scripture quotations are from RLDS editions.

Swenson comments: "From the evidence presented in this little tract, and from much more which might have been presented...we are able to discover how far we really have been led away from the doctrine and the teaching of the Book of Mormon, by the priesthood. This has been done little by little, so that we have not been made aware of the fact until we began to study the book in earnest.

"If you think this could not have been done, remember, that it only required about two years for the priesthood to lead the people away from the new covenant, even the Book of Mormon and the former commandments. This is what history tells us, and there is no guess work about it. The lord told them in 1832, that the whole church (priesthood, prophet and all) were under condemnation for treating lightly the things they had received which vanity and unbelief hath brought the church to that condition. It was the Book of Mormon and the former commandments that God said had been disregarded, and because of this he said, You shall remain under this condemnation, until you repent and remember the new covenant, even the Book of Mormon and the former commandments which I have given them, not only to say, but to do according to that which I have written. (D & C 83:8)

"It can plainly be seen from history that no repentance or turning back to these things spoken of has occurred, for the scourge and judgment pronounced by the Lord, descended on them swiftly. It came in fact the following year, (1833) but as no repentance was manifested it was repeated in 1838. Yet the warning of God was unheeded and as a result the final calamity came in 1844-6, when some of the priesthood, with perverted minds led part of the church west, after it was broken up in fragments...

"The fact that so many contending Latter Day Saint churches are on the scene today is evidence that there is something radically wrong somewhere. All can not be right, but it is possible all may be wrong, by having gone away from the original intent and purpose of God...." (Swenson, C. A., *Seek Ye the Old Path and Walk Therein,* Independence, Missouri, nd, pp. 15-16)

DALTON A. TIFFIN

Listing his address as Cookstown, Ontario, Canada, Dalton A. Tiffin published a tract in 1935 entitled *Is Jesus Christ the True Temple Builder?* Some years later, 1948, he published *The Original*

New Testament Church of Christ of the Bible and Book of Mormon is Defended. Another leaflet, with no date, is called *The Origin of LDS Proxy Baptisms for their Dead.*

Casting aside all of the Latter Day Saint Churches, Tiffin states:

"As a contender for the true original New Testament Church of Christ as proclaimed in the Bible record of the twelve apostles of the Lamb, I find the Book of Mormon to be the greatest support possible on their behalf. It is therefore very gratifying to have both of these uniform records of Christ's words, established in one, to confirm each other in detecting Christ's true church standard of gospel truth, that is destined for the redemption of the whole human family of God's creation. It is not a man, but rather our Creator, God, who is at the head of Christ's Church or Kingdom, when or wheresoever it is truly established throughout His universe..."

SAMUEL WOOD

During the spring conference of the Church of Christ (Temple Lot) in 1926, the first seven of their quorum of apostles were called and ordained. Samuel Wood was one of this body. A resident of California, he was first assigned to missionary work there, but later was reassigned to the European mission of the church.

The conference of the church in April, 1930, called E. J. Trapp, who was the pastor of the church in Gloucester, England, as an apostle and Wood went there to ordain him. According to the history of the Temple Lot Church, "Wood seems to have become imbued with the 'One Person Godhead' heresy, and made that a part of his teaching while in Britain on this, his second trip over there. This resulted in creating a serious division among the membership of that country...A special conference was held by the Apostolic Quorum in Independence, Missouri, and...Apostles Samuel Wood...and E. J. Trapp, who were teaching this new cause of division were dismissed from the Council, and Samuel Wood was disfellowshipped after and Elder's Court Trial..." (Flint, B. C., *An Outline History of the Church of Christ (Temple Lot),* Independence, Missouri, second edition, 1953, page 142)

Wood returned to his native California, settling in Carmel. In the mid-1940s he began publishing *TM*, a magazine dedicated to religious and social reform. Wood died circa 1965.

JAMES ELMER YATES

When he died on April 7, 1954 at the age of 80, James E. Yates had logged almost 60 years as a missionary for the Church of

Christ (Temple Lot). He was called to the apostleship during the April 1928 conference of the church and remained faithful until his death. His field of labor was the Western United States.

From about 1925 until his death in 1954, Yates published a monthly magazine called *The Torch of Truth,* devoted to publicizing the gospel as taught by the Temple Lot Church. (See *Zion's Advocate,* Volume 31, Number 6, June 1954, page 96)

SECTION 3

PUBLISHERS, RESEARCH ASSOCIATIONS AND OTHER ORGANIZATIONS

In addition to the information already presented, there are a large number of other organizations which have sought to promote certain beliefs or to study the Latter Day Saint Movement. In this section a representative selection, particularly of the lesser known organizations, will be presented.

BOOK OF MORMON FOUNDATION (Frank F. Wipper)

After a variety of religious experiences, Frank F. Wipper (see a previous entry: Church of Christ, Independent) and others began publishing a newsletter from Fresno, California in 1951. The Book of Mormon was presented and discussed on an informal and open basis. Frank F. Wipper, James R. Snell and Robert L. Maley published thousands of pages of material over the next several years. In 1951, *Witnesses* began publication. It was replaced in 1958 by *Gospel Fullness Briefs* which ran until 1962. In that year a newsletter *Book of Mormon Foundation* began and ran until 1972. Maley succeeded to the editorship of the newsletter on Wipper's death in 1970. James R. Snell began publishing his own periodical in January, 1970 called *An Open Book.* The Foundation currently is not publishing. The Book of Mormon Foundation is not an organization of believers, it has no leaders and is not a church. The Foundation is an open forum of discussion of the Book of Mormon and its teachings. Wipper felt that in the modern trends of the restoration movement the Book of Mormon was being set aside for other matters. "Whitmerite" Mormonism has provided a strong theological basis for the Book of Mormon Foundation.

Robert L. Maley wrote in 1975: "...we have endeavored to present the Book of Mormon as-is, a capella and encourage all others to do the same. With continued fumings and boilings in LDS churches, heartsickness and disillusionment, we count it to be a mission on our part to offer answers (as David Whitmer did) and assurances to those caught up in a whirl of events they cannot understand. We endeavor to show all that the Book of Mormon is their strength and refuge, not their albatross. We maintain the stance that it is a haven of rest and a wellspring of the gospel of Christ and worthy of all study and examination on a one-to-one basis with an unfettered mind." (Maley, Robert L., *Dear Friend of the Book of Mormon,* Tulsa, Oklahoma: Book of Mormon Foundation, 1975, page 3)

LATTER DAY SAINT FREEDOM FOUNDATION (Douglas Wallace)

Gaining national news media attention, Douglas Wallace, a high priest in the Mormon Church, baptized a black man in a Portland, Oregon motel swimming pool in the spring of 1976 and then ordained him to the priesthood. He was subsequently excommunicated on April 11 of the same year.

Since that time the news was filled with articles about various complaints and law suits Mr. Wallace had filed against the Mormon Church and various leaders within that group. Settled suits were ruled in favor of the church, others were dropped by Wallace or dismissed by the courts.

In a flier calling for contributions issued in 1976, the purpose of the foundation is explained:

"The Foundation has been organized for the express purpose of exposing false doctrine, dogma, and corrupt leadership existing within the LDS church and to assist in litigation expenses that will turn the church away from its presently wrong posture; back to Christ and true Christian ethics and practices. In short, it is intended to overturn the present unchristian posture through whatever legal or equitable remedies that are available.

"The directors of the Foundation include John W. Fitzgerald, Ed.D. and Douglas A. Wallace, J.D. Dr. Fitzgerald has waged a private effort over the past 30 years to bring the false doctrine of black-priesthood denial before the leaders of the LDS Church. His efforts resulted in the church ordering his excommunication. Notwithstanding this, John has persisted in the continuance of his fight against this injustice. Mr. Wallace was also excommunicated from the church following his positive action in ordaining Larry Lester, a black, to the Mormon priesthood in April of this year. Both men are dedicated to continue the struggle.

"At the present time Mr. Wallace is the defendant in an action brought by the Mormon Church against him to permanently bar him from the Salt Lake Temple Square. This effort is waged against Mr. Wallace because he had put the leaders of the church on notice prior to his excommunication that they are imposters and are guilty of improper conduct in office. Mr. Wallace vows that the day will come in which the proper church tribunal will try these men and find them guilty as charged. Mr. Wallace has counter-sued the church for violation of his First Ammendment rights. The action is pending."

For a time the Foundation published a newsletter, *The Millennial Messenger.*

Recent attempts at contact have been unsuccessful. I assume that the Black-priesthood contention is now academic, since the Mormon church changed its policy in June, 1978.

DAVID C. MARTIN

David C. Martin began in 1968 when he published the first issue of a magazine entitled *Mormon History.* Although he was unable to produce it on a regular schedule, he succeeded in publishing several hundred pages of little-known information. In December 1970, *Restoration Reporter* made its first appearance. Over the next few years several issues were published in various formats. The final issue was in November 1975.

Martin was involved in several other publishing ventures, including the revival of the *Nauvoo Neighbor* in Nauvoo, Illinois in 1975-76.

The Nauvoo Neighbor Press, which began actual operation in Provo, Utah in 1974, reprinted a wide series of early Mormon related publications. The series included 9 books and 110 pamphlets. The company published two editions of *Divergent Paths of the Restoration* in 1975.

David C. Martin has made a great contribution to the field of Latter Day Saint studies, and although he is currently not involved in any publishing ventures, he will be long remembered.

RESTORATION FESTIVAL, INC.

Organized circa 1979 by several members of the RLDS Church, Restoration Festival, Inc. is attempting to promote what it views as the original mission and message of the Restored Church.

The policy of the organization was published in its April 1982 report:

"1. The Restoration Festival is a continuing organization.

"2. The Festival should be thought of as a permanent group or movement within the RLDS Church, for it is made up of loyal church members who are striving to preserve the church's original beliefs. Just as there is an archaeological society within the Church, which promotes Book of Mormon archaeology, so there is a Restoration Festival society, which defends and proclaims the original doctrines, ordinances, and practices of the church, as they are found in the Three Books of scripture and the Church history.

"3. The Festival movement is not a church. We have no intention of becoming a church. Our members are urged to attend their local branches, and to be active and devoted members of the RLDS Church.

"4. The Festival has no dominant leader at its head. It is directed by a board of ten men, each of whom has an equal vote. The Board has only a chairman, vice-chairman, secretary and treasurer. There is also a Council of Advisers, consisting of nine men, which gives helpful directions to the Festival movement.

"5. The Restoration Festival holds the same beliefs that the Church has always held—such as are found in the Epitome of Faith which was published by Joseph Smith, Jr., and his son Joseph Smith, III.

"6. The Restoration Festival is opposed to liberalism, and to any affiliation with the World Council of Churches and any of its subdivisions.

"7. The Restoration Festival calls for the saints everywhere to support and uphold the original and fundamental beliefs of the church.

During the 1982 conference of the RLDS Church in Independence, Missouri, the Restoration Festival held its own separate prayer and preaching services in another location.

The First Presidency of the RLDS Church condemned the Restoration Festival in the June 1, 1982 issue of the *Saints' Herald.* They indicated that the Festival was using silenced ministers as their leaders. They stated that "past experience with such groups would indicate they are well on the way to establishing their own church."

REVIEW AND PREVIEW PUBLISHERS

With headquarters in Draper, Utah, Lynn L. Bishop directs the publishing of a number of books relating to priesthood, plural marriage and its history and other Mormon-related concepts. His best known work, written and published with a brother in 1971, is entitled *The Keys of the Priesthood Illustrated.* This work discusses in great detail recent history concerning the various Mormon fundamentalist claims to leadership, etc. and presents Bishop's own belief that a great Indian Prophet now hold all of the keys of the priesthood and will make his presence known when the time is right. Careful documentation makes this work very important.

Several other volumes of significance are also available.

STAR OF TRUTH PUBLISHING

The published name of the individual behind this organization is Joseph L. Jensen. I have been told, however, that this is simply a front for the priesthood group led by Owen A. Allred. Formerly Concerned Latter Day Saints, Star of Truth Publishing has been issuing various proclamations and information regarding the Mormon Church and its "departure from the gospel" since July 23, 1978.

It is asserted that allowing blacks into the priesthood by the Mormon Church is in error. More recent efforts have been devoted to bringing to light current Mormon Church teachings which appear to be in direct opposition to the scriptures and teachings of Joseph Smith, Jr.

SECTION 4

ANTI-MORMON ORGANIZATIONS

Probably no religious movement in the history of the United States has received as much attention as has the Latter Day Saint Movement. From its very inception, mainstream Christians have tried to prove that Latter Day Saint teachings and its various scriptural works are fraudulent.

Various organizations throughout the years have attempted to proselytize the Latter Day Saints and persuade them to come to Christ.

There are probably hundreds of various minstries devoted to preaching against Mormons today. I have selected a few of those which I consider to be some of the more important for inclusion in this section.

MODERN MICROFILM COMPANY

Former members of the LDS Church, Jerald and Sandra Tanner operate one of the best known publishing ministries against Mormonism that exists today. Literally thousands of pages of books of their own authorship have been published, along with an equal number of reprints of early materials.

For a short time, many years ago, after the Tanners left the LDS Church, they were associated with Pauline Hancock's Church of Christ (discussed earlier). At that time, Mr. Tanner penned some of their basic beliefs:

"We believe the Bible and the Book of Mormon to be the word of God.

"We do not believe in holding up any man, but rather in holding up Christ.

"We believe that all mankind are lost through the fall: for the natural man is an enemy to God and has been from the fall of Adam, and will be forever and ever, unless he yields to the enticing of the Holy Spirit, and putteth off the natural man and becometh a saint through the atonement of Christ the Lord.

"We believe that a person must be faithful in Christ until death or he cannot be saved.

"We believe that this life is the only time given to man to prepare to meet God, for there will be no chance for repentance after death." (Carter, *Denominations...,* page 51)

However, in the late 1960s, the Tanners discovered what they felt to be convincing evidence that the Book of Mormon was false, convinced the Hancock group of the same, and have now espoused Christianity and are very fervent in their zeal to present, discuss and refute the doctrines and practices of Mormonism.

Their most widely read book *Mormonism—Shadow or Reality?* was first published in 1963. Since that time it has undergone numerous revisions and enlargements to the point where it has become a hefty volume of several hundred pages. In 1980, Moody Press introduced a revision entitled *The Changing World of Mormonism.* This books is the most definitive work in its field. The authors have gone to original sources and present a very convincing argument.

The Salt Lake City Messenger, a newsletter, has been published for a number of years—46 issues to October 1981.

SAINTS ALIVE IN JESUS

Several years ago, this ministry was founded by Mr. J. Edward

Decker, formerly a Mormon member of the Melchizedek priesthood and active in many church callings. This ministry attempts to reach Mormons, RLDS Church members, Jehovah's Witnesses, etc. Most local associate ministries are known as "Ex-Mormons for Jesus."

A bi-monthly newsletter is published from Issaquah, Washington. It touches on current news of the LDS Church, commentary and news about their own activies.

Several booklets and tapes are published which help reach out to "save" the Mormons.

WALLY TOPE

Wally Tope has been ministering to Mormons for a number of years through pamphleteering and personal contacting. He does not work alone as many people are sincere in wanting to preach Christ to Mormons. His leaflets show up at Mormon Conferences in Salt Lake City and near Brigham Young University campus in Provo, Utah.

Many ministers, such as Mr. Tope, do some of their own writing, but rely very heavily on the available tracts and information from one of the most prominent ministries in the field, the Utah Christian Tract Society.

UTAH CHRISTIAN TRACT SOCIETY

Located in La Mesa, California, the Utah Christian Tract Society has been ministering to Mormons since 1955. Mr. Arthur Budvarson is the President and founder of the society.

In addition to a bi-monthly newsletter, the society publishes more than a score of tracts on various subjects, designed to persuade Mormons of the error of their ways.

UTAH MISSIONS, INC.

John L. Smith, a Baptist Minister, was assigned to a new church in Utah and moved there in 1951. During an almost 20 years sojourn in the state, Mr. Smith became interested in Mormonism and learned as much about the subject as his schedule permitted. Now from Oklahoma, he directs a far-reaching ministry which includes several books, cassette tapes, and personal speaking tours throughout the United States.

His several books include *Witnessing Effectively to Mormons* (1975); *I Visited the Temple* (1966); *Has Mormonism Changed...Now?* (1979); *Thirty-Five Mormons and One Baptist Preacher* (1958); and *Brigham Smith,* an entertaining novel first published in 1969. This book takes the life of a modern-day member of the LDS Church and follows his life through baptism, priesthood ordinations and finally to a calling and ordination as an Apostle, only to culminate in Brigham Smith's conversion to the Baptist faith and total rejection of Mormonism.

ADDITIONAL INFORMATION AND NEW LISTINGS

This section contains new and additional material which updates the entries in the main body of this book. New churches and other organizations that have been founded since 1982, or have some to light since the Third Edition of this work, are also included here. A page number beneath the group's name references the primary entry to be found elsewhere in this volume. An entry without a page number indicates a new listing.

For an understanding of how each group fits into the overall picture, please see the introductory material, the table of contents, the index and the companion volume by the same author, *The Latter Day Saint Churches: An Annotated Bibliography*. The sections and "parts" which divide the following information are consistent with the table of contents.

Dissident Movements Founded Between 1830 and 1844

CHURCH OF CHRIST
(Ezra Booth)

Founded in 1836. No further information available.

CHURCH OF CHRIST
(William Chubby)

Founded in the 1830s or 1840s to provide ministry to blacks. No further information available.

CHURCH OF CHRIST
(Hyrum Page)

Founded in 1842. No further information available.

Non-Extant Movements Founded During the Fragmentation Period, 1844 to Mid-1860s

CHURCH OF JESUS CHRIST OF LATTER DAY SAINTS
(James Emmett)

This information is taken from "The Wi-iyohi" a monthly bulletin of the South Dakota Historical Society, March 1, 1955.

James Emmett was one of a number of church leaders who had been called to migrate to the west by Joseph Smith, Jr. prior to his death in 1844. Emmett's company headed west in the spring of 1845 with about 130 people.

The unpublished LDS Church Journal History records that Emmett joined the church early and by April 1832 was found as a member of the High Priests. In 1841 Emmett became a member of the High Council in Iowa, and on February 21, 1844, was selected by Joseph Smith to explore Oregon and California for a new city for the church. After the death of Joseph Smith, Emmett and a number of church members moved to what is now Clay County, South Dakota.

Reports by church leaders who were sent to visit the Emmett colony in the Spring of 1845 reported serious conditions, and strict enforcement of rigid rules by Emmett. Later visitors from Nauvoo reported much better conditions, but Emmett would not cooperate with them and succeeded in retaining the loyalty of the better part of his company, although many were rebaptized and eventually moved west with the main body of pioneers who followed Brigham Young.

On November 8, 1847, Emmett and those who still followed his leadership were pronounced excommunicated from the LDS Church by the Twelve Apostles in a meeting held at Winter Quarters, Nebraska. Emmett later moved to California.

CHURCH OF CHRIST
(S. B. Stoddard, Leonard Rich, James Bump)

A movement founded in 1845 in opposition to Brigham Young. No further information is available.

CHURCH OF CHRIST
(Hazen Aldrich)

In 1851, after falling out with James C. Brewster (see page 55), Hazen Aldrich formed his own movement in opposition to Brewster's leadership. The movement was short-lived. No further information is available.

Extant Movements Founded During the Fragmentation Period, 1844 to mid-1860s

Part One: Church of Jesus Christ of Latter Day Saints (Strangite)

CHURCH OF JESUS CHRIST OF LATTER DAY SAINTS (STRANGITE)
(Theron Drew) Page 159

It is reported that members of the Drew family have healed their rift and reunited with the main body of the Strangite movement. However, some members of the family continue to remain independent.

The outcome of the legal action was reported incorrectly. The class action suit was judged in favor of the main body of the church, and the properties in question were turned over to officers of the church in the early 1960s.

HOLY CHURCH OF JESUS CHRIST
(Alexandre R. Caffiaux) Page 207

Correspondence from leaders of the Strangite movement reports the following:

"In reference to the Holy Church of Jesus Christ, or Saint Eglise de Jesus Christ, Brother Alexandre R. Caffiaux professed to have been a member of the Utah Church. He came here (to the Strangites in Wisconsin) November 3, 1963 to learn of Strangism, was baptized the following Saturday at Racine, Wisconsin and ordained an elder the same day. He claimed to have received a vision somewhere over the Atlantic ocean on returning to Europe, the vision directed him to go to the east and receive a higher ordination. Notice was received here, posted at Teheran, Iran, that he had been, or claimed to have been ordained under the hands of the Archangel Raphael, near Meshah, Iran, on January 22, 1964.

"He returned to the U. S. about June 25, 1964, a council of High Priests was called for June 28, 1964, the consequences were he was sustained in the calling where unto God had called him (be it Elder or Prophet no one could determine). Within a short while after returning to Europe most of the correspondence from him was submitted and written by his son Roger Y. Caffiaux, and finally was discontinued altogether—the letters were too brief and contained no enlightenment. About 1967 two publications were issued for the Holy Church of Jesus Christ—the first number of a bilingual newspaper *The Gospel Informer* about 16 pages, 4" x 6" as I recall, and *The Call and Ordination of A. R. Caffiaux*, about 30 pages extremely well done, also about 4" x 6"—both now rare. The second listed publication was entirely in English as I recall. I do not know how many of each were printed, but I believe about 500, perhaps 1000.

"We have no other information excepting his testimony, have seen no evidence per se that A. R. Caffiaux was ever connected with the Utah Church, he had no copies of the Book of Mormon in either French or English....He was a personable man and enjoyable in conversation, he professed to have no English, but conversed readily in German, French, Spanish or Latin—also Flemish, a singularly strange or very peculiar individual."

The temple, referred to in the primary entry, is not a temple in the Latter Day Saint sense. The French word for a protestant meeting house, or church, is "temple."

In 1966, shortly after Caffiaux's contact with the Strangite movement, a supporter, Stanley L. Johnston, produced a small booklet entitled, "The Call and Ordination of Alexandre Roger Caffiaux." This booklet contains a brief history of Caffiaux's involvement with the church, and his first-hand (translated) account of his visit with the angel Raphael. (*Restoration 2,* October 1983, p. 4; *Restoration 6*, January 1987, p. 28)

REUBEN MILLER

One of Strang's first important converts, Reuben Miller was also one of the first to leave the new church. In 1846, Miller published *James J. Strang, Weighed in the Balance of Truth and Found Wanting. His claims as first President of the Melchizedek Priesthood Refuted.* Apparently a few followed Miller out of the church. Miller eventually united with Brigham Young.

CHURCH OF JESUS CHRIST OF LATTER DAY SAINTS (STRANGITE)
(Albert Norman Ketchum)

Due to an error in record keeping, this church co-existed with the main body of the church for several years, beginning with conference action in 1924. Ketchum was disfellowshipped from the main body of the church about 1905 at Monte Vista, Colorado. This was during the period of time when many of that branch were in the process of moving to New Mexico. Although Ketchum made satisfaction and was reinstated, the record of his reinstatement was lost or mislaid. During the Strangite conference of 1924, the disfellowshipment was acknowledged and a number of church members from the Kansas City, Kansas area who had joined the church through Ketchum's ministry were declared not members of the church.

The issue was resolved in 1955 during the church's general conference. Ketchum's membership and priesthood was acknowledged as having been reinstated in 1905 and an apology was issued to those church members who had been excluded for 30 years. (Personal correspondence from Bruce R. Flanders, in possession of the author.)

HOUSE OF EPHRAIM AND HOUSE OF MANASSEH OF THE CHURCH OF JESUS CHRIST OF LATTER DAY SAINTS
(Jerry Sheppard) Page 220

A 1979 newspaper article, forwarded by a correspondent but unfortunately without identifying the specific newspaper (although it is from the Michigan/Wisconsin area), provides information on this group.

Jerry Sheppard and about 30 other people moved to Beaver Island in Lake Michigan and in September 1979 were attempting to build a mission house on a 10-acre site in Peaine Township, about 4 miles south of the old Strangite village of St. James.

Sheppard, from Colorado, claimed to be the presiding elder, and that he was commanded by Christ to move to the island and build a church. Besides a place of worship, the mission house will also be the means by which Sheppard and others will be able to tell the world about Strang. All the members of this group have been excommunicated from the main body of the Strangite church.

According to the article, Sheppard claims that he and his brother have created their own religious movement, adhering to the doctrines of the main body of the church. The reason for their excommunication, according to Sheppard, was their disagreement with the church over the doctrine of marriage, as well as the church's reluctance to permit them to move to Lake Michigan. *(Restoration 2,* October 1983, p. 4)

CHURCH OF JESUS CHRIST OF LATTER DAY SAINTS (STRANGITE)

The Strangite Church has been fragmented in various groups, divided over doctrinal issues and administrative procedures. This segment of the Strangite movement has as one of its key promoters John Hajicek. Members are located in Wisconsin and other areas. One prominent question is the ability of a church organization to exist without the office of prophet being filled—as has been the case since Strang was assassinated in the 1850s. (*Restoration 2*, October 1983, p. 5)

STRANGITE BELIEVERS IN PENNSYLVANIA

A correspondent has furnished information regarding a group in Pennsylvania which professes a belief in Joseph Smith, Jr. and James J. Strang, but apparently have no other connections with the Restoration by way of baptism or ordination. They are said to practice polygamy and are attempting to build a community in the northern part of the state. No further information is available. All attempts at contact have been unsuccessful.

priesthood members have since been silenced or expelled from the RLDS Church.

The split thus created a division in the church members there, with many following Fishel's leadership. Although they initially attempted to continue to function under the RLDS name, legal requirements forced them to incorporate under the name, "Church of Christ Restored." The new group purchased property and built their own church building in the Vancouver area. From 1978 to 1988 the church published a bi-monthly newsletter named "New Life."

In a letter from Fishel, he summarized the position of the church as follows:

"We did not leave the church...We firmly believe in the church organized by Joseph Smith and five others April 6, 1830 and because of transgression, reorganized April 6, 1860.

"We continued to register our newly baptized members with the RLDS Church (through 1977) until they notified us they would no longer accept them; since then, we record them locally. We believe that any member of the RLDS Church baptized by any elder of the church who continues to teach the principles of the gospel of Christ is a member of Christ's Church.

"The division resulted from the introduction of new doctrinal teaching which are contrary to those taught by the church as reorganized. They were first introduced in the 'Position Papers' in 1969.

"It is not our intent to set up a new Restoration Church. We have no plan to select 12 apostles or a prophet. We know that God is the only one who can do that and we are confident that he will in his own way and in his own time do just that." (*Restoration 4*, July 1985, p. 7)

LAMANITE MINISTRIES FOR CHRIST

Renamed *New Covenant Ministries for Christ* in May 1984, this was formed early in 1984 or the latter part of 1983. Its stated purpose was not to form a new church, but to take the Book of Mormon to its "divinely directed recipients, without the attachment of any facet or faction of Mormonism." The name was changed to indicate that the efforts of the group were directed to all who might benefit from the Book of Mormon and not just the Indians per se. Current status of the group is unknown. (*Restoration 3*, April 1984, p. 4; July 1984, p. 2)

JOSEPH T. LONG

"Joseph T. Long, 55 years old (in 1983) who claims some Lamanite ancestry, claims to have met with God, Jesus Christ, Joseph Smith, Jr., Elijah and Moroni at various times. Mr. Long visited Wallace B. Smith [RLDS Church President] and advised him that he was to step down and announce Mr. Long as his successor....Mr. Long acknowledges that he has had leukemia and says this was cured by administration—but his health does not seem to be very good at this time and Mr. Long says his visits with the above dignitaries came during the time he was taking treatments and medicine for his leukemia. Mr. Long worked for Herald House [RLDS publishing company] some years ago. Mr. Long seems to claim he now has the rod of Moses, which gives him his power and informs those he speaks to that something major is to happen between now and May 15—that Christ will make it known. Although Mr. Long currently is attending Enoch Hill [RLDS congregation in Independence, Missouri], ... his transfer from Blue Valley Stake has not been made, and Stake President Roger Bauer has sent a letter of silence to Mr. Long dated March 2, 1983." (Reported in *Watchman of Zion no. 39*, Independence, Missouri: March 1983, p. 3)

RESTORATION BRANCHES MOVEMENT

With the 1984 announcement by Wallace B. Smith, RLDS Church President, of a revelation permitting women to hold the priesthood, some in the church unable to accept this began to look elsewhere for their religious expressions.

Believing that the RLDS Church is the true church, many of these dissatisfied people have organized branches outside the laws of the church, at the same time claiming to be the RLDS Church. These separatist movements are led mainly by men who have been removed from priesthood ministry by the RLDS Church—the legality of the actions being denied by the promoters of the separatist agenda. As yet no unified movement has been effected, with various independent branches and associations functioning essentially on their own. Some attempts at unification have failed, such as the International Elder's Conference, which held a special conference at Independence beginning on April 5, 1985. However, at its third meeting, held in 1986, the conference fell apart when John Cato was introduced as a prophet.

The Cato contingent left the meeting to start their own church, which will be introduced later.

Another group, composed of fifteen independent branches, formed "the Association" on October 25 and 26, 1986 in Independence. Those in attendance selected a committee of five to lead the group. The first issue of a newsletter, the *Restoration Messenger*, was issued in January 1987. Current status of the group is unknown. There were rumblings of internal contention.

Many in the "fundamentalist" camp believe they are in a similar position that the original church found itself in after the death of Joseph Smith, Jr. in the 1840s and 1850s. (*Restoration 4*, April 1985, p. 5; *Restoration 5*, April 1986, p. 3; July 1986, p. 28; *Restoration 7*, July 1988, p. 28)

CHURCH OF JESUS CHRIST, THE LAMB OF GOD

(A. Lee Abramson)

The August 1985 issue of the "Restoration Foundation" newsletter reports the organization of this group which has broken with the RLDS Church over doctrinal issues.

"Many of the saints in Beals [Maine] have been steadfast in their support of the Restoration Gospel. Approximately 45 saints meet together on a regular basis for worship services. They have organized as a branch under the leadership of a presiding elder, as well as utilizing the leadership of six other priesthood. Some of the priesthood have been silenced because of their support for the restoration.

"...they have incorporated under the name of the "Church of the Lamb of God." Former RLDS Seventy A. Lee Abramson has emerged as a key leader in this church, which now claims several branches across the United States. Although the branch initially felt it should remain faithful to the RLDS Church, Abramson now believes that by remaining within the RLDS organization is supporting it. Abramson acknowledges that the Spirit of God has used him from time to time, but he does not claim to be a prophet. In 1988 Abramson and his church were exploring legal arrangements to unite with the Church of Christ Restored in Vancouver, Washington. (*Restoration 4*, October 1985, p. 5; *Restoration 7*, January 1988, p. 18)

THE CHURCH OF JESUS CHRIST, ZION'S BRANCH

(John M. Cato)

Organized shortly after the breakup of the International

Elder's Conference in April of 1986, John M. Cato emerged as the prophet of this new church, headquartered in Independence, Missouri. Several revelations were issued by Cato in 1986 and 1987 as this church was in the process of developing, but in October of 1987 the family joined the Mormon Church where as of February 1991 they remained actively involved in various roles. (Verified by Julie Cato, February 11, 1991). The church issues a monthly newsletter, "The Voice." In the spring of 1989, the church issued a statement that they no longer believed in the office of president or of high priest. In essence, this aligns them with the Temple Lot movement.

Doctrine

Statement of Purpose

This statement of purpose was published in 1988:

"Having a sure knowledge that Jesus Christ is the only Begotten Son of God we, as members of the Church of Jesus Christ, by reason of the covenant we have made with God in the waters of baptism, in order that His will might be done and that His Kingdom might again become a reality upon the face of the earth, feel it wisdom in Christ to herein state our beliefs and purposes of existence in order to better secure a more organized and beneficial promotion of His precious Gospel and Doctrine. Without this gospel, man has no hope of attaining that which he was created to be, even sons of God.

"I. We believe in God the Eternal Father and in His Son Jesus Christ and in the Holy Ghost. We have but one Grand Head, He being Jesus Christ, the Savior of men. He being begotten of God because He was conceived of God, and He being the Son because He was born of the flesh, and He being our Lord because he has received a fullness of the glory of His Father, even the Eternal God.

"II. We believe that the Church of Jesus Christ is eternal in nature and that the eternal gospel of man's salvation through Jesus Christ has been restored to mankind for the last time. (RLDS D & C 26:3a-3c).

"III. We believe in the Inspired Version of the Holy Scriptures and the Book of Mormon, both of which were revealed through Joseph Smith, Jr., a prophet of the Living and Eternal God. We also accept as divine guidance the Doctrine and Covenants, so far as it is consistent with past revelation and history. We herein attest to these as being holy and sacred scriptures and willingly bind ourselves for time and eternity to the doctrine of Christ contained therein; and to the articles of faith as adopted by the early Church of Jesus Christ under the guidance of Joseph Smith, Jr.

"IV. We believe and are prepared to defend the Church of Jesus Christ as restored in 1830, and according to the covenants and commandments of God at its Reorganization in 1860, which today exists only where the servants of God have disassociated and abstained from the ordinances by that organization which once bore the name of Christ in purity, but now finds itself apostate and abhorrent in the sight of Almighty God.

"V. We of Zion's Branch have existed in a state of waiting...hoping to see an indication of repentance on the part of the leadership and membership of the RLDS organization and a commitment to once again represent Jesus Christ and the fullness of truth before the world. We have reached an understanding that the RLDS organization has not, nor appears ever will, return to the Holy task for which it was established, for their pollution of the Holy Priesthood was culminated as of April, 1984.

"The responsibility of the remnants of the Lord's House is to seek to establish themselves in righteousness and bring to pass His Holy and Divine Will, which includes the re-establishment of the full structure of Christ's church.

"VI. We believe that it is our purpose, through the covenants we have made with Almighty God, to see that our priesthood authority is used in its Holy and Sacred power in concert with the commandments of God to bring to pass righteous execution of all the ordinances of the Church of Jesus Christ in order that a righteous environment might be fostered, that our lives might be so ordered as to become living temples, that God might be glorified.

"VII. We, as a remnant body, do declare our intention to do all in our power to call mankind to repentance, to a firm faith in God and the sure knowledge of Jesus Christ as the beloved and only begotten Son of God.

"VIII. We recognize that it is our responsibility to take the gospel of Jesus Christ to a world in need, and therefore vow to see that this is done in all deliberateness and with singleness of purpose in order that God might be glorified and men might have the hope of Celestial glory.

"IX. We recognize that Independence, Missouri shall be the place of the gathering of the Saints and the place of Zion, as commanded by God. Our commitment will be to bring about such a condition of righteousness among men that this promise will be fulfilled...to the eternal blessing of all the earth.

"X. We recognize the infallible and eternal nature of Almighty God and therefore recognize His unchangeability. We therefore bear public record of our willingness before God to carry out all His commandments as they are made manifest, yesterday, today and from this time hence, through His duly ordained channels, and will seek not to council our God or place our wisdom above His Divine Will and His revealments to us thereof.

"XI. Our hope shall be steadfastly anchored in God's promise to Enoch that: 'When thy posterity shall embrace the truth, and look upward, then shall Zion look downward, and all the heavens shall shake with gladness, and the Earth shall tremble with joy, and the general assembly of the Church of the Firstborn shall come down out of heaven and possess the earth, and shall have place until the end come' (IV Genesis 9:22, 23)." (*Restoration 7*, October 1988, pp. 27, 28)

CHURCH OF CHRIST

(David B. Clark)

Founded at Oak Grove, Missouri in November, 1985 by a former member of the RLDS Church, David B. Clark and his wife. The following statement was issued by the church in a letter to the author:

"The Church of Christ is established by God. Its rock and foundation is Jesus Christ, and the fullness of his gospel doctrine, as found in the Holy Bible (The Record of the Jews) and Book of Mormon (The Record of the Nephites).

"The Church of Christ was established by the Lord among the Gentiles in May of 1829, when the ministerial 'order of the Son of God' was bestowed upon two men, Oliver Cowdery and Joseph Smith, Jr., and they baptized one another. Those two, along with David Whitmer, were inspired to 'build up' the Church of Christ, which the Lord has established by giving the 'fullness of the gospel' (the Book of Mormon) and the priesthood to the Gentiles.

"The doctrines and beliefs of the Church of Christ are based solely upon the Bible and the Book of Mormon (the Lord's standard in the latter days), as was the Church of Christ described in the Book of Mormon, and as was the Church of Christ that was established in 1829. The early leaders of the Church of Christ established in 1829 were gradually led into errors, and added several doctrines and practices that are contradictory to both Bible and Book of Mormon. We believe that, for many reasons, including their failure to use the Book of Mormon as their 'standard,' the Church of Christ fell into apostasy. Although the organization known as the Church of Christ fell away, the Lord preserved and blessed a small remnant of humble members because of their righteousness, and in order to fulfill his purposes. The 'Church of Christ' continued, in spite of the fact that the institutional 'Church of Christ' fell away.

"This present day Church of Christ is built up just like the Nephite Church of Christ and the Church of Christ as it was originally founded among the Gentiles in 1829. We proclaim the same gospel, we teach the same doctrines, and have the same ministerial offices (elder, priest, teacher) as those previous churches. The ministerial 'authority' within the Church of Christ comes from God.

"This Church of Christ has much in common with the Church of Christ that was founded by Alma I. As a result of intensive study of so-called 'restoration' church history, and earnest study of the scriptures, it became apparent to David Clark that the Latter Day Saint churches were very dissimilar to the Church of Christ that was established in 1829, and had all evolved from it over the years, adding spurious offices, doctrines and ritual ordinances. He discovered that Latter Day Saint doctrines are rooted in the teachings of Joseph Smith and his various successors, and have very little in common with the doctrine of Jesus Christ as proclaimed in the Book of Mormon and the Bible. In a sense, the Bible, Book of Mormon, and David Whitmer's *Address* were to David Clark as Abinadi was to Alma. As the result of much study, fasting and prayer, the Lord drew him and his wife, Gwyn, out of the RLDS Church. In November, 1985, organized Sunday morning scripture studies began to be held regularly. The Lord eventually led David to build up a Church of Christ, in a manner similar to Alma I.

"The Church of Christ is not an 'off-shoot' of any of the 'Latter Day Saint' churches; it is not a 'dissident protest group'; in other words, it is not a 'modification' nor a 'reorganization' of any of those existing church organizations....

"The Church of Christ publishes *The Return*, a monthly newsletter which is targeted toward the person who has a Latter Day Saint background, or is at least familiar with the Book of Mormon. The first issue of *The Return* appeared on May 8, 1987. *The Standard* is a newsletter publication for the person without any familiarity with the Book of Mormon...."

The church issues several tracts explaining its beliefs. (*Restoration 5*, October 1986, pp. 4, 17; *Restoration 6*, April 1987, p. 8; *Restoration 7*, January 1988, p. 18; October 1988, p. 2)

INDEPENDENT CHURCH OF JESUS CHRIST OF LATTER DAY SAINTS
(Christopher C. Warren)

Organized in November, 1986 at Oxford, England. Christopher C. Warren, a former member of the LDS Church who joined the RLDS Church, resigned from that affiliation on November 30, 1986 to take up official duties in the new movement. The church has effected some ties with Sons Ahman Israel (reported previously) in the United States. In 1988, Warren moved the church headquarters to Oslo, Norway, where the church has seen success in attracting new members. The *Messenger and Advocate* is the official English-language publication of the church, and through its pages readers may learn of the teachings and organizational structures of the church. Space does not permit reprinting the lengthy articles of faith which have been published by the church and contain more than 40 paragraphs.

Warren has received several revelations, many of which have been published. The church argues that two latter-day apostasies were foretold. With the death of Joseph Smith, the original church was rejected and Brigham Young introduced heresies into the church. The RLDS Church, then, originally taught the truth, but it, too, since 1958, has shifted into apostasy.

The scriptures used by the church include the Inspired Version of the Bible, the Book of Mormon, the 1835 edition of the Doctrine and Covenants (which includes the Lectures on Faith), several additional revelations of Joseph Smith, and the revelations of Joseph Smith III, Frederick M. Smith and Israel A. Smith. Various apocryphal writings are accepted, as is the translation by Davied Israel (see page 266) of what is claimed to be the sealed portion of the Book of Mormon plates. (*Restoration 5*, October 1986, pp. 22, 28; *Restoration 6*, April 1987, pp. 12, 13; July 1987, pp. 2, 5; *Restoration 7*, July 1988, p. 11)

Part Five: The Church of Jesus Christ (William Bickerton)

REORGANIZED CHURCH OF JESUS CHRIST
(Allen Wright, et. al.) Page 114

Some sources indicate that each of the various leaders involved in this separatist movement later split and each formed his own church organization. No further information has been located.

PRIMITIVE CHURCH OF JESUS CHRIST
(James Caldwell) Page 115

The legal name of this church, as was registered with the Commonwealth of Pennsylvania, was "The Church of Jesus Christ with headquarters in Erie, Pennsylvania." It is now defunct. The roots of this small group began with the Primitive Church of Jesus Christ which was founded by James Caldwell in 1914 in Washington, Pennsylvania. This group followed, for the most part, the beliefs of the parent organization: the main Bickerton movement. Caldwell was succeeded in leadership by his nephew, Laurence C. Dias, who had moved into the Erie, Pennsylvania area in 1920. Dias was born in Homestead, Pennsylvania in 1888, the son of McCandles and Jennet Caldwell Dias. In 1930, he formally organized the church and served as its pastor. Services were held in private homes until 1940 when the church erected its own church building in the Brookside area of Erie, where they met on Sundays to worship and partake of the sacrament. Dias was totally committed to his church and its members. Several tracts were published. The membership of the church never totalled more than 10 people. Laurence's son Frederick became the leader of the group on the death of his father in 1963.

The Dias family were never members of the main body of Bickertonites. Their teachings on the Godhead were different, the Dias group being Unitarian in belief. The First Vision of Joseph Smith was rejected by this group.

Sources indicate that Laurence Dias proclaimed a revelation sometime before his death to unite with the Bickerton church, but members of his family prevailed upon him to refrain from so doing. The church declined, a few members uniting with the Bickerton group, but none of the Dias family members are carrying on the work begun by Laurence nor are any of them apparently members of any Latter Day Saint church. The little church building, which was located at the corner of Dias Street and Hereford Road in Erie has since burned.

Part Six: The Church of Christ (Temple Lot) (Granville Hedrick)

THE CHURCH OF CHRIST WITH THE ELIJAH MESSAGE
(W. A. Draves) Page 143

The date on page 144, third paragraph, fifth line, should be June 1944.

CHURCH OF CHRIST
(Pauline Hancock) Page 152

The date on page 155, second paragraph under the heading "Publications", second line, should be 1971.

This church voted to disband in March, 1984. Diminishing numbers made it increasingly difficult to find leadership, and for some time had been receiving the ministry of a Nazarene church pastor. Church members sold the property of the church and dispersed to other Christian fellowships in the Independence area. (*Restoration 1*, April 1982, p. 7; *Restoration 3*, January 1984, p. 3; July 1984, p. 2)

CHURCH OF CHRIST
(Leighton-Floyd/Burt) Page 174

Howard Leighton-Floyd, who is no longer affiliated with this group, provided the following information in a personal letter to the author:

"In your book in speaking of the separation from the Draves church you indicate it was only due to Draves incorporation of the church under another name. That was only one point. The main problem for me and many others was that on August 15, 1964 a message was received. In the tenth verse it stated, 'Fear not and worry not about the temple of the Lord, for the Lord can choose the place, etc.' Message 80:20. When I read that statement on the morning it was received I asked Brother Draves if possibly he had misunderstood the messenger. He said no, that the messenger had repeated that statement, it was as the messenger gave it.

"Well, I recalled that back on March 29, 1929, in the Tenth Message it states, 'the building you have staked is set ten feet too far to the east and if you will move the stakes then it will stand upon the place that was pointed out by the Finger of God.' They moved the stakes, dug down and found the stones placed by Joseph Smith and six others. Church history relates how the spot was pointed out by the finger of God. I found I could not accept the 80th message and that...was the main reason for my part in the 1965 division in the Draves church." (*Restoration 3*, April 1984, p. 4; *Restoration 5*, April 1986, p. 5)

CHURCH OF CHRIST
(P. A. Ely)

Philip A. Ely, a member of the Church of Christ (Temple Lot) by transfer from the RLDS Church in the 1920s, followed Otto Fetting in 1929 when Fetting's movement separated from the Temple Lot group. Ely was selected as the business manager of the new church paper, *The Voice of Warning*. About 1931, calling himself "Philip of the 100" Ely published his own manuscript in the church paper without the authority or approval of the church editorial staff. Ely's manuscript related various dreams and visions he had claimed to receive. Ely was fired and ultimately faded from view. Whether or not he had a following and what have become of them is not known. (*Restoration 5*, July 1986, p. 27)

CHURCH OF CHRIST
(C. W. Humphrey)

C. W. Humphrey was pastor of the Lamoni local of the Fetting Church in 1929. He had transferred his membership from the RLDS Church to the Temple Lot church in 1927, then left with Fetting. Apparently he received revelations and attempted to lead the church of his own accord; some tracts were published. What became of him is unknown. (*Restoration 5*, July 1986, p. 28)

CHURCH OF CHRIST
(Paul C. Hilgendorf)

The July 1942 issue of *The Voice of Warning* (paper of the Fetting church) contains the following information:

"Yesterday we received a six-page pamphlet put out by one Paul C. Hilgendorf, of Salt Lake City, a former minister in the Church of Christ, advocating this strange doctrine [the one-God doctrine as opposed to the trinity of the Godhead]. True, Mr. Hilgendorf has a right to do here what he could not do in his native country, namely, exercise the right of free speech, but this same pamphlet bears a false and misleading stamp on the bottom of the last page, to wit: '1829-Church of Christ-1929, Headquarters, Independence, Mo., 2040 1/2 So. 11th East, Salt Lake City, Sunday Services 2:30 P.M. & 3:30 P. M., All Welcome.'

"This stamps the writer as a representative of the Church of Christ, and assumes that the public will receive this doctrine as a doctrine of the Church of Christ. That makes it false and misleading. Years ago it was provided by the Assembly that all literature put out in the name of the church must be approved by the Board of Publication. Inasmuch as no such approval has been given, this man is, to put it mildly, out of harmony with the church he claims to represent, but which, instead he misrepresents."

No further information is available. (*Restoration 4*, April 1985, p. 5)

FLOYD DENHAM

For a number of years Floyd Denham of Missouri and other family members and associates have been independently doing missionary work in Mexico. The male members of this society, which apparently has no formal organization or ritual, are said to grow long beards. They have published an edition of the Book of Mormon in Spanish.

No further information is available.

STEPHEN BROWN

Originally a Baptist, Stephen Brown and his wife joined the Latter Day Saint movement later in life. For nine years they lived in Holden, Missouri attending two different Latter Day Saint churches, one which met on Saturday, and the other the Leighton-Floyd/Burt group, which worships on Sundays.

Sometime during his experiences, Brown was apparently called and ordained an apostle with the Fetting group located on East Gudgell Street in Independence, Missouri, but on July 25, 1979 Brown wrote to the quorum of apostles, of which he was a member, proclaiming his separation. Brown declared that he had received a revelation that the Lord was calling out a new council of twelve apostles. He issued several revelations. Brown died in the early 1980s. (*Restoration 4*, July 1985, p. 4)

CHURCH OF CHRIST—RESTORED GOSPEL 1929
(Robert and Laura Miller)

The first information received about this church is a letter dated June 14, 1985 which proclaims a revelation dated May 23, 1985. The Millers, according to leaders of the Church of Christ with the Elijah Message, former members of that organization. This church accepts only the 30 messages received by Otto Fetting, and in 1987 voted to accept several messages issued by a Mr. Collins. The Millers reside in Yuma, Arizona, and the address there is the only one ever determined, except that claims are made that headquarters of the church is in Los Angeles, California.

No further information is available. (*Restoration 4*, October 1985, p. 4; *Restoration 6*, April 1987, p. 12)

LATE INFORMATION

WYCAM CLARK
(Page 21)

The "Kirtland Township Trustees Record" mentions Clark by name as early as 1818. He was an early settler of Kirtland, arriving long before the Mormons arrived. There is a microfilm of this volume in the LDS Church Historical Department.

AUSTIN COWLES
(Page 56)

I. H. Bishop, listed as Cowles secretary, is Isaac Hyde Bishop, an older brother of Francis Gladden Bishop. He was a member of the church in Kirtland where he was inspector of roads, and later a member of the Springfield stake presidency during the Nauvoo era.

FRANCIS GLADDEN BISHOP

(Page 28)

Bishop joined the church in 1832 and soon after received a vision that identified him as the branch referred to in Zechariah. He was soon coopted and brought back into the faith. From 1832 to 1842 he served as a missionary over the eastern US, signed the articles of the Kirtland Safety Society, was tried for heretical teaching in 1832, 1835 and finally 1842 when he was excommunicated. After trying vainly to gather a following together (beginning in 1847) he went to Voree where he encountered Strang. He later moved to Kirtland, where in 1851 he began a brief publishing career promoting his beliefs. In 1854 he traveled to New York attempgint to preach his gospel to the Jews. Unsuccessful at this he returned west, eventually reaching Salt Lake City, where he died in the winter of 1864. His church, *The Church of Jesus Christ of the New Jerusalem*, was organized June 11, 1854 at Council Bluffs, but fell apart soon after he left for the east.

APPENDIX
The Twelfth Message

Otto Fetting, an apostle in the Church of Christ (Temple Lot) received this message on July 18, 1929. It was to become the source of the tremendous contention which shook the church for several years and was one of the prime factors in Fetting's organizing his own church which later became the parent of several other Latter Day Saint groups.

This revelation was first published in Zion's Advocate, Volume 6, Number 10, October, 1929, and it is from that source we quote:

REVELATION ON BUILDING THE TEMPLE
Twelfth Visitation

The Messenger came to me for the twelfth time Thursday night, July 18, 1929. He came and went three times, remaining each time until I was weak from his presence, then he would leave me for a short time so I could regain some of my strength. The Divine is so much stronger than the human, that the presence of the Messenger makes a person weak in body. This time I had the first opportunity to ask him a question, which I did. I asked him if our work which we have done has been accepted of the Lord, to which he answered, Yes.

I hope that whosoever may read these messages that they may make it a matter of prayer and fasting in humility before God, that they may know for themselves that God has again spoken and revealed His mind from Heaven.

The Words of the Messenger

I have come to you from time to time, to instruct you as to the work of building the Temple, and the organization of the Church of Christ, and re-establishing it again in its fullness, that the church may again receive the power and Holy Ghost as in the days of old, and that as on the day of Pentecost, the servants of the Lord may be filled with the Spirit of God, that they make take the message of the Gospel of Christ to the nations of the earth, for the Lord has reserved unto Himself this remnant on the Temple Lot, to set the church in order. I have come to you in your own language that you may understand, and impart it to the children of men, and that the message might be understood by all people, in its plainness, that they may have no excuse at the judgment day, for verily these things shall come to pass.

The Lord has looked upon you and your brethren, and has seen the humility of your souls, and your desire to carry out the instructions that the Lord has given you from time to time, and thus far your work has been accepted of the Lord, but remember, you must remain very humble before God, and do the things He has, and will command you to do, or the spirit and light that the Lord has given you will be withheld from you and your minds will become dark, and doubt and fear will enter your souls. Therefore, seek the Lord often in prayer and in the humility of your souls the work that the Lord has commanded you to do will come before you. Contend with no man, only contend for the truth, for the truth will make you free. Contentions will darken the mind and the spirit of God will not dwell in the hearts of men who are contentious.

The plans as drawn by your brethren are correct as to the foundation, that is, as to size, but let the pillars be added to the outside, 4 feet, 8 inches in length, and 2 feet, 8 inches in depth, and let the pillars on each corner be the same size. Dig the trenches, and bring the foundation to the level of the basement floor, and your steel 15 inches above the grade level. Let your fabricating be done, so that your work may continue from there, for behold, many important things shall come to pass, and many things shall yet be given, but I will come from time to time to instruct you, that the work will not be delayed.

Behold, the Lord has rejected all creeds and factions of men, who have gone away from the word of the Lord and have become an abomination in His sight, therefore, let those that come to the Church of Christ be baptized, that they may rid themselves of the traditions and sins of men; preparing themselves, that they may be fit and worthy for the spirit and power of the Holy Ghost, and as the greater power shall come, that they may be ready to receive it with joy. For this is the time of the restitution and restoration of all things, and this must come to all that shall be permitted to dwell in the presence of Christ, for sin cannot receive the glory of God, nor the power of the Holy Spirit.

Let not the building of the Temple hinder the preaching of the gospel, but let those that have been appointed and set apart for the Temple work, see that all things be done after the patter which I shall give. And let those that have been called and set apart to carry the gospel message to the nations of the earth do their work as they have been instructed. Let them preach the things as they are found in the Bible and the Record of the Nephites; let them take the message to Jew and Gentile, to all classes, tongues and peoples. Let the men who have been placed in charge and appointed to look after and receive the tithes, offerings and oblations, be mindful of their work, that the monies so received are spent wisely. Let them give an accounting to the church, that all things may be done in justice to all, always being mindful that they are ambassadors for Christ and the church, and that they will be without excuse to God, for everyone must be faithful to their trust for this is the Lord's work, and so shall it be required of him in the last day.

Remember, the Lord committed to Joseph Smith a great work in his day, and power and authority to re-establish the Church of Christ in his day as in the days of old. He gave them the pattern to establish it as in the days of the apostles, and restored the priesthood and authority of the Son of God to the children of men. Yet, because of pride and the love and praise of men, he sinned before God, and much of his work has been destroyed, but he will be saved as by fire, and will be numbered with the prophets of old. Again, the Lord has called others to prune His vineyard, to bring the gospel of peace, to establish His Church as in the days of old, that the power of the priesthood may be again enjoyed as in the days of old.

Behold, the Lord changes not, again he has sent me to instruct the children of men as to the building of the Temple, the size thereof, the inner court and the outer court, the construction of the building, the time to begin the work, the time to complete the building of the Temple, the material it shall be built of, and I will come from time to time to instruct you, for thus was I commanded to instruct Joseph Smith, but because he was not true to the trust, this was withheld from him. Remember, you have been intrusted with this work, therefore be humble that you fail not in your work.

And as I laid my hands upon Joseph Smith, so now I lay my hands on you, that greater power and light might come to you, and to set you apart to do the work intrusted to your care and in your day. Remember, the priesthood was not and will not be taken from the earth since I conferred it on Joseph Smith, but the greater power of the priesthood has been withheld because of the transgression of those who have been intrusted therewith, therefore, see that all things are done after the pattern I will give you, that in all things you may please the Lord your God. Be true to the trust that has been placed upon you and your brethren, each one in his place and calling, for the Lord will hold each one responsible in their work that must be done and will require it at their hands in the last day. Some will fail because of the temptations that shall come to them, but they will suffer loss. But, remember, Christ is at the head of the church and will direct His work; He is the great high priest of His people and he will direct the work as in days of old. I therefore bless you in the name of Christ, and admonish you to seek not the praise of men but be humble before God, and the people of the Lord, and our brethren. The priesthood and authority that was placed upon you by the servant of the Lord will never be taken from you unless you deny the Lord your God, but if you are not true to the trust imposed upon you, you shall suffer loss and lose your crown. The Lord will reveal to you from time to time the things pertaining to the building of the Temple and the work that must be done by the Church of Christ, that the people of the Lord might be instructed of the things that shall come to pass. Amen.

Let C. A. Spilsbury be set apart among men to fill the vacancy in the Quorum of Twelve, that the work may not suffer, for this is a day of haste as I have told you. Let him take the field with the gospel message, as he is not burdened with the cares of life as some are. Let the elders who are not burdened with the cares of life go from place to place and prepare to take the message to other nations, but let those go to the far off fields that are not burdened with the care of children, and let their companions go also. Use wisdom in these matters, be careful in your expenses, while and where you labor, that more may be sent into the harvest field.

Let your work on the Temple continue, working as fast as the monies come in but keep out of debt, contract no debt with any man, for this work must be done by sacrifice and not by promise. For behold the people of the Lord are glad to help in this work of the Lord, by tithes and by offerings for thus did the people in the days of old, which was pleasing unto the Lord, for this was the law in Abraham's day who paid tithes and the Lord blessed him, and the Lord will bless in your day all those that shall keep His law. Therefore pay your obligations to the Lord in all things that your work may be accepted of him, so that when trying times are upon the earth your works might stand the test. Let the gospel be preached, let the poor be provided for, let the Temple be built, that in all things you may be the children of God.

Those that will heed the warnings that I have given to them in the past will be blessed; those that will not believe will lose, nevertheless, take the message to them, and the honest in heart will accept it.

I am John the Baptist that prepared the way before Christ and I will prepare the way before him again, and a people to receive Christ when he comes. Send this message to your brethren, the Twelve first, then send it to the nations of the earth with all the rest now in print, but the things I have shown to you in vision, keep that only for your brethren, give not that to the enemies that seek to hinder the work of the Lord.

I will come from time to time until the work is finished after the pattern. Be humble, and the Lord will bless you by His Spirit, and men will be blessed by the message in time to come. Amen.

BIBLIOGRAPHICAL NOTE

Source material for the information contained in this volume is found in thousands of publications issued by the various organizations mentioned herein, and others. In addition, the author has amassed thousands of pages of correspondence with church leaders and members, other researchers, etc. Major collections of material may be found at Yale University, Brigham Young University, and the headquarters of both the LDS and RLDS Churches.

Published source materials are cataloged in Steven L. Shields' *The Latter Day Saint Churches: An Annotated Bibliography* (New York and London: Garland Publishing, Inc., 1987). This 300 page volume, a companion to *Divergent Paths of the Restoration*, contains the more than 1500 items used as source materials. Each entry is briefly annotated.

INDEX